Praise for *Original Intelligence*

"*Original Intelligence* describes the architecture of human cognition, from *mental modules* to *pedagogy* to a *theory of mind*. By defining the nature of intelligence, the Premacks also reveal a blueprint for the evolution and development of human cognition. *Original Intelligence* is an adventure for anyone captivated by brain and mind."

—Ira B. Black, Professor and Chair,
Neuroscience and Cell Biology,
Robert Wood Johnson Medical School,
and author of *The Dying of Enoch Wallace:
Life, Death and the Changing Brain*

"*Original Intelligence* provides a cornucopia of insights into our origins, how the human mind unfolds during development, and how our minds differ from those of our nearest cousins."

—Terrence Sejnowski
Howard Hughes Medical Institute
Salk Institute for Biological Studies

"This is an extremely stimulating book. Can animals or young infants entertain abstract concepts, draw analogies, or think up a sentence? What do they understand about physics, biology, or morals? Page after page, the Premacks draw on their in-depth knowledge of animal and infant cognition to propose tens of new ideas for experiments, always with great wit, clarity, and concision. This book is a seedbed of experimental designs waiting to be tried out."

—Stanislas Dehaene
Unité INSERM, Cognitive Neuroimaging Unit,
Service Hospitalier Frederic Joliot, Orsay, France,
and author of *The Number Sense*

Other Books by the Authors

Why Chimps Can Read, by Ann J. Premack

Intelligence in Ape and Man, by David Premack

Gavagai: The Future History of the Animal Language Controversy, by David Premack

The Mind of an Ape, by David Premack and Ann J. Premack

Causal Cognition: A Multidisciplinary Approach, edited by Dan Sperber, David Premack, and Ann J. Premack

ORIGINAL INTELLIGENCE

Unlocking the Mystery of Who We Are

David and Ann Premack

McGraw-Hill

New York   Chicago   San Francisco
Lisbon   London   Madrid   Mexico City   Milan
New Delhi   San Juan   Seoul   Singapore
Sydney   Toronto

McGraw-Hill

*A Division of The **McGraw·Hill** Companies*

1 2 3 4 5 6 7 8 9 0   AGM/AGM   0 8 7 6 5 4 3 2

ISBN 0-07-138142-2

This book is printed on recycled, acid-free paper containing a minimum of 50% recycled de-inked fiber.

Contents

Acknowledgments

Several old friends—ethologist Peter Marler, and the ethologist-psychologists Marc Hauser and Robert Hinde—read early versions of chapters some years ago; Marler read five, Hauser three, Hinde one. Robert "complained" that an idea from the chapter he'd been asked to read had kept him awake all night. More encouragement than we had counted on! But it seemed only fair to protect him from his susceptibility to ideas by not pressing any further chapters on him.

The philosopher of mind Fred Dretske read and largely approved of the chapter on Belief, an unexpected pleasure, for the topic is not one on which "eye-to-eye" thinking comes easily. The prehistorian Alan Walker not only introduced us to his field, guiding our reading and answering our questions, but checked the fruits of his labors by reading our summary of human prehistory which is included in the Introduction.

The inferences we draw concerning what the bones and artifacts of prehistory have to say about the human mind are very different from those drawn by prehistorians. This is not a surprise, since prehistorians are not cognitive scientists. In studying bones and artifacts, prehistorians, however, have a goal that intersects with that of cognitive science: They wish to reconstruct not only the body of the human but the human mind itself. The field of prehistory is not alone in spilling over into psychology. All the life sciences—biology, economics, linguistics, philosophy of mind, sociology, anthropology—do the same. They cultivate their own competences, and then overflow into cognitive science, making unwarranted assumptions about the human mind.

Economics, in studying market trends (among other things), offers us largely unexamined assumptions about human decision making: what causes people to buy, invest, save, and so on. Evolutionary theory, though hailed for illuminating human social behavior, cannot possibly do so. The model of human cognition it has adopted is so painfully simple it fails even to contemplate the crucial underpinnings of human social competence: theory of mind and meta-cognition (see Chapter 7 and the Conclusion).

Is this inadequate use of cognitive science a problem that could be solved? Easily! Simply by increasing the integration of, especially, the life sciences. Virtually all sciences have become ecumenical these days, even as cuisine has become "fusion." But while the physical sciences have managed the problem of integrating knowledge, the life sciences remain desperately in need of deeper integration. Since all the life sciences lie in the shadow of the human mind all feel qualified to make pronouncements about it.

* * *

Although we asked only a few people to read parts of the book, we asked questions of many people, relying heavily on email to do so. Since the book was largely written in locations where people were not available, email was vital. Moreover, it was not to colleagues that we needed to speak, but to strangers—to experts in fields other than our own.

Requesting information on the phone can cool your ardor for new knowledge, especially if you are not certain of the words and phrases to use in framing your question. Email turns us into heroes, and seems to have a salutary effect on recipients, by making it easy for scientists to carry out what most of them wish to do, that is, to share knowledge.

Russell Doolittle, Carl Gerhardt, and Harry Jerrison were generous in sharing their biological knowledge with us, often sending us reprints as well as answering our questions. We were, however, "unkind" to an old friend, Ellis Englesberg, tearing him away from his newfound interest in art and music and returning him to his roots long enough to have him explain regulatory genes to us. The physicist (now neuroscientist) Michel Kerszberg explained Galileo so lucidly that it was easy to envision how his ideas could be taught to three-year-old children, through animation (see Conclusion). Given Einstein's well-known gifts for imaginal thinking, another half-hour with Michel is probably all one would need to write a comparable program for teaching Relativity to toddlers.

We suspect that the molecular neuroscientist Ira Black actually enjoyed speculating on the many issues we peppered him with over a period of four or five years (see Chapter 10, for example), for he never failed to reply. His answers were so well rounded we never even considered giving him a rest by questioning other neuroscientists.

Many colleagues upheld our confidence in email by providing lucid discussions, crisp answers, and prompt reprints. Among them are Susan Carey, Leda Boroditsky, the late Peter Jusczyk, Stanislaus Dehaene, Roger Thompson, Doris Bischof-Kohler, and Terry Sejnowski.

Richard Hecht and J. Campo, of the UCSB Institute of Religious Studies, while declining to answer our questions, did recommend books that they thought would provide answers. The field of history evidently does not yet have the tradition of sharing knowledge (except perhaps among the historians themselves) that is found in the sciences, for most historians did not reply.

Several people played the role of good samaritan by helping with library cards, making contact with intermediaries who subsequently put us in touch with the appropriate experts, and providing computer assistance, office space, and research facilities. Marc Hauser shared more than knowledge—he shared his time. References, forgotten names, and articles poured in from Boston in answer to requests. Each exchange was enlivened with vigorous discussions that sprang up around a reference. Such collegiality as he extended shines a bright light on the sometimes gray academy.

Keith Holyoak was unendingly helpful, pulling library cards out of thickets of red tape. The child developmentalist Henrietta Bloch did the impossible by providing us with office space in Paris. Only because we took so long to finish the book did we succumb to the relentless smog that finally stole our view of the Eiffel Tower. Henrietta introduced us to the many able women who run the crèches of Paris, ideal locations for infant research. Finally, we are indebted to the MacDonnell Foundation and to Paris Cogniseine for supporting our research with infants.

In writing any book, it is essential to be in a location that will help keep your "dickey up." Books have a way of taking far longer than anticipated. They may make a mockery of the original "plan" by not "revealing" what it is they have in mind until the very last chapter. Such a book requires a location that uplifts the *esprit*. Paris, where much of the book was written, is such a place; but so is California, where the book was completed. A great city, Paris! But let us not sell Nature short. Take a mountain view and several acres of semitropical orchards in which to rediscover dawn and twilight, and one is amazed how well one can hear the mind of a book.

ORIGINAL INTELLIGENCE

Introduction
Once Were Hunter-Gatherers

Early Relatives

Chimpanzees and humans emerged from a common ancestor that walked on all fours with palms flat on the ground, had a modest brain volume of about 400 cc, and the appearance of a combined ape and monkey. About 6 million years ago, for reasons that are not clear, a division occurred in the population: The species split into two groups which subsequently became sexually isolated and increasingly distinct from each other. One of the groups evolved into the chimpanzee; the other, into Australopithecus, the first creature directly in the human lineage.

As descendants of a common ancestor, chimpanzees and australopithecines initially shared a number of features, including bodies and brains of similar weight. But their spinal columns were different: Australopithecines stood upright. We know this from the routine reconstructions of fossil remains and from a happy accident. About 3.6 million years ago, a lucky combination of fresh volcanic ash and a subsequent rainfall left an impressionable bed through which several australopithecines happened to walk. The footprints they left show a bipedal, human gait.

Australopithecus disappeared about 2.5 million years ago, to be replaced by the *Homo* lineage, *H. habilis* and our immediate ancestor, *H. erectus*. A second hominid species, the Neanderthals, lived in a partly overlapping period with *H. erectus*, but DNA studies show that the Neanderthals are not part of the human lineage. Yet anatomists, perhaps with tongue in cheek, have suggested that a Neanderthal dressed in modern clothing who happened to ride the New York subway would not be singled out as strange. Others, however have countered: Is this a comment on Neanderthal, or on the New Yorker?

1

Homo erectus evolved along a number of lines, the most important being the enlargement of their brain; this reached a volume of 870 cc, about 87 percent of the size of the present human brain. The brain placed a heavy burden on the species. It was a greedy feeder, demanding a greater share of the nutritional load than any other organ. And it made serious meat eaters of *H. erectus*. On the one hand, the brain induced the need for a protein-rich diet that only meat can provide; on the other hand, it provided *H. erectus* with a mentality that was capable of obtaining meat.

Figure I.1 presents a more complete account of human evolution, showing its characteristic nonlinear branching. This standard tree diagram of human evolution is found in virtually all textbooks on prehistory.[1]

First Signs

What are the earliest signs of human intelligence, and when did they first appear? Both Australopithecus and *H. erectus* give answers to this question, the one suggestive, the other more definitive.

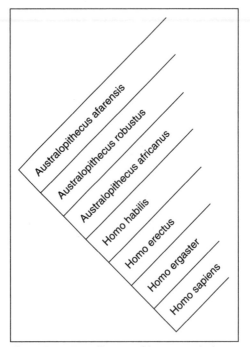

Figure I.1 Tree diagram of human evolution.

Although the Australopithecus brain was about the same size as that of the chimpanzee, it apparently was organized differently, for the australopithecines used, and may even have fashioned, simple bone (perhaps even stone) tools. Cut marks found on animal bones recovered among the fossils of Australopithecus suggest that these tools were used to cut meat from bone, and removing meat from bones with a tool rather than one's teeth is an important step in the humanizing of an animal. Tool marks on animal bones do not narrow intelligence down to a specific capability, however; they are merely a general comment on intelligence. It is *H. erectus* who provides us with evidence that points to specific capabilities.

While the earliest tools associated with *H. erectus* were primitive (a single tool being used for everything), later tools—scrapers, awls, handaxes, burins, and the like—clearly were designed for specific purposes. These tools were impressively uniform. Tools that are both specific and highly uniform strongly suggest imitation, one individual copying another.

Further, the tools designed for specific tasks were clearly the product of a complex process, far different from the simple chipping of a stone that had produced the first tools. Can we estimate the complexity of the process? French anthropologists developed an ingenious way to answer this question. They established a laboratory in an area where *H. erectus* had lived, and, using the same type of stone that *H. erectus* had used, tried to duplicate the tools. Their work revealed the unexpected complexity of the process required. They found the necessity for a five-step sequence, starting with the selection of the stone best suited for the tool.

This requirement for a multistage process suggests that *H. erectus* had gone beyond imitation, for it is difficult, if not impossible, to reproduce multistage sequences by simple observation. Imitation is a limited process. Even when an object is simple, the copy the novice makes of it is generally imperfect. Teaching, in which an experienced individual guides the novice in making an accurate copy, is the most effective method of correcting a nonexpert's errors.

In order to instruct the novice, must the teacher have language? Strictly speaking, no. But, it is interesting to note, *H. erectus* probably did have language. Endocasts of the skulls of *H. erectus* indicate the presence of Broca's area, a principal area of language in the human brain. While not essential for teaching, language can greatly increase the efficacy of teaching. Teaching, we assume, evolved before language—and by adding to the advantage that language confers, further contributed to the evolution of language. Probably it is not a coincidence that there are no species that teach but do not have language; nor are there any that have language but do not teach.

The combined evidence suggests that *H. erectus* was already armed with three cognitive capacities that mark the human: imitation, teaching, and language. These abilities form the nucleus of human social intelligence and are the very devices that enable the human to transmit knowledge from one generation to the next.

The Flexible Human

The popular assumption of a closeness between human and chimpanzee intelligence, based on a misreading of the overlap of 98.4 percent in DNA of the two species, overlooks the fact that the brain of the chimpanzee has remained at about 500 cc while that of the human has advanced to about 1300 cc. Species whose brains differ to this degree cannot possibly overlap in intelligence.

The story of how humans acquired genes has not been properly told. All human genes came from yeasts and followed an evolutionary path leading to bacteria, then to the lower animals, and only later to humans. Thus, while humans share 98 percent of their genes with chimpanzees, they also share about 60 percent with sponges, and over 80 percent with flatworms! Obviously there is no linear relation between genes and intelligence: the chimpanzee does not have 98 percent of human intelligence, the flatworm 80 percent, or the sponge 60 percent.

How then might a difference as small as 1.6 percent—the difference in chimpanzee and human DNA—have produced so vast a difference in brain and intelligence as that between chimpanzee and human? Probably it was the work of regulatory genes, which have an effect out of proportion to their number. By suppressing or activating major metabolic pathways, pathways that have multiple branches, even a single regulatory gene, can have an overpowering effect on development.

Geneticists have recently pointed out that it is what genes *express*, what they actually do, that accounts for the difference between species. The number of genes that species share is not of paramount importance. Gene expression is not uniform. In blood and liver, the pattern of gene expression is very similar in both chimpanzee and human. In the brain, however, the pattern is similar in monkey and chimpanzee but different from that of the human. The authors "found five times as many differences in gene expression . . . in the human brain than would be predicted by evolution." It is clear that the difference between human and animal intelligence is beginning to yield a definitive explanation.

The linchpin of human intelligence is flexibility. By contrast, animals are specialists. Beavers are remarkably adept at building dams, bowerbirds at constructing nests, the nuthatch at remembering the location of thousands of caches of acorns that it has hidden, the bee at performing dances indicating the location of food to other bees (as well as to humans who have deciphered its dance!). But each of these species is imprisoned by its adaptation. None can duplicate the achievement of the other. Bowerbirds cannot build dams, bees do not have an unusually keen memory for hidden caches of food, beavers cannot send messages, and so on.

Not only can humans send messages, build dams, and record the hiding places of innumerable objects; they can duplicate the performance of every species that evolution has so far produced: the radar of the bat, the deep sounding of the whale, and so on. Indeed, humans can produce the "performances" of species that have not yet evolved, for example, species that are capable of interstellar travel, of visiting the moon, and so forth.

Human intelligence and evolution are the only endlessly flexible processes on earth, capable of producing solutions to the unceasing problems that living creatures confront. Recently, humans have added to their ability to duplicate evolution by developing models that simulate evolution itself!

Hunter-Gatherers Are Us

Humans, having migrated from Africa, appeared in every corner of the world from the desert to the arctic, always in the same form: nomadic groups of about twenty to sixty. Chimpanzees, unable to produce a technology that would permit migration, have never left Africa.

Hunter-gatherers, the name given to these earliest human groups, tended to be egalitarian. Every member of a hunting party was given a share of the kill, which he then divided among members of both his family and that of his wife. Does this suggest that humans originally were more altruistic? And that our modern environment has destroyed the altruism, replacing it with self-aggrandizement? In actuality, the egalitarianism of the hunter-gatherer was the result of a precarious food supply. Since no one hunter could predict when his family would be without food, sharing was a necessity. A cynical interpretation of such sharing would be ill founded, however; hunter-gatherers show us that under the proper circumstances, small groups of humans can form stable societies based on sharing.

Like the modern human, hunter-gatherers had culture. They had belief systems based on supreme beings and on their own origins. They had theories of disease and death. Unlike the modern human, however, they had no history. History is a record of the changes a group undergoes over time, and hunter-gatherers did not change. They remained permanently in the Stone

Age. Each generation repeated the activities of the previous generation. Modern humans, because of developed technology which continually transforms the environment, do change from generation to generation.

Hunter-gatherers are, of course, biologically equivalent to us, gene for gene. The radical transformation of the hunter-gatherer, from denizen of the Stone Age into modern human is a curious phenomenon. While the difference between chimpanzee and human is biological, that between hunter-gatherer and modern human is due to cultural or environmental "accidents."

Homo erectus has given us evidence of three major forms of human cognition: imitation, pedagogy, and language. Hunter-gatherers give us more. Research of the past twenty years or so has revealed that human infants have modules—learning devices that enable the infant to acquire the competences on which adult mastery of the world depends: language, arithmetic, theory of mind, music, etc. Were these modules present in hunter-gatherer infants? The research was not conducted with the infants of hunter-gatherer groups; nevertheless there is indirect evidence of modules at work in the behavior of the adult hunter-gatherer.

A study of the grammars of the languages spoken by hunter-gatherers shows them to be comparable to those of modern languages. Hunter-gatherers explain how others behave by attributing "mental" states to them in accounting for their behavior; they engage in arithmetical calculations; they use causal reasoning; they perform music. These are competences shown to originate in the infant modules.

Evidence for the attribution of mental states can be found in the hunter-gatherer's method for obtaining termites. The chimpanzee is known for its elaborate technology for extracting termites: It enlarges the orifice in the termite mound, inserts a straw, gives it a twirl, and carefully removes the straw, which is now covered with termites. Hunter-gatherers obtain termites using a psychological rather than a physical technology. The termites emerge spontaneously.

Termites can be most easily harvested during their mating season when, triggered by showers, they emerge from the mound. The clucking sound produced by the hunter-gatherer as he kneels over the mound causes the termites to emerge because, presumably, within the mound the clucking resembles the sound of falling rain. Only a species that can take the perspective of the other one, attributing mental states to the other—hearing, for example—is likely to invent a technology of this kind.

On a visit to the Kalahari San, a hunter-gatherer group, we found, accidentally, that hunter-gatherers engage in arithmetic. In an attempt to check how often they are successful in their hunting, we devised a simple, non-verbal procedure for posing the question. We represented each day with a row of marks in the sand, and added a small stick in the mark if hunting had occurred on that day. If the hunt was successful, the stick was set in the upright position. Our translator explained the system to the informant, who smiled broadly. Seizing the sticks, he dropped to his knees on the sand. He laid a stick on each mark (indicating that he hunted daily) and then he set every fourth stick in the upright position!

What did this mean? That he actually succeeded on every fourth day? Not too likely. What it meant was more astute. It was his way of "saying" that he succeeded about a quarter of the time. The San, like other hunter-gatherers, have names for only a few numbers. But this limitation does not affect arithmetical calculations, these not being limited to named numbers.

The San have fashioned musical instruments (see Figure 1.5). They sing, beat time on percussive devices, and dance to the music. Modern humans sing lullabies to their infants; probably hunter-gatherers do the same.

Music, arithmetic, language, theory of mind (or the attribution of mental states to others) are some examples of the major competences that originate in the infant modules. Almost certainly they have the same origin in the hunter-gatherer.

The adaptation of the hunter-gatherer to his environment was highly successful. It afforded considerable leisure for gossip, chatting, and discussions around the campfire about hunting and the distinctive wiles of animals. All humans adopted this form of living. Why did they abandon it?

Probably because they ran out of food. They killed game at a greater rate than it could be replaced. The hunting prowess of the hunter-gatherer is not revealed by his primitive weapons. Behind the Stone Age spear, behind the bow and poisoned arrows, lay human cognition. Behind the weapons there lay tracking combined with causal reasoning—a knowledge of the wiles of every animal, a knowledge that was continually shared, updated, and discussed.

Yet it was human cognition itself that produced a rate of kill which imperiled not only the species that lived with the hunter-gatherer but the hunter-gatherer himself. This may have been a maiden voyage for human cognition: the first time in human history that human intelligence placed all species, including the human, at risk. It would not be the last.

Although losing one's food supply as a consequence of excessive intelligence is unique to humans, the loss of a food supply has been a recurring problem for many species. Typically the loss has come as a consequence of changes in climate, of competition with other species, and the like. Probably many species that suffered such a loss did not recover. Those species that did recover were rescued by evolution; over the course of hundreds of generations, these species adapted to a new diet.

The hunter-gatherer did not adapt to a new diet. He was not rescued by evolution. He survived in an entirely novel way. He retained his old diet, and, rather than gather plants and hunt animals, he now planted the former and domesticated the latter. In other words, he invented a new technology. The cognition that originally had imperiled him, now saved him.

The new technology of agriculture set in motion an uncanny sequence of events that in one way or another brought about the invention of writing; the emergence of economics; and the beginnings of such social institutions as state, church, and army. These institutions replaced the informal, personal governance of the hunter-gatherer band. Changes of this kind were brought about by the principal consequence of the conversion from hunting and gathering to agriculture: the steady increase in population.

We now have the first true evidence of the power of environmental or cultural change. In lifting the hunter-gatherer off the desert floor and out of the Stone Age, cultural change was producing a transformation equal to anything previously produced by biology.

The Invention of Writing

Successful agriculture produced vast surpluses of goods that needed to be stored and credited to their owners. This led to the development of recording systems which, over the course of thousands of years, developed into writing.[2] The effect of writing has been extraordinary. It is fair to speak of two human minds: one before and another after writing.

Humans have symbol systems other than writing, of course—language and images—but they are innate. Writing is the first invented symbol system. Memory is stored (in the human mind/brain) by means of innate symbols. But by using the invented symbols, humans could, for the first time, take stored, private knowledge and make it public and permanent. The resulting written documents overcame the limitations of short-term memory and of the innate symbols of the mind. The written documents could be examined, poured over, reexamined, revised, added to, subtracted from by a single individual, working feverishly through the night; or by groups of individuals who, in discussing the documents, could produce, in a short period and over successive generations, documents so changed that only historians can trace them to their original source.

None of these changes could have been accomplished without writing. Hunter-gatherers, for example, had an astounding fund of informal knowledge; but because they did not invent writing they could not subject what they knew to successive waves of editing and revision. As a consequence, the character of what they knew never changed. Knowledge remained informal. Similarly, the oral stories of the hunter-gatherer, constrained as they were by short-term memory, never acquired a complex plot or a panoply of characters, prerequisites for transforming simple oral tales into written sagas, narrative poems, and drama.

The Greeks were the first to divide the syllables (in the syllabries), of which all written systems then consisted, into vowels and consonants, that is, into the first true alphabet. The Greeks were first to use writing not merely to record goods, but to represent their ideas and knowledge. They converted "folk" knowledge into systematic knowledge. They turned oral stories into literature and turned the calculations used in building and in marketing into geometry and arithmetic. Daily argument and bickering became logic. And speculation, at which humans excel, became philosophy. Having been the first to attach writing to mind, the Greeks changed the character of human knowledge forever. Our modern human mind consists of the mind of the hunter-gatherer plus this addition—writing. Writing has enabled the human to leap from the Stone Age into an age of space travel.[3]

The Emergence of Economics

Economics, perhaps the strongest determinant of human behavior, did not exist in the life of the hunter-gatherer. Ownership, a precursor of economics, always existed among humans. Even protohumans probably owned their tools. But look at a different form of ownership, one that does not consist merely of the possession of personal artifacts: the ownership of land itself and of its resources. No such ownership existed in the day of the hunter-gatherer. The earth and all its resources were available to everyone. Mild restrictions existed. For example, water holes were claimed by given bands, but even these were shared with other bands in the same core group.

Agriculture changed ownership. Farmers claimed land as individuals. Yet even personal claims to land did not constitute a true economic factor until increased population had made land scarce and introduced one of the principal novelties on which economics rests, permanent scarcity. Although hunter-gatherers had known seasonal shortages of plants and animals (caused by natural rhythms of climate), they had never experienced permanent shortages caused by competition from other peoples. The scarcity of land and the ever-increasing population led people to claim not only land, but its resources—water, salt, timber. While there was little point in owning a salt mine when salt was plentiful, when salt became scarce because of an increase in population, the ownership of resources such as salt became economically attractive.

Agriculture divided the world into rich and poor, a condition unknown among hunter-gatherers. The rich owned the land, and increasingly, the resources of the land, thus setting the stage for the single most powerful economic factor—work.

The possibility of work arises from a simple situation: An individual is in a state of preference but does not possess the goods that can satisfy this preference. This preference could be satisfied by a second individual who owns the goods in sufficient supply. This disparity makes it possible for an owner to require a nonowner to work, to carry out a set of tasks in order to obtain the goods that will satisfy the preference.

Economics and Culture

Biologists, and even some anthropologists who should know better, have mistakenly equated culture with behavior that is "socially acquired." A field-worker who looks at several groups of chimpanzees and finds differences among the groups, differences that cannot be explained by either genetic or environmental factors, assumes that the differences must have been learned, and learned socially, because the behavior is seen in all members of the group. From this assumption comes the conclusion that the differences are cultural. But many socially acquired behaviors are trivial.

Driving on the right side of the road rather than on the left, definitely a socially acquired practice, is one trivial behavior that has no cultural significance. When, on a given date and hour, Swedish drivers reversed to driving on the other side of the road, Swedish culture did not change one whit. (Neither did the accident rate.) Suppose, however, that on the same date and hour, Sweden had converted to capitalism, selling off all its government-owned companies, or had converted to Roman Catholicism or Orthodox Judaism, replacing its Lutheran ministers with priests or rabbis?

Why is it that the religion Sweden observes, or the economy it practices, is incontrovertibly part of Swedish culture, whereas the side of the road on which Swedes drive is not? If we follow the biologists and misguided anthropologists in defining culture as "socially transmitted behavior" we cannot even properly raise this question. To do justice to the question, we require a concept of culture that recognizes the difference between socially acquired behaviors that are and are not significant.

When we look closely at the behaviors that the fieldworkers have called culture—chimpanzees in some groups hold hands when grooming, solicit sex by stripping leaves, and so on—we see that all their examples are trivial, analogous to driving on one side of the road or the other. What might constitute a nontrivial social practice in these animals?

Among chimpanzees, it would be nontrivial if animals that hold hands when grooming are found to deal more kindly with one another, or if males that solicit sex by stripping leaves are found to cajole females rather than force them into compliance. These consequential changes, though originating in trivial acts, might be found to develop slowly across generations. But long-term observations of chimpanzees have thus far revealed nothing of this sort. Acts that began as trivial, remained trivial; they did not develop into attitudinal changes of a kind that verge on culture.

Cultural differences among humans depend on belief systems and economic forces and express themselves with special clarity in the treatment of the weak by the strong. The strong—the rich, educated, free, majority members—and the weak—the poor, uneducated, slave, minority members—and the division of power they represent are found in every human society. And in every society the strong oppress the weak. The exact form of the oppression and the rationalizations offered for it are determined by the culture of the society.

Thus, criminals are punished in all societies but in very different ways, each culture offering a justification for the way it has chosen (be it whipping, cutting off hands, or lethal injections). Women suffer economic infringements in all countries, even the most "advanced" democracies, but those infringements are far greater in some countries than in others. A Muslim woman who defies her father's choice of husband risks physical disfigurement or even death. This abuse appears to arise from the Muslim belief system, which gives women a lowly status (and men an impunity unknown in the West), but in fact, as in many cases of cultural difference, the underlying factor is economic. The daughter's disobedience denies her family a connection with a carefully chosen family that could have advanced its cause economically and socially. Economics and culture, both uniquely human developments, go hand in hand.

Social Institutions

In a typical hunter-gatherer band of thirty or forty, everyone knew everyone else personally. Many were kin. There was no rich, no poor, no economic hierarchy. There was not even any formal social organization, and social power (like the kill of the hunting party) was shared more or less equitably.

But the steadily mounting population put an end to the small bands, forcing the establishment of ever larger social units. The sharing of social power came to an end when the governance of personal relations was displaced by a variety of institutions, culminating in today's state and church.

With the advent of the church and state people were used in a way they had never been used by a band. From their inception, states have used people to fight their battles—to conquer other states or to avoid being conquered by them. Those who live within the territory of a state belong to the state. They are its automatic members. But the church, not having any "real" territory had no automatic members. It needed to inculcate members; it did this by appealing to people's "minds," converting people to a belief system capable of creating and holding its members together.

A band did not use people in order to perpetuate itself. A band was not an external organization, an organization that existed independently of its members, as were both church and state. Indeed, a band *was* its members.[4]

The equity of the hunter-gatherer band did not eliminate sexual rivalry or prevent males from occasionally killing sexual rivals for women. It did not prevent hunter-gatherers from fighting border skirmishes where the point was to bloody the neighbor, nor from attacking another group to right a wrong and returning home safely, suffering as little damage as possible. The "natural" hostility that all human groups feel for other groups sometimes flares into violence; but it was not until the church and state activated simple intergroup hostility with their belief systems that hostility became vicious, and humans avenged themselves on infidels or sacrificed themselves for a higher glory.

Belief systems, like intergroup hostility, are innate, or nearly so; one cannot picture humans without belief systems (see Chapter 6 for further discussion). But belief systems as such are not inherently evil; they are no more vicious than simple intergroup hostility. Hunter-gatherers had both without massacring one another. Only when these elements were joined in a spurious way by the church and state did their combination become lethal.

The Core of the Book

To understand the sweeping consequences of the accidents that befell the human, we must understand not only the accidents, but the mind that reacted to them. Had similar accidents befallen another species, the outcome is almost certain to have been totally different. If chimpanzees, for example, were to lose their food supply, starvation would be a more likely consequence than agriculture. The invention of agriculture depends on causal reasoning, on recognizing that seeds grow when planted in the ground, and causal reasoning is not part of the chimpanzee's thought processes.

In order to obtain a clear account of the mind that reacted to the accidents, we turn to the core of the book, the ten chapters that follow. Chapter 1 discusses the infant's modules, the innate learning devices that provide a framework for what ultimately develops into adult knowledge.

Chapters 2 through 5 focus on imitation, pedagogy, and language. They describe competences whose ancient origins can be discerned in our ancestor, *H. erectus*. Theory of mind, or the attribution of mental states to others, claims a chapter because it is the cornerstone of an elaborate human social competence. An ancient competence too, for as Chapter 6 shows, rudiments of theory of mind can be found in the chimpanzee.

In belief or conviction (Chapter 7), we encounter for the first time a competence that is uniquely human and not of ancient origin. Conviction can be produced only through a special use of language.

With causal reasoning and analogy (Chapters 8 and 9), we depart from the social side of the human and turn to the need to understand and explain. "Why did this happen?" "How did it happen?" The answer to these questions occurs when the human can say what *caused* the event to occur. Science is the incredibly sucessful system invented to satisfy the human need to understand and explain. The system benefits from analogies but leans heavily on causal analysis. These two chapters are laid side by side because causal and analogical reasoning are complementary processes. The first explains the world by dissecting its processes into their particulars; the second, by uniting parts of the world, by finding similarities in disparate events. The human propensity to discover metaphoric connections and similarities in unexpected quarters goes well beyond analogies; it is so far reaching that an entire chapter, equivalence, is devoted to the topic.

These ten chapters, which contrast the social and nonsocial sides of the mind and introduce the modules that are the initial directors of human learning, present the major components of the human mind.

In the Conclusion, we return once more to cultural change; this time, however, we examine change produced not by environmental accidents but deliberately, by the individual. Humans who understand their minds, who understand the competences that they command, are in a unique position, one with little historical precedent. They can knowingly change themselves, though perhaps not so much themselves as their children, by changing the educational process that molds these children.

The world longs to improve the education of its children, and perhaps nowhere more so than in the United States. And the American commitment to education is serious: People are willing to pay for it. But the discussion of how to improve education—making classes smaller, giving more time to reading and science, improving teachers' salaries, perhaps giving education over to business—has not kept pace with the commitment. While most of the proposals offered are reasonable, they are not substantive. Substantive changes depend on content, not on the size of the class but on what is taught there.

Content depends on a theory of education that can be derived only by understanding the mind that is to be educated. The modules are the original "teachers," guiding the initial learning of the infant. They are remarkably effective educators, laying the groundwork for language, arithmetic, theory of mind, music well within the first five years of life. Schools cannot hope to duplicate the achievement of the modules. But education as a *cultural* process can take a cue from education as a *biological* process.

What has evolution prepared the child to learn? Of the topics for which the child is prepared, are there any that are overlooked? Or are not taught at all? Are there topics for which evolution has not prepared the child but which must be learned nevertheless, and could be more readily learned if they were linked to topics for which the child has been prepared? Finally, is evolution as flawless as the impression given, or has it failed on occasion, and endowed the child with false intuitions that need to be corrected?

If what the child is taught is based not on tradition, but on what evolution has prepared the child to learn, the cultural process of learning will come far closer to the process biology has itself provided to every child.

Notes

1. The original theory of human origins proposed that today's human population migrated from Africa about 100,000 years ago and replaced the early populations inhabiting Europe and Asia. A more recent theory suggests not one but two distinct waves of migration. These groups, rather than replacing the existing populations, interbred with them "for hundreds of thousands of years." This view proposes that the genes of today's humans carry vestiges of the genes of extinct branches of the human family, including those of the Neanderthals.
2. While other events could have led to the invention of writing, they did not. In the course of human history, only surplus goods have led to writing. Not every group that adopted agriculture went on to invent writing, but no group that did *not* adopt agriculture ever invented writing. The Mayans are a partial exception to this generalization, not because they invented writing without having developed agriculture—they never invented writing—but because they invented another

symbol system, a system of representing numbers by means of knots tied in rope, and this system did not arise from agricultural surpluses. The Mayans may have the distinction of being the only group that developed a complex society that was not based on writing.

3. The development of knowledge depended on writing, though not on an alphabet, for systematic knowledge developed in China as well. The Chinese too had writing, but their system was based on ideograms, not on an alphabet.

4. In all likelihood women enjoyed greater social equality when living as hunter-gatherers than at any time since. When the governance of hunter-gatherer groups passed from personal relations to institutions—church, state, and army—women were the biggest losers. Although physical strength can be a determinant of status among men, it is not such a determinant between men and women. Men have always deferred to women on a personal basis.

The sharing of social power came to an end when personal relations were displaced by institutions because the church and state were composed exclusively of men. And though when acting individually men tended to share power with women, they did not do so when acting as a group. The all-male institutions enforced regulations highly detrimental to women.

Chapter 1
Modules
The New Infant

Infants are highly visual. When shown events they do not expect to see, they are puzzled and look at them longer than at events they do expect to see. But what do infants expect to see?[1] Expectancies can come from either of two sources: personal experience or the experiences of one's ancestors. Personal experience is easy to explain. If an infant sees a sequence of events that is repeated, and the sequence then changes, the infant's expectancies will be violated and she will look at the changed sequence longer than usual. For instance, an infant is shown a bird that flies repeatedly into its nest and feeds its fledglings. One day it flies into the nest without feeding them. The change will surprise the infant, who will look longer than usual.

Infants can also inherit expectancies from their ancestors, expectancies that were vital for the survival of the species. An example of such an expectancy is illustrated in the following experiment. Two groups of infants of about four months of age are shown a ball which is supported by a platform. The platform is removed and one group is shown that the ball falls; the other group that the ball does not fall. The infants in the second group look longer, indicating that they saw an event they did not expect to see. This observation suggests that the idea of "gravity," that unsupported objects will fall, is one that infants inherit from their ancestors.

Over the past twenty years research has shown that infants have inherited expectancies not only about how physical objects "act," but also about psychological and biological objects, about language, number, spatial navigation, and music. Indeed, infants have inherited expectancies in all the domains into which human problem solving can be divided. These expectancies are an integral part of the infants' modules.

Modules are innate devices that guide the infant's learning in all domains that are basic to human knowledge. Although every module is unique, shaped to solve a specific problem, all modules operate in the same general way: They act only when stimulated by the information relevant to the problem for which the module was designed. By monitoring the information to which an infant can react, the module protects the infant from distracting information and from entertaining false hypotheses. The module's action, like that of all reflexive devices, is fast and certain. Modules process information at great speed because they do not "think" or weigh alternatives.

An infant's modular intuitions develop as the infant ages. In our example drawn from the physical domain, the four-month-old infant is surprised when the platform is removed and the unsupported object does not fall; but what the four-month-old accepts as "support" is merely that the platform make contact with the side of the object. The five-month-old, however, requires more—that at least part of the object be supported from below—and the eight-month-old increases his demands, requiring that the entire object be supported from below. The requirements of the eight-month-old infant are comparable to those of the adult.

Not all of an infant's learning is governed by modules. There are hosts of events in the world that do not concern the problems for which modules were designed. These events are learned by *domain-general learning*. For instance, the surprise that the infant shows when a bird flies into the nest and does not feed its fledglings is based on domain-general learning.

Ordinarily, modular and domain-general learning do not interact; they go their separate ways. But there may be cases in which a module will interfere with domain-general learning. In these cases the infant would not learn something that she might otherwise learn. While an older child could learn that objects sometimes "fall up" (when blown from below, for example), it is doubtful that an infant could learn such a relation. Probably the infant's physical module would inhibit the attention to objects that fall up.

But why would the module not prevent the older child from learning that objects sometimes fall up? Modules are not permanent. They operate during a critical period only and cease functioning thereafter. That modules have this character is shown most clearly in the language module.

Children learn their native language with amazing ease, acquiring the fundamentals of adult grammar between their third and fourth years. Adults, by contrast, have great difficulty acquiring a second language, presumably because they have lost the advantage of the language module. Evidence for the transitory influence of the language module also comes from clinical studies. Language, normally acquired in the left hemisphere, suffers a loss when this hemisphere is damaged. The loss is permanent in the older child. But in the younger child, because the language module still functions, the loss is not permanent. He can reacquire language in the right hemisphere.

Since the best evidence for modular learning comes from the language domain, it is no surprise to find that the idea of modularity was proposed originally by the linguist Noam Chomsky. He based his argument on the kinds of rules that children learn as they acquire language. Their learning does not depend upon feedback (reward or punishment), a prerequisite for domain-general learning. Nor do children acquire language by imitation. The distinctive characteristics of learning that Chomsky unearthed in the child's acquisition of language have since been generalized to become the basis of all modular learning.

Later, the philosopher Jerry Fodor and the cognitive anthropologist Dan Sperber elaborated Chomsky's distinction, as have many others. Fodor made the reflexive nature of a module clear, proposing specific mechanisms by which a module works; Sperber set the idea in the context of evolution, demonstrating the unexpected compatibility of modules with cultural novelty. Today, the idea of modularity—some version of an innate reflexive device that guides infant learning—is deeply entrenched in cognitive science.

Human and Animal Modules

The seminal paper by J. Lettvin and his associates, "What the Frog's Eye Tells the Frog's Brain," describes the effect that a certain visual pattern has on the frog's brain. Objects of a certain size that move in a "quick, jerky pattern" cause the coiled tongue of the frog to unfurl; if the animal were in the field and not the laboratory, it would almost certainly catch an insect.

In the honeybee, a modular component adjusts the orientation of the bee's dance to changes in position of the Sun that occur during the bee's return flight to the hive. The bee's computation, though more complex than that of the frog, is no more interpretive. The bee does not react to the position of the Sun, nor does the frog react to the position of an insect. Neither frog nor bee has the concept of "object" of which Sun and insect are examples. The bee reacts to a luminosity in the sky, just as the frog reacts to a "quick, jerky pattern." Animals like these do not have the cognitive capacity for concepts.

The infant's modular processes, too, are reflexive, but they do not culminate in motor reactions. The infant's modules are a mental device. They guide the infant's acquisition of the basic competences of the species, those that enable the human to cope with the world.

The Physical Module

How does an infant identify a physical object? The extensive research done by the developmental psychologist Elizabeth Spelke and her associates indicates that features such as color, shape, and size are of little importance to the infant in the identification of a physical object. What does matter is how the object moves.

Infants expect a physical object to move in a smooth continuous straight line, not to stop and start, not to disappear and reappear, not to come apart as it moves, and not to pick up—or adhere to—other objects. When an object departs from these regularities infants are surprised, and look longer than usual.

At the age of four months, human infants have already formed preliminary ideas about all the basic physical relations—not only support, but also containment, launching, and so on—and progressively refine these ideas over the course of the next few months. The developmental psychologist Renee Baillargeon finds that infants achieve a nearly adult level of understanding of all basic physical relations by about their eighth month.[2]

The Psychological Module

Research in the psychological domain lags behind that in both the language and physical domain. Thus, in discussing the psychological module we will speak not of established findings but of a model and theory. The model has been tested and tacked down at key points in some cases.

Motion is no less central in the psychological domain than it is in the physical. The two principal grounds on which infants distinguish psychological and physical objects both concern motion. Physical objects move only when acted upon. Psychological objects, by contrast, move spontaneously, starting and stopping their own motion. In addition, psychological objects show a unique form of movement, goal-directed action. A goal-directed object often follows a consistent path, one that converges on a "target" such as another object, the top of a hill, or a break in a wall. However, the goal-directed object does not always follow a consistent path. Sometimes its target will be another self-propelled object which changes its location. The goal-directed object will then track the other object, changing its path in doing so.

An infant who sees an object that is both self-propelled and goal-directed automatically interprets the object as intentional (Figure 1.1). And when two intentional objects interact, the infant interprets the interaction in terms of value+/− (Figure 1.2). Infants use one of two criteria in assigning value: intensity or intervention. Low-intensity contacts—caressing, licking, or patting of one object by another—are coded "positive," while high-intensity contacts—hitting, biting, or kicking of an object by another—are coded "negative."[3]

Further, an action is coded positive when one object "helps" another to achieve its goal, and coded negative when one object "hinders" another from achieving its goal. The model predicts, and tests confirm, that infants will find an equivalence between gentle actions and "helping," on the one hand, and between harsh actions and hindering, on the other.

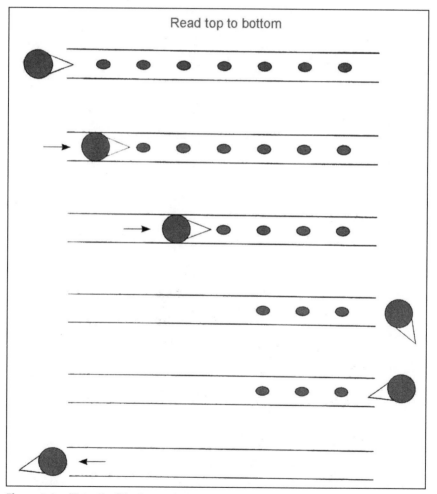

Figure 1.1 "Intention" is shown when a creature returns for food that it has overlooked. *(Courtesy of Marc Wexler)*

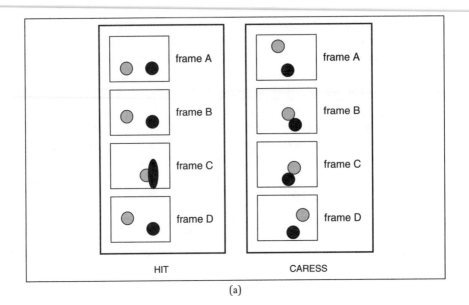

(a)

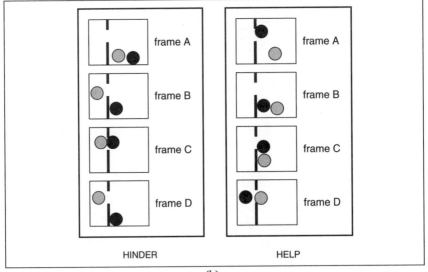

(b)

Figure 1.2 Computer-generated interactions of figures illustrating (*a*) hit and caress and (*b*) hinder and help. These animations were used in our test of the infant's psychological module.

The model assumes that infants also have an idea of reciprocation. An infant who has observed an object being caressed or helped, hit or hindered, will expect that object to retaliate. And the infant will expect the object to retaliate with an action that has the same value+/−. In other words, the infant expects the hit object to return the hit, the caressed object to return the caress.

Intentional objects that move together freely are, the model assumes, seen as a *group;* infants expect members of a group to act positively on one another and to coreciprocate. By contrast, when one object forces another to move, the infant sees the forced object as the other's *possession.* Possession has interesting consequences with respect to the attribution of value+/−. Normally infants assign value to the actions of intentional objects only; they do not assign value+/− to the kicking or caressing of a stone, for example. An infant who sees a stone as a possession, however, will assign value+/− to actions directed at the stone.

Let us suppose that an infant, having lost interest in looking at the positive events of caressing and helping, is shown a negative event, say hitting. The change produces dishabituation, and the infant's interest is renewed in looking. Ordinarily dishabituation means no more than the resumption of responding. The concept of value+/−, however, introduces the possibility of a new view of dishabituation, one we will call *dynamic dishabituation.* Dynamic dishabituation may produce a hidden effect, one that can be shown by taking a step that has never been taken: returning the infant to the originally habituated condition.

When we do so, however, we may be in for a surprise: The infant's interest in the original condition has been restored, the infant having regained an interest in looking at positive events! In looking at hitting, and thus habituating to negative value+/−, the infant is no longer habituated to positive value+/−.

While dynamic dishabituation is strictly a speculative hypothesis, the effect of dynamic dishabituation on a two-valued, bipolar system like that of value+/− would be highly advantageous. An infant, habituated to positive value+/−, dishabituates when shown negative events. In looking at the negative events, however, the infant's reactivity to positive events is restored. Conversely, an infant habituated to negative value+/− dishabituates when shown positive events; but looking at positive events will restore the infant's reactivity to negative events. The advantage of dynamic dishabituation is that an individual's responsivity to the value+/− system cannot be shut down.

There may be systems for which continued responsivity is of no particular advantage as well as systems which, because of their makeup, cannot be shut down. Number is a system that cannot be shut down. An individual who has been habituated to some group of numbers can always be shown a new number; the infinitude of numbers makes it impossible to shut down the reactivity to number. Color, on the other hand, is perhaps a system that can be temporarily inactivated. Habituating an organism to all the wavelengths to which it is sensitive should render the individual insensitive to color. While such an outcome is unlikely, the point is that any system composed of finite members (like color) and governed by ordinary dishabituation could be shut down—in this case, leaving the individual temporarily color blind.

The inactivation of the value+/− system could be harmful to the individual. A system that enables an individual to code social interactions as either positive or negative, which controls, among other things, the disposition for reciprocation, is one that may need to be protected from shutdown. Dynamic dishabituation would prevent the value+/− system from ever closing down, even temporarily.

The Biology Module

The developmental psychologist Susan Carey insists that the infant does not have a biological module; what appears to be biological knowledge is actually psychological. Carey points out that young children understand hunger to be an unpleasant psychological state and regard eating as a way of relieving their discomfort. Children do not grasp the physiological consequences of eating until they are about ten years of age, when they learn in school about digestion, the circulation of blood, respiration, and the like.

If Carey is right, the science of biology differs from that of physics and psychology in that the latter two fields are derived in part from primitive notions that are an integral part of the infant's modules. And yet the claim that the infant does not have a biological module is still warmly disputed. The developmental psychologist Frank Keil and his associates, for instance, have demonstrated numerous biological distinctions that are understood by young children, among them the difference between communicable and otherwise acquired conditions: One can catch a cold from someone else, but not a sprained ankle.

Larry Hirschfeld, a cognitive anthropologist, claims that children discriminate between adopted and natural children, recognizing that adopted children, though living with "parents" for a long time, never come to resemble them; natural children, in contrast, despite living apart for long periods, do resemble their parents.

The cognitive anthropologist Scott Atran sees an entirely different content for the biological module: the heirarchical classification system which every traditional society imposes on its surrounding plants and animals, a system that bears a striking resemblance to scientific taxonomy.

All these proposals are well documented, and important in showing the rich and unexpectedly diverse lines along which biological thinking develops in both children and adults. But as counterproposals to Carey, they suffer from a common defect: Unlike the findings that support the physical and psychological modules, they are not findings from infants. The findings of Keil and Hirschfeld come from children who are three and a half years of age and older, while those of Atran come from adults.

However, the early age at which children grasp the biological ideas of inheritance and contagion is puzzling. How can children grasp such ideas, if they have no evolutionary precursors? And what might such precursors look like?

Notice that contagion and inheritance both concern the same basic process: the transmission of a condition from one object to another. A condition such as skin color or shape of eye—is permanent in inheritance but transitory in contagion; contagious diseases typically are not permanent.

Perhaps the precursor of the idea of inheritance takes this form: Infants expect small objects that are "looked after" by large objects to "grow" and come to resemble the large objects. An expectation of this kind could have arisen in the Pleistocene, because most children grew up to resemble their parents. There were few adopted children. Only, however, if infants, when tested, are surprised when small objects do not grow to resemble their "parents," can we take this speculation seriously.

The evidence for contagion is appreciably less direct, and therefore the child's conception of contagion may depend more on learning. One could test for the possibility, however, that an infant has a precursor in the case of contagion. We show the infant two objects that share some transitory condition, such as coughing. We show the infant that in one case the two objects previously had been in close contact. Will the infant expect to see the transmission of coughing in this case, but be surprised at the transmission of coughing in the case where two objects had not previously been in close contact?

The biological module may have a content different from that of both the physical and psychological modules because biological events lack the perceivability of both physical and psychological events. The fall of unsupported objects, the launching of one object by another, one object hitting another—all are highly perceivable. So are the sounds of language. This is not true, however, of the biological domain.

Many fundamental biological processes—for example, digestion, impregnation, respiration, and circulation—are not perceivable. Neither are many fundamental biological objects—blood corpuscles, ova, genes, and the like. Invisible events cannot lead to evolution. When events are visible, however, individuals can react to them in different ways, and some will react to them in a way that will lead them to outreproduce others.

Because the form or shape of an animal *is* highly perceivable, the biological module could contain the elementary body plan of the animal. The plan could consist mainly of bilateral symmetry and a gradient of sensitivity ranging from head to tail. Characteristics such as these could be "taught" to the infant by the module.

When an infant is shown an asymmetrical form, such as the circle with a beak seen in Figure 1.3, the infant may treat the protruberance as the "head," attributing special sentience to it and perhaps even an ability to "see." That the infant treats the protruberance in this way can be tested by passing the "asymmetrical form" through a baffle.

When traveling "head first" the object should pass through smoothly (because it can "see" the baffle), but when traveling tail first it should bump the baffle. If the infant takes this outcome for granted (head first, smooth sailing; tail first, bumpy), but is surprised by the opposite (smooth sailing, tail first; head first, bumpy), this would support the hypothesis that infants attribute visionlike sentience to the "head" and that the biological module may not be empty after all!

If infants did indeed distinguish a sentient from a nonsentient end, this could help explain why three- to-four-year-old children are better informed about the head than the tail of animals. For young children *do* know far more about the heads of animals. This can be shown by cutting toy animals in half and requiring children to put the fronts and backs together again.

In one test with children we used ten varieties of such toy animals—dogs, cats, camels, lions, and so on—all of the same size and color. Shape was therefore the only cue available for the children. Children were shown the animals in the context of a series of match-to-sample tests in which, in half the tests, the front of the animal was the sample and the rears of two animals served as alternatives, while in the other half of the tests the rear was the sample and the fronts of two animals were alternatives. (See Figure 1.4.)

Three- to-four-year-old children consistently failed the tests of placing, for example, the head of a sheep with the back of a lion and the back of an elephant with the head of a dog. While this might seem to suggest that children have little knowledge of animals, the truth is far more interesting: Chil-

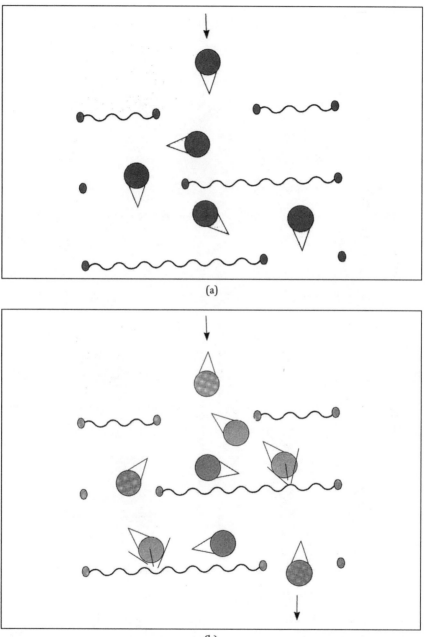

Figure 1.3 An infant who attributes "seeing" to the head will expect the head to (*a*) pass smoothly through a baffle when traveling head-first, but (*b*) blunder when traveling backward.

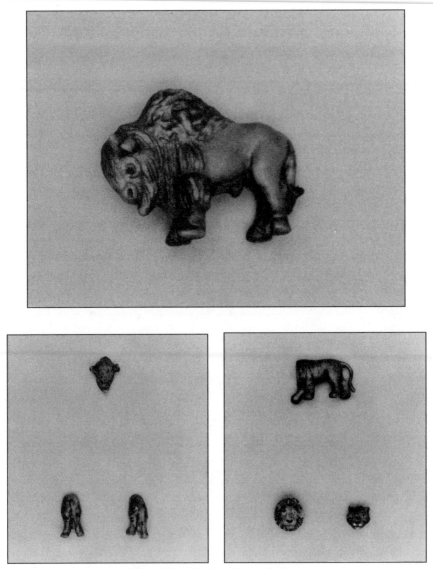

Figure 1.4   Matching up the heads and tails of toy animals.

dren know more about one end than the other! And this can be demonstrated by using the names of the animals as the sample and either the heads
or backs as alternatives.

   If you say "cow" to children, while offering the choice of a head of a cow
and that of a lion, they will do well. But if you say "cow" while offering the

choice of the *back* of a cow and that of a lion, they will fail the test. Three-to-four-year-old children matched names to the front halves of the ten animals at about the 85 percent correct level, but they performed at chance level when matching names to the back halves.

And why do children know so much more about the front of animals? Perhaps children spend little time looking at the backs of animals. But if so, why? Could it be because the infant's floor plan of an animal assigns special sentience to the head, making the head salient and thereby causing it to capture the infant's attention?[4]

The Number Module

There was a time when the number faculty was seen as part of language, or more specifically, as an interaction between language and the handling of objects and collections. Consequently the need for a separate number module was never considered; number was just another of the endless competences that could be milked from that most provident of cows, language! And number, too, was seen as setting humans apart from animals. All of this has changed.

When number is used for the counting of objects, numerical quantity appears to be digital or discontinuous. But the discovery of an analog representation that underlies numerical quantity has transformed the "number faculty" from a digital to an analog system. Moreover, the "number faculty," rather than being limited to creatures who speak, is found in preverbal infants and animals.

Building on the work of many distinguished predecessors, the cognitive neuroscientist Stanislaus Dehaene has summarized evidence that shows convincingly that animals, preverbal infants, and human adults all share a common number sense. This number sense consists of a mental line, a representation of numerical quantity that is found in the brain. This idea of a mental line, proposed many years ago, now is seen as being right at the foundation of our sense of numerical quantity.

The numbers that humans use when counting and doing arithmetic calculations—1, 2, 3; I, II, III; one, two, three—are mapped onto the mental line so as to divide it into pieces. Although modern humans use arabic or word numbers when doing arithmetical computations, their computations do not actually start with such symbols. They rely on the mental line.

The main evidence for this claim comes from the finding that the discrimination between two numbers improves as the numerical distance between them increases, the so-called numerical distance effect. This effect is seen when humans compare the numerosity of two sets of dots, and also when they process arabic numbers or number words.

Even a rat or pigeon, when required to indicate which of two numerical quantities is greater (or whether two quantities are the same or different), will show the numerical distance effect. When the quantities are close together, animals are slower to respond and make more mistakes. The fact that adult humans show the same effect when numbers are presented in the form of a symbolic notation suggests that the human brain automatically converts the symbolic form of numbers into an analogical form, that is, into the mental line.

If the format in the brain were indeed digital, were a sequence of discrete pieces, there would be a "decade effect." An adult would find 59 smaller than, say 65, as quickly as finding 50 to be smaller than 65. Actually, however, this is not so. There is no decade effect. The mind of the human adult works more slowly when comparing 59 to 65 than when comparing 50 to 65.

Number size, a second effect, also supports the argument for the mental line, the idea of an underlying, continuous representation of number. A human adult's discrimination of any two numbers that are equally far apart worsens as the numbers increase in size. It takes more time (and the likelihood of error is greater) for a human adult to decide whether 9 is larger than 8 than whether 4 is larger than 3, for the time it takes to traverse the number line increases with the size of the number. The adult shows this effect whether the numbers are presented as sets of dots or written as arabic or word numbers.

Animals show the same effect. Pigeons discriminate between, say, forty-five and fifty pecks more quickly and accurately than between fifty and fifty-five pecks. These data add to the suggestion that the human and animal representation of number is comparable, namely that the underlying representation is continuous and gets "fuzzy" or difficult to deal with as quantity increases.

Preverbal infants and animals can discriminate numerical quantity. An infant habituated to the quantity 2 will dishabituate when shown the quantity 3 or 1, and the habituation/dishabituation can be shown to be controlled specifically by numerical quantity. If two rabbits are changed in color or size, or are replaced by two toy cars, or their position is changed, the infant will not resume looking. Only when the two rabbits are replaced by three rabbits or by one rabbit will the infant dishabituate, that is, recover her interest in looking.

The same outcome can be demonstrated in chimpanzees, though in their case we use the match-to-sample test. When given a sample that consists of, say, three objects, and alternatives consisting of three and four objects, chimpanzees immediately select the correct alternative. Their choice is not affected by changes in the color, size, composition, or position of the objects.

Does this mean that infants and chimpanzees are counting? Counting—as originally formulated in the seminal work by Rochel Gelman, a developmental psychologist, and Randy Gallistel, a comparative psychologist—is a competence that presupposes several subcompetences. The first of the subcompetences is that of one-to-one correspondence, the placing of a "counter" into correspondence with each object. Children do this spontaneously, when about two and a half years of age. Chimpanzees do not. When given marbles to be placed in correspondence with each block in a long row of blocks, chimpanzees place one marble by some blocks but two by others, and they move marbles from block to block.[5]

Another subcompetence is the ability to use a consistent sequence of spoken numbers such as are used in counting. Also perfectly acceptable are such idiosyncratic sequences as 2, 5, 9 or 1, 3, 6 (which some children use), provided that the child uses the sequence consistently. Cardinality, the final subcompetence of counting, is the recognition that the last number used in counting a set represents the quantity of the set.

Natural systems for counting and arithmetical computations are confined neither to the human brain nor to the brains of higher primates. Natural systems for dealing with numerical quantity are to be found in the nervous systems not only of rats and pigeons but also, certain evidence suggests, of bees and other invertebrates. Clearly, counting and arithmetical operations are exceedingly primitive.

Pigeons and rats count not only their own responses but external events such as light flashes and bursts of sound. Recently several psychologists (J. Gibbon, R. M. Church, and W. H. Meck) employed a model in an attempt to explain just how such counting occurs. The model they proposed consists of a pulse former, a gate, and an accumulator. When the animal perceives an event to be counted, the pulse former sends a burst of pulses through the gate; the closing of the gate registers in the accumulator, increasing the magnitude by one. The last magnitude in the accumulator—which occurs when nothing remains to be counted—represents the numerical quantity of the set and is deposited in long-term memory.

Recently, the primatologist Tetsuro Matsuzawa and his student N. Kawai reported on an ingenious test in which a chimpanzee that had been taught visual names for numbers up to 9 was able to arrange any five numbers in an ascending order from memory. The numbers were shown on a screen in a random order—say, 1, 4, 2, 9, 6—and the animal's task was to touch the numbers in an ascending order. Once the animal chose the first number the other numbers were covered, and the animal had to recall the subsequent numbers from memory. The animal was slow to make its first response after the covering of the first number—say, 700 seconds—suggesting that the animal first memorized the position of all the numbers on the board, then made its subsequent choices more rapidly.

These striking results add to the growing evidence that humans and animals deal in a comparable way with numerical quantity. But while they may use the same mechanisms, even the same parts of the brain, how far up the line does the similarity go?

The chimpanzee can produce ascending orders from memory—even doing so perhaps in a human fashion—but does the animal comprehend the concepts of ascending and descending? A match-to-sample test will give us a quick answer.

The animal can be required to match ascending sequences, such as 2,4,8,9 and 1,3,5,7, and descending sequences, such as 7,6,3,1 and 8,5,4,2. If the animal comprehends ascending and descending order, it is appropriate to ask whether it also comprehends the concept of monotonic order. Could the animal match an ascending sequence to a descending sequence rather than to a scrambled or disordered sequence? Tests described later (in Chapter 2) demonstrate that three-year-old children comprehend monotonic order but that young chimpanzees do not.

Infants as young as four months of age are sensitive to the operations of simple addition and subtraction. An infant is shown, say, one or two toy rabbits standing on a stage. A curtain then is dropped, concealing the rabbit(s), and as the infant watches, an experimenter reaches behind the curtain to remove or add a rabbit. The curtain is then drawn to reveal a stage on which there is one rabbit, in some trials, two, in others.

If the infant is shown two rabbits originally, and the experimenter removes one of them, the infant shows surprise if, when the curtain is lifted, two rabbits remain on the stage. If the infant is shown one rabbit originally, and the experimenter adds another, the infant is surprised if, when the curtain is lifted, only one rabbit is on the stage. We owe these informative experiments, which have been replicated many times, to Karen Wynne, a developmental psychologist.

The number module is one of only two—the language module is the other—for which there is supporting neural evidence. A location in the inferior infraparietal area of both hemispheres appears to be dedicated to numerical computation; adults who have suffered damage to this area cannot perform normal numerical tasks. When the damage is confined to only one side of the brain there is no impediment, because the other hemisphere can still carry out the necessary task.

It is certainly supportive of the idea of a module to find a brain area dedicated to a task. A biological "entity" that serves to process the comprehension and production of a particular kind of knowledge *should* be located in a specific area of the brain, and ideally, homologous areas in animal brains should be found. Parts of the brain that control monkey calls have been shown to be homologous with parts of the brain that control the human motor behavior involved in speech production. It is hoped, of course, that language and number will not long remain the only modules for which dedicated parts of the brain have been identified.

The Module of Space

When it comes to spatial problems, one can say this: A creature needs a representation of its spatial geography, as well as an ability to locate its own position within that geography. A wasp seems to meet these requirements, because after having completed a burrow, it travels a distance many times that of its own body (equivalent to more than a 100-mile trip for a human), stuns a caterpillar, and then drags the caterpillar back to its burrow where it conceals the caterpillar and implants it with its eggs. But how does the wasp figure out how to return to its burrow?

The wasp's search for a caterpillar, like that of many animals in search of food, often involves a most circuitous path, with many changes both in direction and distance. Yet the wasp and the animals that take circuitous paths when foraging for food are able to return home on a straight path. They do this by dead reckoning, which is to say, integrating twice over the values of the outgoing path, a mechanism so impressive as to seem improbable. Yet the mechanism is found even in "lowly" creatures such as certain rodents and ants and wasps.

Note that finding a mate generally does not depend on solving spatial problems; every creature carries a built-in stimulus—typically an odor, sometimes a call, occasionally both—that identifies its gender. Males (and sometimes females) go in search of the identifying stimulus at certain times of the year. The searching individual simply homes in on the identifying marker, requiring neither a representation of space nor a knowledge of its own location in space. Perhaps mating is too important to the survival of a species to be left to anything but a most simple mechanism.

Species can combine a knowledge of geography with identifying stimuli. The rat offers a nice example, for it forms a mental map of the location of foods in the area and combines it with food odors it encounters on the body of returning conspecifics. When the rat encounters a food odor, its map guides it directly to the location of the food. The chimpanzee too may have an internal representation of the location of foods in the area, and use it in combination with the food calls of its conspecifics.

The space module has all the advantages and drawbacks of other modules. It provides an efficient mechanism for solving certain problems, but is blind to other alternatives. This blindness is dramatically shown in how the module copes with disorientation.

Rats solve the problem of disorientation by using strictly geometric cues. In a study done by the comparative psychologists Ken Chang and Randy Gallistel, rats first were shown the location of food in the corner of a parallelogram-shaped box, then disoriented by being rotated in the dark, and finally returned to the box. When the rats made errors in their search, by going to the wrong corner, the corner was not just any wrong corner but one diagonally opposite to the one that had been baited—the corner geometrically equivalent to the baited one. Even when offered conspicuous landmarks—black versus white walls, the smell of licorice versus that of peppermint—the rats ignored the perceptual cues and relied instead on the geometric properties of the box.

Elizabeth Spelke and her student, Linda Hermer, have found that young children, when disoriented, respond as rats do: The children they studied ignored landmarks in favor of geometric cues. Toddlers also erred by searching in the corner diagonally opposite the correct one. Older children and adults combine both geometry and landmarks in their search. The researchers argue that children and adults use words to rehearse the location of the landmarks; they confirmed their point by showing that adults failed to use landmarks while searching for the target, when required to repeat a sentence out loud (thus interfering with the rehearsed words).

A Module for Music

The evolutionary origins of music remain a profound challenge. Recently, the cognitive psychologist C. L. Krumhansl argued for the importance of experience in the composition, performance, and even the appreciation of music. Formal training in music improves the ability of children (as well as adults) to perceive and retain music. Researchers who emphasize the role of experience point to the striking differences among the musical traditions of the world. (See Figure 1.5.)

More recent discussions of this question, undertaken by the developmental psychologist Sandra Trehub and her associates, make a strong case

Figure 1.5 Kalahari San (Bushman) playing a musical bow. *(From R. B. Lee and I. De-Vore, Kalahari Hunter-Gatherers, Harvard University Press, 1976)*

for the role of innate factors. Although the musical traditions of the East and West are indisputably different, certain kinds of sequences turn up in all music. Chinese music is based on two-valued scales, as is western music. Indeed, there is no music that is not built on such a scale.

Trehub et al. build their case for innate factors by identifying human auditory predispositions. Biases found in the processing of auditory sequences by adults are also found in the infant. Like adults, infants show a preference for small intervals and can better discriminate pitch changes in a two-valued than in a one-valued scale. These biases appear very early, long before the infant can possibly have learned them.

Humans, infants as well as adults, are sensitive to the contour and rhythm of melody. Changing the pitch or tempo of a melody does not change the melody for human listeners. Monkeys, by contrast, identify melodies on the basis of specific pitch and tempo, absolute rather than relative factors. A human infant, when played the same song at different tempos or in different keys, recognizes the equivalence; the monkey does not.

Aesthetic and emotional factors are integral to music. Fortunately, the universality of lullabies represents a hopeful way of our someday integrating the biases of human auditory processing with the emotional and aesthetic factors. When asked to sing to an infant, children and adults alike adopt a special musical style—one that even infants can distinguish. Moreover, listeners can tell when the singer is actually singing to an infant, rather than merely pretending to sing. Infants prefer those songs that are actually being sung to other infants. Infants recognize the lullaby, young children produce it, and the style is universal—factors suggesting that the lullaby is an innate mode of communication in humans.

Not only the melodies but also the lyrics of lullabies are universal and take one of three forms: They urge the baby to sleep, praise the baby for sleeping, or warn the baby what will happen if it continues to cry. The mother sings in a sweet, soothing voice of the fate that awaits her wakeful child: being devoured by a witch, torn apart by wild animals, dropped on rocks! Interestingly, it is the mother (or female caretaker) in every human culture who sings the baby to sleep; males (even when full-time caretakers) never sing, or even hum, to the infant!

The intonation of lullabies is the same as that of baby talk or "motherese"—speech that both adults and young children adopt when addressing infants. Whether an adult's use of baby talk helps the child to acquire language has been a controversial topic for years. What is not controversial is that young children like baby talk, and the psycholinguist Ann Fernald has shown that the musical component of baby talk—the intonation pattern that also identifies a lullaby—captures the young child's attention.

Every cultural institution, from labor union to college football team to religious group, relies on music to fire the zeal of its members, to lift the spirits of a flagging group. Religious services are chanted or sung, never conducted in everyday speech. Musical intonation is a sound infants prefer, and it may bind them to the caretaker. Musical intonation increases the salience of speech; lullabies soothe crying infants, often putting them to sleep. And music of a proper kind, more than any other event, produces dedication and exaltation in a large proportion of the population. Perhaps these are the "problems" whose solution led to the evolution of music.

Notes

1. The developmental psychologist Peter Eimas initiated one of the first methods for studying habituation, dishabituation in infants. Using nonnutritive sucking time (rather than looking time), Eimas arranged for an infant to hear, for example, the phoneme *pa* each time she sucked on a nipple. Once the infant had habituated on *pa* and her sucking had declined, Eimas changed *pa* to the sound *ba*, and the infant's sucking recovered.

2. Female infants typically acquire an understanding of physical relations several weeks in advance of males. The best explanation of this difference is that testosterone slows the development of the brain of the male infant. It has been found that testosterone injected into infant female monkeys slows their brain development.

   Is the female infant's advancement in the acquisition of physical relations found in other domains? It is not found in language, probably because the acquisition of language occurs later, between the eleventh and thirty-sixth month. By that time the development of the infant male's brain has caught up with that of the female.

3. "Intentional" and "animate" are distinctly different concepts. While both are expressed by self-propelled movement, the nature of the movement is quite different. Intentionality is expressed by movement in space, animation by movement in place. A classical example of movement in place is that of respiration, easily simulated by an object whose sides alternately expand and contract. However, such a strongly "breathing" object may strike one as being "alive," that kind of movement does not meet the terms of goal-directedness and therefore cannot be interpreted as intentional. Only those objects that move in space are interpreted as intentional.

   The distinction between stalking food and ingesting it by chewing and swallowing illustrates the same point. Only stalking meets the terms of goal-directedness and can be interpreted as intentional. It may be asked, "In order to be intentional, must the whole object move in space? Or is it sufficient for just a part of the object to move?" Provided the movement meets the terms of goal-directedness, partial movement of the object is sufficient. A stationary object that reaches for an apple could qualify as intentional—but not a stationary object that merely "stretches," as though yawning.

4. One could argue that the head is perceptually more complex or interesting than the back, and that therefore the child knows more about it. This hypothesis could be tested by adding some new perceptual detail to the sides of toy animals for one group of children and for another group adding the heads—and then teaching both groups new names for the animals. Which group will associate the names with the new features? Our prediction is that the "head" group will associate the names with the new features far more readily than will the "sides" group. In the child's pretheoretical conception of "animal," the head counts for more than the sides; the sides have no more functional importance than do the tails. The head is the seeing or perceptually sentient end; it "steers" the animal, and explains why animals walk head, not tail, first.

5. Although in children one-to-one correspondence develops prior to counting, there is no evidence that one-to-one correspondence is requisite for counting. Chimpanzees do not develop one-to-one correspondence, yet they can be taught to count.

Chapter 2
A Disposition to
Repeat the Past
Imitation as Rerun

Everyone knows what imitation is. Don sticks his tongue out, lifts his cap, unfurls his umbrella; Roger does the same, sticks out his tongue, lifts his cap, unfurls his umbrella. When Roger does what Don does, this is imitation. The developmental psychologists Andrew Meltzoff and M. K. Moore report a most striking example of such copying: A forty-minute-old infant watches an adult protrude his tongue, and then promptly sticks out his own tongue!

Imitation has traditionally been regarded as the copying of motor acts. In this chapter, we present a new view of imitation, one that does not dispute but rather enriches the traditional view. Oddly enough, it has grown out of an attempt to examine representational art in the chimpanzee.

Humans draw representations of the world. The objects that humans inscribed on cave walls over 30,000 years ago—some captured in the midst of motion—are immediately recognizable as representations of animals and humans. Why then do chimpanzees confine their art to scribbles and splashes of color? Why don't they produce representational art?

Our initial purpose in addressing this question was to eliminate the possibility that chimpanzees are prevented from drawing by such trivial impediments as a hand that does not function well as an instrument for "art" or confinement in a geographical niche that does not afford material for drawing. We thought that if we reduced the motor requirements and provided more structured material for the chimpanzee, their undiscovered cognitive competences might be expressed and they might then demonstrate a capacity for representation that field investigations have thus far failed to uncover.

A Faceless Puzzle

Since the face is one of the first items drawn by children, we wondered if the chimpanzee too could "draw" a face, provided that the motor requirements for drawing were reduced. So we prepared a large photograph of a chimpanzee's head, blanked out the face portion, and offered three of our chimpanzees facial pieces—two eyes, a nose, and a mouth—with which to reconstruct the blanked-out face.

Two of the chimpanzees played with the puzzle much as two-and-a-half-year-old children do, stacking the facial pieces in a tower or arranging them along the border of the face. But the third animal, Sarah, did not engage in play; she immediately reconstructed the face. Sarah, who was about 8.5 years of age at the time, did as children do between three-and-a-half and four years of age, placing the facial pieces in their correct topological position: eyes across from each other toward the top of the head, mouth at the base, and nose nicely settled between the two.

Sarah, much to our surprise, went beyond simply reconstructing the face. A few days after the test, she began to transform it (Figure 2.1). That is, after reconstructing the face she disassembled it, moving the nose toward the top of the head. One day she transferred the mouth to the top of the head, then placed the nose on top of the mouth! Another day, after assembling the puzzle in the proper way, she rescued from the floor of the cage some banana peel that had been dropped from lunch, and draped it on the top of the head.

It began to look as though Sarah was trying to give the photograph a hat. But why? Why was she making these changes? And why was the goal always the same: to add something to the top of the head?

About 5 percent of children between the ages of five and ten also make changes in the puzzle, transforming the face after constructing it veridically. Their changes, however, are entirely different from those made by Sarah. The children "squash" all the facial pieces into the center of the face, or they place the eyes one above the other, Picasso style, on the same side of the face; while doing so, they make eye contact with the adult, smiling, eyes twinkling, as though sending this message: You know I know better and am just playing!

In Sarah's case, however, transformations were consistently directed to a specific location; there was no evidence of play. She seemed to be involved in a serious attempt to construct a representation of something that was missing. Fortunately, a quick inquiry resolved the riddle. In the same period during which Sarah was engaged in reconstructing the face puzzle, she also was being motivated to learn new words for her language lessons.

(a)   (b)

Figure 2.1   (a) Sarah's reconstruction
of the face; (b) Placing both the inverted
mouth and nose on the head. (c) Placing
banana peel on the head.

(c)

A caged animal runs out of things to "talk" about, so we often enlarged
Sarah's world by offering her new experiences to "discuss." Hats and a mirror provided those new things. A bag lady's treasure trove of hats, of every
size and type, was purchased at the Salvation Army. The chimpanzees and
their trainers had a field day primping in the mirror as they modeled the
hats (Figure 2.2).

Our point here is that Sarah did not transform the face puzzle until
after she had had the experience of modeling hats. Before being given the
opportunity to model hats, she made no transformations to the puzzle. Her
normal baseline for transforming the puzzle was zero. But whenever she
had tried on hats no more than twenty-four hours prior to being offered the
puzzle, she went beyond merely constructing the face. She transformed it
by giving it a hat.

Moreover, as we later discovered, Sarah would transform the face even
when she did not see herself in the mirror—simply donning a hat was sufficient impetus. We soon broadened Sarah's sartorial experience, giving her

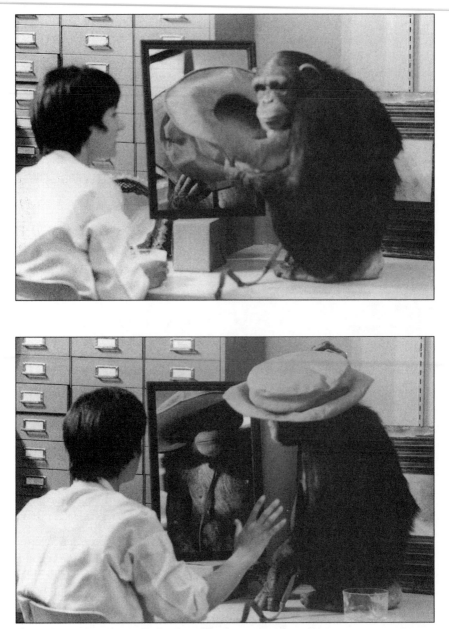

Figure 2.2   Chimpanzee viewing herself trying on hats in a mirror.

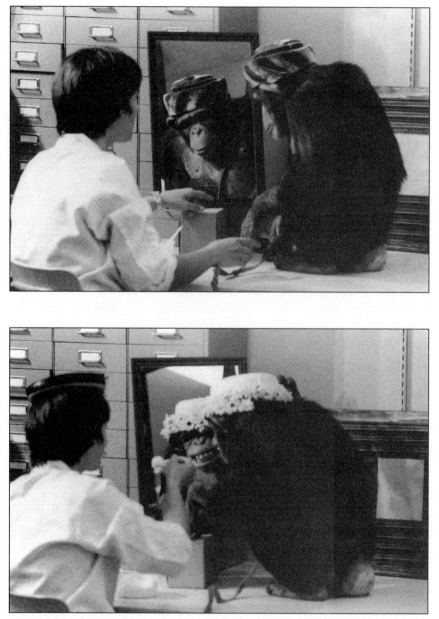

Figure 2.2 *(Continued)*

the opportunity to adorn herself not only with hats but with eyeglasses and necklaces as well. Would she respond similarly to these ornaments? She did.

To examine Sarah's capacity for these fancier improvisations, we first introduced her to modeling clay. We demonstrated for Sarah the plasticity of clay by rolling, flattening, and compacting it—motions that are within the range of a chimpanzee's manual dexterity. Sarah particularly enjoyed rolling the clay out with her palm, and when portions of it extruded on either side of her hand, the change excited her and she sought eye contact with the experimenter. She also ate bits of the clay.

After introducing Sarah to this transformable material, we gave her the new adornments—glasses and necklaces as well as hats. Plus we made a slight change in her tests. We still offered her the photo with the blanked-out face, but we did not provide the missing facial pieces. Instead we gave Sarah a generous wad of clay. Sarah made immediate use of the clay by applying it to the puzzle in the location that corresponded to that of the adornment.

After trying on hats she applied the clay to the top of the head; after wearing glasses, she applied the clay in the vicinity of the eyes and after wearing the necklace, to the bottom of the face. In each case she pressed the clay forcefully in the appropriate area (Figure 2.3).

When offered the puzzle without being given a twenty-four hour-earlier experience with the adornments, Sarah tore the clay into two to four pieces, then pressed the pieces onto the blanked-out face puzzle, more or less in the position of would-be facial elements (Figure 2.4). Although the placement of the clay pieces was now decidedly less veridical than her placement of the original puzzle pieces, it nevertheless suggested that her objective was to construct a face.

Something in Sarah's unusual activity was reminiscent of imitation. We detected a sense in which Sarah was copying herself. Not her previous *action*, but her previous *experience*. For in transforming the face—relocating the nose and mouth, adding banana peel to the top of the head, placing clay in appropriate areas—Sarah was literally "recreating" a physical condition "like" the one she experienced earlier. On day X, for instance, either she or the trainer would wear a hat, glasses, or necklace; on day X + 1, she would remodel the face so that it corresponded to the one she had previously experienced. Is there a relation between copying motor acts, the traditional view of imitation, and Sarah's reconstruction of her past experience?

To Repeat the Past

Traditionally, we judge whether imitation has occurred simply by noting whether an observer has carried out the act of a model. But Sarah, in plac-

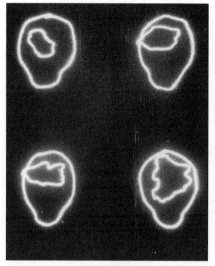

(a)

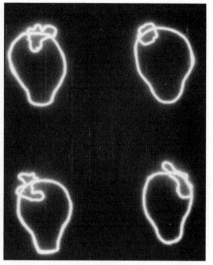

(b)

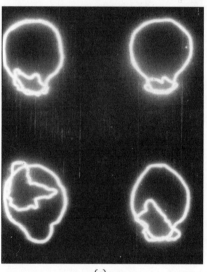

(c)

Figure 2.3 The face puzzle, adorned with wads of clay by Sarah after having tried on (*a*) glasses, (*b*) hats, and (*c*) necklaces.

ing clay or other adornments on the face, was not doing anything of that kind. Thus, if one is to construe Sarah's transformation of the face as "imitation," one must agree that this is a case not of imitation of the act of a model, but rather of self-imitation. But that is not a problem. Self-imitation has long been recognized as a legitimate form of imitation. The Swiss psychologist Jean Piaget even argued that self-imitation is more primitive than

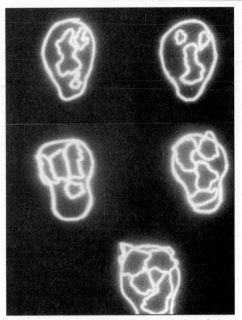

Figure 2.4   Sarah's baseline placement of clay.

imitation of the other one; indeed, he was among the first to recognize that an infant, in repeating some of her acts, is imitating herself.[1]

Thus we see that self-imitation remains completely within the purview of imitation as traditionally formulated. There is no change in what is viewed as the goal, which, in the traditional view, is the copying of a previous act whether the act is one's own or the act of another. Let us suggest, however, that the copying of a previous act is only the *apparent*, not the real, goal of imitation.

What then is imitation, and what is its real goal? If, in transforming the face puzzle, it is Sarah's goal to recreate—as best she can—her previous experience, is her performance not a description of imitative acts in general? When an individual observes a model carrying out an act, and then proceeds to carry out the act himself, there is no denying that the individual copies the model. In doing so, however, the individual inevitably also recreates his previous experience—the experience of having perceived the model carry out an act.

What is an individual really up to when he copies the model? Does he have a disposition to copy the model, or does he have a disposition to repeat the past? And can we distinguish between these differing views of imitation? It is, in fact, impossible to distinguish between the two views of imitation as long as we continue to use the standard test for imitation.

One Button versus Multiple Buttons

In the traditional test, a model carries out some act—takes up a spoonful of sand, slides a doll down a slide, puts rouge on the cheek of a doll, and so forth—and then, in effect, makes one "button" available to the child. The child can either desist or push the button. If the child pushes the button, the material used by the model is made available to the child who can then copy the model. Our test requires a second button. If the child pushes this second button, the *model* will repeat the previous act.

In this new test design, if the child chooses the first button, she will be able to copy the model, but if she chooses the second, she will be able to watch the model repeat his previous act. In both cases, the child will "reexperience" the original event. An approximation of it in the first case, a "replica" in the second. Undeniably, copying the act of another with one's own body is distinctly different from observing another repeat his own act; nevertheless, both satisfy the same goal since both provide the repetition of a previous perceptual experience.

This goal can be realized in a far greater number of ways than just the two we have mentioned. For "copying the model" or "requiring the model to repeat the action" are but two of a large set of alternatives. For example, a child, having observed the model put rouge on a doll's cheek, could have the experience repeated to some degree at least in several ways by

1. Applying the rouge on the doll (the one case that tradition has considered).
2. Requiring the model to repeat the action (the new case we have introduced).

In addition, the child could

3. Apply rouge to her own cheek, to the cheek of her little sister, to that of a doll, and so on.
4. Induce someone else to copy the model,
5. Look at a picture in a storybook in which rouge was being applied to a doll's cheek.

Clearly, when imitating, the child achieves the goal of copying the model. It is equally clear that when imitating the model, the child inevitably recreates the past. So, which of the two goals is primary?

A Pilot Test with Children

The following pilot test not only helps to answer this question but clarifies our enriched view of imitation.

Ten five- to six-year-old children observed a model place a doll on the top of a slide and guide it down. The children then were given two buttons, and shown the effects of operating each of them. Pushing one button made the doll and slide available to the children, enabling them to copy the model; pushing the other button led the model to repeat his previous action.

Each child was given eight trials; during each of these the model, after having guided the doll down the slide, offered the child the opportunity to select between two buttons. Of the ten children only two exclusively chose the first button and copied the model. Four chose the second button exclusively, leading the model to repeat his previous action. Four children alternated their choices.

These results do not favor the traditional view of imitation. If merely copying the model is the main goal in imitation, no child should have selected the second button, for selecting it meant that the child could not then imitate the model. If, however, the goal of imitation is viewed more broadly as a disposition to reexperience the past, then both buttons, one as well as two, permit that goal to be realized.

A child who elects to copy the model may do so, in part at least, because she enjoys using her own body, a disposition perhaps independent of either goal. The child may, in fact, find some acts simply irresistible to copy.[2]

The Echolalic Child

Some number of autistic and retarded children are echolalic, that is, they lack normal speech and simply repeat what is said to them. These children may appear to be exotic cases, but in fact such children have something important to teach us about imitation in general.

The first question one needs to ask about the echolalic child is this: Is the child's imitation confined to speech alone, or does it extend beyond speech? Put differently, is echolalia a pathology of speech or a more general pathology? Our specific question was this: Do echolalic children repeat speech only, or other acts as well? To answer this question we used the match-to-sample paradigm, probably the most incisive test with any creature that lacks speech. Notice that a correct response in the traditional match-to-sample test can itself be considered a form of imitation, since the subject who responds correctly chooses the alternative that matches the sample, thus copying or repeating the sample. And since this is the way normal children respond, imitation or repetition is perfectly correct under the right circumstances. How then are we to differentiate "good" imitation from "bad"?

We can rephrase the question thus: Are there actions that an echolalic child will, but a normal child will not, imitate? It turns out that there are, and the differences in the actions are not just individual quirks but belong to a category that is fundamental. For the imitation of normal and echolalic children pivots on objects that, respectively, are and are not intact. Certainly such a category could not be more fundamental!

In match-to-sample tests, both echolalic and normal children select alternatives that "match" the sample when the sample is an intact object. But what if the sample is not an intact object? More specifically, what if the sample is a headless doll and the alternatives offered the child are a doll's head and another headless doll? Echolalic and normal children now part company. The echolalic child selects the headless doll, the alternative that duplicates or matches the sample. The normal child selects the head of the doll, the object that restores the integrity of the doll. Echolalic children repeat, normal children complete, distorted objects.

The incompleteness of an object need not be as dramatic as a headless doll. It can be a completely prosaic item—a teapot without a lid, or a tube of toothpaste without its cap. Even separating a saucer from a cup or a hairbrush from a comb will produce the diagnostic effect. The normal child will match a hairbrush to a comb, a saucer to a cup, whereas the echolalic child will match a saucer to another saucer, a hairbrush to another hairbrush.

Two fundamental points emerge from this simple study. First, the normal child has an extremely potent disposition to restore "distorted" objects to their former integrity. But while most past researchers treated the restoration of the integrity of an object as the opposite of imitation, is it really? In our new view of imitation, isn't restoring an object to its previous form equivalent to repeating the past? Perhaps so; but one still must ask, with respect to this case, what constitutes the "past": the complete or the incomplete form of the object.

And the answer is: the complete form—the intact apple, the doll with a head, the whole horse. These are the forms from the past, forms the child previously experienced on numerous occasions. Therefore a normal child who selects the alternative that completes the object is simply reproducing a perceptual experience that conforms to her past images of the objects.

By contrast the echolalic child, who selects the object that duplicates the sample—the headless alternative, in the presence of the headless doll—is repeating not the past but the present. The child selects the alternative that coincides with her *immediate perception*.

In the normal child, memory and its long-term representations, its past images, take priority over perception. In the echolalic child it is quite the opposite: Perception takes precedence over memory. The results of these tests lead us to an unexpected conclusion: The normal child appears to be driven by memory, the echolalic child by immediate perception, reflecting the fact that echolalia clearly represents more than just a pathology of speech.

The Power of the Past

Imitation, in its traditional formulation, has been accommodated into evolutionary theory on the grounds that "copying the model" has obvious adaptive value—it helps the novice to acquire adultlike skills. An equally compelling argument can be applied to the present view of imitation. The recreation of previous perceptual experience permits a review of what may be a complex act. Repetition builds up a representation, making it more accurate and complete. It can build redundancy, duplicating representation in the brain.

Do we find signs of repetition in the mind of the human? We suggest that if the human brain could be "unfolded," laid out chronologically so as to disclose its history at a glance, we would be struck by repetitions. When spread out in time, a human life resembles a necklace whose beads appear and reappear. It was not Beethoven alone who repeated and elaborated themes; every human life contains such repetitions and elaborations. When two people cohabit for years, they share themes, doubling them. If we could decode their brains, translating neural connections into experience, we would be astonished to find that one partner's neural connections appear in the brain of the other, and vice versa.

In addition to its effect on the life of an individual, repetition benefits the social group. In her work entitled *Walbiri Iconography*, the anthropologist Nancy Munn describes the visual symbols that Australian hunter-gatherers use when telling stories to one another. Gathering in the shade of the afternoon, the women verbally repeat the content of their day, embellishing their stories with visual symbols which they draw in the sand. Each woman implants the events of her day in the minds of the others. To describe these stories Munn introduced the provocative term *rerun*, observing that both language and visual iconography are exceptionally powerful rerun devices, which is to say, tools for recreating the past.

Reproducing a Concept

Children, upon reaching a certain age, recognize the *concept* inherent in a model's action, and copy the concept rather than repeat the motor behavior of the model.

For example: After watching a model place three dolls in a horizontal line—the largest doll first, the intermediate next, the smallest doll last— children copied the model's concept and thus revealed their knack for *monotonic order.* The actual arrangements of monotonic order used by the children differed from that of the model, and varied among themselves. Indeed, as Figure 2.5 reveals, the children used thirteen different arrangements to represent the concept of monotonic order.

Arrangement	Frequency	
	Old	Young
 ▮▮▮	1	0
 ▮▮▮	13	4
 ▮▮▮	1	8
 ▮▮▮	1	2
 ☰	1	0
 ▮	1	1
 ☰	1	0
 —•—•—•	1	0
 —•—•—•	1	0
 ☰	0	1
 ∿	0	1
 ☰	0	1

Figure 2.5 The various physical arrangements the children used to depict the monotonic order of three different-sized dolls.

The fact that children imitate at the conceptual level alone can be seen when they play a simple game in which we divide objects into categories and invite children of from two to four years of age to do the same. We place a number of toy animals and plants (carrots, apples, dogs, cats, horses, oranges, and so forth) in a large bowl, making sure there are many duplicates of each. We then select pairs of animals, placing them in a red bowl, and pairs of plants, placing them in a green bowl.

Sometimes we select such identical pairs as two lions or two apples; at other times nonidentical pairs such as a dog and a sheep or a tomato and an orange. Even two-year-olds imitate the model successfully. When the model places a cat and sheep in the red bowl, the child places a dog and a pig in the red bowl, copying the correct bowl and category but not the exact category members. Further, when the model selects two carrots, the child may select an apple and an orange, once again copying the category but not the exact category members.

In placing objects in the bowls, the children do not copy either the motor actions of the model or the exact token/category member selected by the model. Thus we see once again that children imitate at the conceptual level alone.

The Child's Imitation of Grammar

It is not possible to give a sentence to an eighteen-month-old child, and then ask him, "Can you say that?" much less, "Is that a good sentence?" To obtain a *grammaticality judgment* from a young child requires a different strategy. The one we adopted was that of imitation.

We arranged to have mothers record what their children said for a week, and used these simple protocols to construct a grammar of the child's speech. This was not difficult, since children between eighteen months and two years of age have a simple grammar. We used the child's grammar to generate two kinds of sentences, one compatible with the child's grammar, the other not. All the sentences we generated consisted of either two or three words and were "new," never having appeared in the child's protocol.

Our hypothesis was that the child would not imitate the "sentences" that were incompatible with its grammar. By and large, the results bore out the hypothesis. When given sentences compatible with their grammar the children repeated them, or some part of them, 30 to 40 percent of the time, as opposed to less than 5 percent of the time when given sentences incompatible with their grammar. Except for one child! This young boy imitated both kinds of sentences, and at a level higher than those of any of the other children—close to 50 to 60 percent. Are we compelled to say that he disproved our hypothesis? No, for the child still behaved very differently depending on whether the sentences were or were not compatible with his grammar.

Here was his delightful surprise: When a sentence was compatible with his grammar, the child imitated it word for word. But when a sentence was incompatible with his grammar, he delivered his curve ball. With a little smile he produced a sentence as incompatible with our sentence as ours had been incompatible with his grammar. We rush to some clarifying examples.

When given our incompatible, pure-nonsense sentence, "Doggy red byebye," the child replied playfully, "Home green daddy." He did not however play this game when simply imitating the grammar-compatible sentences. We did not at first understand what was happening. And when we did, we were bowled over. For this child was imitating on both levels, both the motor and the conceptual. When sentences conformed to his grammar he imitated on the motor level, producing, word for word, what the model had said. When sentences did not conform to his grammar he imitated on the conceptual level, producing the sentence anomalies he took to be our goal! For what else could have led us, he must have reasoned, to say such funny things as "Doggy red byebye"? Surely we were jesting, or playing, or whatever a highly precocious twenty-month-old child assumes of an adult who is "breaking" grammatical rules.

When a Child Does Not Understand a Concept

Since animals and plants are primitive categories, even two-year-old children can imitate a model's choice of these categories. But what if the child has no innate preparation for a category? In such a case, children can neither imitate a model's choice nor learn the category. A good example is seen in the categories of same/different.

We place two cats and two oranges, members of the category "same," in the red bowl, and a dog and a goat as well as an apple and an orange, members of the category "different," in the green bowl. We also use a camel and a grape, another example of "different," placing them in the green bowl.

In other words, all cases of same—the alike animals, the alike plants—are placed in the red bowl, and all cases of different—the different animals, the different plants, a plant and an animal—are placed in the green bowl. Four-year-old children are now unable to imitate the task. They place all the plants in one container and all the animals in the other.

So we change the contents of the large bowl, introducing a new variety of objects—spoons, bottles, erasers, and the like—including many duplicates of each. We again place pairs of alike objects in one bowl and pairs of unlike objects in another. Two spoons, two bottles, two pencils in the "same" red bowl; an eraser and a car, a pencil and a marble, a sponge and a doll's shoe in the "different" green bowl.

These changes do not help the children. And since in both tests they fail to imitate the concept of "same" and of "different," their failure cannot be blamed on interference from the plant/animal distinction.

Children are surprisingly late in mastering the concept of same/different; most children do not grasp the distinction until they reach the age of four. Even at four, many children cannot match a pair of alike objects (A A), say two shoes, with another pair of alike objects (B B), say two hats; nor can they match a pair of unlike objects (C D), say a shoe and a hat, with another pair of unlike objects (E F), say a purse and a belt. In other words they cannot match one instance of same with another instance of same and cannot match one instance of different with another instance of different.

Children are unable to imitate conceptual behavior when it instantiates distinctions that they do not draw spontaneously. Conversely, when the model performs an action that instantiates a concept the child does understand, the child will imitate the concept. Thus children will imitate a model whose action exemplifies the concept of monotonicity, or the concepts animal/plant, but they will not imitate the model whose action exemplifies the concepts same/different.

Infants Copy Motor Acts

Children copy motor acts spontaneously, imitating novel as well as familiar motor acts on the first trial. Meltzoff demonstrated that fourteen-month-old infants can copy the motor actions carried out by a model on novel objects even after a delay of one week! When for instance a model shows a very young human infant three or four novel objects, each of which the model manipulates in a distinctive way, the infant will, upon the model's return a week later, manipulate each object just as the model did—nice evidence of imitation where "imitation" means copying motor acts. In point of fact, however, the infant's grasp of imitation may go well beyond mere copying. A quaint episode suggests that the infant may not only imitate but also "like to be imitated."

An eleven-month-old infant grimaced when his mother, while carrying him, touched a green olive to the infant's lips. After three or four such experiences and the passage of about a week, the infant began to grimace spontaneously, without the benefit of the olive. In other words as soon as the adult picked him up he would grimace on his own. (Incidentally, this is also a nice illustration of the passage of a response from its involuntary to its voluntary form.) In short order, when the infant grimaced the adult tended to grimace as well. Each time she did the infant laughed, wriggled vigorously, and grimaced again. The infant seemed to be trying to induce the adult to copy him, and to enjoy it when she did.

While an incident such as this proves nothing, it suggests that we may underestimate the infants' disposition to control or cause events. When infants imitate, they are controlled; if and when they induce you to imitate them, they control. Psychology has thoroughly explored the infant's disposition to be controlled, to imitate; it is time to look at the other side of the coin.

Imitation in Animals: Motor Action versus Object Choice

Most tests of imitation in animals do not actually measure the copying of the model's motor action; they measure the copying of the model's *choice of object*. In a typical imitation experiment, a hungry pigeon, after observing a trained model peck a red (versus a green) key and obtain food from a hopper, will peck the red key. A hungry rat, too, after observing a model press a small (versus a large) lever and obtain food, will press the small lever. The pigeon and rat are imitating, we say, but the question remains: Precisely what are they copying: the model's choice of object or the model's motor action. Unfortunately, it is not possible to decide, since all pigeons peck a key in a species-specific way, and the same holds true for the rats' pressing of a lever.

Well then, let us train models to carry out idiosyncratic actions—train a pigeon to strike a key with its wing, a rat to press a lever with its nose—and then repeat the experiment. In other words, in the previous type of experiment we could be confident that the observing pigeons and rats would select the correct objects; but will the pigeon now strike the key with its wing, the rat press the lever with its nose? Or will both animals continue on with their species-specific forms of responding?

There is little likelihood here that either rat or pigeon will copy the motor action, for copying motor acts requires a unique mechanism, one different from that needed for copying object choices. The mechanism is found in human infants, as shown above, but is not likely to be found in rats or pigeons. Even human-reared adult chimpanzees have difficulty copying the motor responses of a model, as has been shown in a careful recent study. The primatologist Tetsuro Matsuzawa and his student Masako Myowa-Yamakoshi demonstrated a small number of simple acts to each of several chimpanzees: placing a ball into a bowl, wiping a lid with a towel, hanging a hose around a stool. Acts of this kind, which involve the directing of one object toward another, were imitated quite accurately.

But the chimpanzees were downright poor at copying pure motor patterns, even when the patterns were simple. A pure motor pattern is one in which the position of the limbs or the body is changed without making any contact with an object—as when raising or lowering the arms, making a fist, turning the head, or any combination of these patterns. And most difficult of all was the copying of "novel" motor patterns. To produce copying of these acts by the chimpanzees the model had to do several repetitions, passively guide the chimpanzees through the acts, and even reward them for "copying."

Keith and Cathy Hayes, early researchers who conducted the original language study on the chimpanzee Viki, reported that she could imitate at least "ten completely novel acts." More recently the primatologists Custance, Whiten, and Bard found that two four-year-old chimpanzees, when shown forty-eight novel acts, reproduced thirteen and twenty of them, respectively. In both the above studies, however, the young animals had been specially trained, from youth, to copy. By contrast, the chimpanzees in the Matsuzawa and Myowa-Yamakoshi study were appreciably older before training began. The latter authors speculate that there may be a critical period for acquiring imitative skills, and that their animals lay outside this period. At any rate, we can safely conclude that while chimpanzees, like other species, require no training to copy a model's object choices, they do require training to copy the motor actions of a model.

Imitation in the Wild Chimpanzee

Do chimpanzees in the wild imitate? Once again we turn to the Japanese researcher Matsuzawa, who recently completed extensive filming of nut cracking in wild chimpanzees. He has traced the infant's acquisition of this skill from six months to ten years of age, a definitive record. The seven to ten mothers in the group under his observation place nuts on root anvils and pound them with hand-held rocks. Their infants play in the vicinity, observing the nut cracking on occasion with intense interest.

While an act by a mother sometimes triggers a similar act on the part of an infant, the motor behavior of the mother does not affect the form of the infant's motor act. In other words, the infant does not crack the nut in exactly the same way the mother does. Adult chimpanzees crack nuts ambidextrously: placing a nut on the anvil with one hand and cracking it with a rock held in the other hand. Infants use the same hand (either right or left) to both place a nut and to strike it; they do not alternate hands until their third or fourth year.

The Converter: From Perception to Action

It is not difficult to understand why few species are able to copy the motor actions of a model, or why even the chimpanzee needs special training to do so. In copying motor actions the observer must form a representation of the model's motor action and "reproduce" it with her own body. But how does one translate "pictures" of the actions of others into one's own performance?

Another question: What might an observer need, to carry out this translation of images into actions? A "converter" would do nicely. The newborn human infant evidently already has such a converter, for when a model sticks out his tongue, opens his mouth, or purses his lips, the infant's perception commands his motor system to produce the acts of the model. How might this converter work?

Perhaps we are supplied with a partial answer to this puzzler by "mirror" neurons. These neurons, recently discovered in the monkey, discharge under two conditions: (1) when the monkey itself produces a particular act, and (2) when the monkey simply observes another individual produce the same act. Neurons that discharge under both the observation and production of an action may be the first step in the formation of a converter, a device that transforms perception into action.

Monkeys are capable of intermodal sensory equivalence, which is to say, of matching objects that have been placed in their mouth with objects they are shown. The capacity to make equivalence judgments of this kind, like the mirror neuron, may be another step in the development of a converter. However, both these mechanisms—the mirror neuron, and intermodal equivalence—can be no more than first steps in the formation of a converter, for monkeys are incapable of copying motor actions. "Monkey see, monkey do" is a false adage.

Simulation, or mental trial and error, may be another process that facilitates the copying of motor behavior. No doubt individuals who are adept at picturing motor acts in their minds will be adept at copying them. The capacity to simulate permits an individual to "see" an act without necessarily having either observed or produced it before.

Wolfgang Kohler has claimed that chimpanzees are adept at solving problems by simulation. He speaks of animals that when shown bananas that were placed high up and out of reach, "pictured the table under the food" and then moved the table to the appropriate location.

But Kohler's account does not jibe well with the actual behavior of the chimpanzee. While the frustrated animal does sit still momentarily, and may even appear to puzzle over the situation, when the animal "acts" it is likely to hurl objects, including the table, around the cage. Sometimes the table ends up in the vicinity of the food. When this happens, the animal jumps onto the table and seizes the food. The next day, however, rather than move the table under the food, the animal merely repeats its hectic activity. Not until about the fourth day does it calmly move the table to a proper position and take the banana.

Parrots may be an exception here, since they are capable not only of the auditory mimicry for which they are justly famous (see T. F. Wright, a biologist, for an account of auditory mimicry) but also of visual imitation. The psychobiologist B. R. Moore reports that his parrot spontaneously imitated several of his gestures. Though this is only a single case, it is an impressive one; if it can be duplicated, it looks as though parrots, unlike most species, can imitate motor action.

Neither vocal nor auditory imitation presents the problem posed by visual imitation. Species that are capable of vocal imitation—such as birds, cetaceans, and humans—have built-in devices which enable them to voluntarily produce any of a large set of sounds. Chimpanzees, lacking such a built-in device, do not engage in vocal mimicry—they have little, if any, voluntary control of their auditory system. Their cries—food grunts, clicking of the tongue, or buzzing of the lips when grooming, hooting when excited, screeching when upset—are all reflexive. Whenever Sarah wished to attract the attention of trainers who were passing in the hall, she never called out to them but instead pounded vigorously on a resonant surface.

Simulation and the Conception of Time

Both the sequence in which events occur and their duration depend on the ability to picture events in the mind. The chimpanzee, owing to its inability to simulate or imagine motor actions, suffers from an impaired conception of time.

In order to remember the sequence in which events occur, humans employ spatial metaphors. They envision a mental line—horizontal in the case of English speakers, vertical in the case of speakers and readers of Mandarin—onto which remembered events are laid out. Recent events occur at the bottom of the vertical line for speakers of Mandarin, to the right of the line for speakers of English.

Duration, which also depends on simulation, is judged somewhat differently from sequence. Activities such as eating an apple, polishing a car, or raking a yard consist of a sequence of actual dynamic movements. The mental images of actions are equally dynamic, organized as a representation of a sequence of movements. Both the actions and the image have a duration. While the action and the image are not of equal duration—an hour of raking may be represented by an image that lasts a mere second—the duration of the image is proportional to that of the action, so that it is possible to rank-order the duration of different acts by comparing the durations of their images.

It is our view that four-year-old children are using such a procedure when solving the following problem. After watching an experimenter hide two cookies (one frosted, the other plain) and then reappear eating a cookie, the children consistently go to the location that holds the cookie *different* from the one the experimenter is eating. Evidently the children assume that the cookie the experimenter is eating is the same as the one he had hidden. When however the cookies are wrapped in layers of tissue paper before being hidden, the children no longer head for the location containing the cookie different from that being eaten by the experimenter.

Here, by mentally simulating actions, the child is able to conclude that unwrapping the cookies takes so much time that the cookie the experimenter is eating cannot possibly be the one he had hidden. In notable contrast, chimpanzees fail at this problem. They continue to head for the location holding the cookie different from the one that the experimenter is eating.

Animals cannot simulate sequences of events or their durations, but they can take into account experienced duration and, to a certain extent, sequence. When even rats or pigeons are rewarded at, say, three-minute intervals, both species quickly learn to suppress their desire to respond shortly after being fed, responding instead shortly before the third minute.

Chimpanzees can compare the sequences of events provided that they have had the chance to experience the sequences. They can judge whether the order of three elements in two temporal sequences is or is not the same. More impressive still, they can compare temporal and spatial sequences, judging whether the temporal order of items in one sequence is equivalent to the spatial order of items in the other sequence. But the chimpanzee's difficulty with time is dramatized when such events must be simulated.

Future events must be imagined since they have not been experienced. This is true as well of past events; they too must be imagined. One cannot recapture the order of events simply by remembering time; one must translate time into space, and picture events arrayed on a mental line. The price of being unable to image events is high, costing the chimpanzee the concepts of past and future, and thereby making it highly unlikely that the animal can plan.

Why Copy Motor Behavior?

There is nothing in chimpanzee technology that requires the copying of motor acts. The motor actions of a model in termite fishing, the sponging of water with leaves, or the cracking of nuts are all acts that are within the repertoire of any chimpanzee. The central act of termite fishing, inserting sticks in holes, is species specific and part of routine chimpanzee play. The pounding of a nut placed on an anvil is an act that virtually all young chimpanzees master in due time through simple observation. The level of complexity of chimpanzee technology does not require special instruction; any chimpanzee can manage to produce the technique in time.

What, then, is the importance of copying motor behavior? The value of copying emerges once we reach a level of complexity that is found in human technologies. Technologies of a complex level are of ancient origin, found in prehistory, and continue today in human cultures. The Kalahari San for instance, produce jewelry by cracking ostrich eggs into hundreds of quarter-inch fragments. The edge of each fragment is ground into a circular form, and the center of each fragment then is pierced to accommodate a leather thread which joins each fragment to form a necklace, bracelet, or other piece of jewelry.

Modern technologies require a sequence of complex, precise motor acts. Blowing glass, weaving lace, transplanting hearts—even separating the yolks of eggs from the whites—all require carefully orchestrated acts, a set of unique motions tailored to the task. Only a species capable of copying motor acts could learn technologies of this kind.

The Limitations of Imitation

The power of imitation is severely limited on both the motor and conceptual sides. On the motor side, we know, curiously, that observing a model does not assist the baboon in carrying out termite fishing. Baboons observe chimpanzees obtaining termites by inserting straws into holes in the termite mound, but they do not benefit from the observation. They continue to simply scrape up fallen termites from the ground. And unlike chimpanzees, baboons do not spontaneously insert sticks or straws into holes and thus cannot copy models that do so. For as we note here, an observer can reproduce the motor response of a model only if the act is one he could have produced spontaneously. Imitation does not induce novel acts.

On the conceptual side, a model cannot teach an observer to imitate a distinction that the observer himself does not draw. Children who do not spontaneously discriminate between instances of same and different do not benefit by observing a model who does so. Unless the observer spontaneously engages in action that instantiates the distinction, the model's example will be of no benefit.

Humans are particularly disposed to repeat previous experience. Such a disposition is highlighted by the way Australian aboriginal women recall the events of the previous day with stories embellished by visual symbols drawn in the sand. Because humans have the capacity for speech, they are especially well endowed to repeat previous experience. No device has a greater capacity for rerun than speech.

But neither the repetition of previous experience nor the imitation of motor acts contributes to novelty. These limitations on imitation severely constrain the effect that imitation can have on social change. In humans, the principal contribution made by imitation is in the transmission of existing traditions; it is not a consequential vehicle for the introduction of new traditions. It cannot be: for any act that an individual imitates is also one that he could already have performed spontaneously.

Limits on imitation set the stage for pedagogy. It is pedagogy which is the major vehicle of social change. Pedagogy overcomes both the motor and the conceptual inadequacies intrinsic to imitation. Pedagogy on the one hand helps to introduce new motor actions, new technologies that an individual cannot design on his own. And on the other hand it sparks new ideas, ideas that the individual might never develop independently.

Notes

1. Self-imitation need not precede imitation of the other one, for as already noted, infants imitate the other one within forty minutes of birth.
2. We must entertain the possibility that when causing the model to repeat his prior act, the child's principal interest is to control the model rather than recreate the past. We can assess this possibility with an experiment in which the model performs not one motor act but three different acts. So we now offer the child not two buttons, but three.

   For example: The model performs the following acts: guides a doll down a slide; stirs sand into water; pounds a nail; marks a small chalk board. Button 1: All materials used by the model are made available to the child, and she can copy the model. Button 2: The model repeats his immediately prior acts. Button 3: The model carries out an act that does not repeat any act in the series. (Of course, one must control for the preferences children may have for the different acts).

Variations in the children's patterns of response can be used to diagnose their motivations. For example, children whose primary aim is to control the model should avoid button 1, in which the model does not act. By contrast, children whose primary goal is to repeat the past should avoid button 3, in which the model does not repeat a past act.

Chapter 3
Pedagogy
Rooted in Aesthetics

The qualities that constitute a "beautiful" face obviously differ profoundly from one culture to another. In some cultures bones inserted into the nasal septum, lips distended by disks, skin intricately scarred and tattooed, and necks and earlobes unnaturally elongated are considered beautiful. Yet when photographs of these scarred and tattooed faces are shown to judges from other cultures, not one of them selects as attractive a woman, for example, whose nose is penetrated by a bone. Can we claim a universal sense of beauty in the presence of such human diversity?

We do see some signs of universality. When required to select the most attractive woman in the group favoring the characteristics just mentioned, Western males choose the very same one chosen by males who are members of that cultural group. Thus, members of the group and Western judges both prefer the same faces, so presumably a Western male confined to living in that particular non-Western culture would have to compete with other males in the group for the same females.

Preferences of this kind are found not only with respect to faces but in aesthetic judgments of non-Western artifacts as well. Western judges often do not evaluate highly the pottery produced in certain regional cultures; when required, however, to confine their judgments to this pottery, they and the natives prefer the same pots. Thus, had the Westerners sought to buy the pottery, they would have found themselves in competition with the natives for the same pottery.

Agreement in judgment of beauty is not confined to faces and pottery but extends to all forms of human expression: song, dance, poetry, dress. In each case, while individuals prefer their own tradition, when asked to judge the forms of another culture their preferences will agree with those of individuals who belong to the other culture.

Further, the human judgment of aesthetics "penetrates." While stimulated by the "outside," it soon moves "inside." From the aesthetic judgment of face and voice, of movement and style, it moves to the unseen, to a judgment of character or morality—from a judgment of beauty to a judgment of "good" and "bad." For every human culture links aesthetics with morality.

Beauty Is Truth

The human predilection to link beauty and morality is made explicit in the writings of the nineteenth-century German romantic, Friedrich von Schiller. Schiller proposed that physical and spiritual beauty march together, that a beautiful face is the expression of a noble soul. Though lofty and mystical as portrayed in Schiller's writing, the thesis was given a decidedly pedestrian turn when taken into the American laboratory and tested on college sophomores.

Students were asked to judge photographs of male and female faces for intelligence and morality, and to predict their success in career and marriage. The faces were not picked out of a hat, but had been judged and ranked in advance for attractiveness. Certainly Schiller would have been deeply gratified by the outcome. While never having heard of his thesis, the students nonetheless embraced it, producing a purely Schillerean outcome. They judged that morality, happy marriage, and career success all "marched" with physical beauty.

Schiller's thesis is supported by studies of yet another kind. College sophomores were asked to judge the occupations of male and female faces that, once again, had been prejudged for attractiveness. No student objected that it was absurd to make such a judgment from photographs of complete strangers! Instead they all willingly identified the faces as those of minister, teacher, and doctor, or thief, rapist, and so on, linking "good" occupations with attractive faces, criminal ones with unattractive faces. This widespread acceptance of Schiller's thesis does not mean, of course, that it is correct, namely, that people with attractive faces actually are more intelligent, happy, or moral than people with less attractive faces. However, people with attractive faces *are* more successful. They actually do earn more money, have fewer divorces, and spend less time in prison. But is their success owed to superior intelligence or morality?

The success of physically attractive people, rather than being due to any special virtues they possess, is owed to their appearance alone. It is owed to the enormous influence of beauty. Humans are irresistibly drawn to attractive people. A pretty or handsome face provides advantages. Not only the decisive advantages that operate once or twice in a lifetime, in acquiring a mate or in obtaining professional advancement, but in the quotidian niceties: being served promptly by clerks and waitresses, welcomed by smiling doctors and dentists, excused for small or even serious blunders. Welcomed by a world that cannot get enough of an attractive face.

Mate Selection

The evolutionary origins of aesthetics are as mysterious as are those of music. There are biologists who argue that the evolutionary origin of aesthetics lies in mate selection. This makes the female the crucible of aesthetics because mate selection typically is her business: She has access to innumerable males but selects only one. It is the rare species in which we find the reverse, males that have access to innumerable females and select but one.

A simple rule appears to govern choice of mate: The gender that feeds and cares for the young has the privilege of selecting the mate. There are a few species in which the female leaves the nest shortly after parturition, makes no contribution to the care of the egg or young, and philanders by taking on multiple mates. In these species it is the male that exercises mate selection. In the majority of species, however, the female is the caregiver and exercises the choice of mate.

The basis on which the female chooses her mate remains largely a mystery. Females seem to prefer colorful to drab, large to small. With respect to mating song, she prefers loud to quiet. There is even evidence that females prefer brave to timid, favoring males that dare to approach a predator over those that linger in the distance. Symmetry is another factor biologists have proposed, and this factor is easily related to aesthetics.

Frequently symmetry is lodged in exaggerated features, such as the tail of the peacock or the elk's towering antlers. These features have been exaggerated as a result of having been selected for sexual attraction. Symmetry is also seen in the bilateral construction of the body. Feet, hands, breasts, legs, eyes, and so on come in pairs, and often show small random deviations from perfect bilateral symmetry. An overall measure of this deviation, designated FA, has been observed to play a role in mate selection. Females seem to prefer a male with a small FA. The biologist Randy Thornhill reports that female scorpionflies prefer males whose wing lengths have a low FA, that is, are symmetrical. The female is not required to measure the male's wings, because the sex pheromone the female prefers happens to be extruded by males whose wings are symmetrical.

The biologist Diane Scutt and her colleagues have linked high FA to breast cancer in humans. Asymmetrical organs, or high FA, is thought to be a developmental outcome of stressful environments. It disposes a woman to cancer. There is no evidence, however, that this factor also is linked to male preference, that is, that males prefer females whose breasts are symmetrical.

As a possible criterion in understanding aesthetics, symmetry has the advantage of being general. It can be applied to all categories that humans judge: faces, movements, artifacts, and so forth. Further, a preference for a symmetrical mate could have evolved because of an association between low FA and fitness, low-FA individuals being healthier, more likely to survive and procreate. Yet aesthetics cannot be reduced to any single factor. Even the most generous account of symmetry is no more than a beginning in explaining the origins of aesthetics.

Early Evidence for Evaluation

Infants at ten or eleven months of age already distinguish certain forms of action as positive or negative. As we mentioned earlier, when shown ball-like figures that interact on a computer screen, infants not only attribute goals to their actions but assign value +/− to their interactions. In doing so the infants use two criteria: a simple evaluation based on the *intensity* of the motion and a more complex one based on the functional equivalent of *helping* or *hindering*.

A ball-like figure that contacts another with gentle motions ("caress") is coded positive, while a ball-like figure contacting another with harsh motions ("hit") is coded negative. An object that assists another in attaining a goal ("helping") is coded positive, while one that prevents another from attaining a goal ("hindering") is coded negative. These positive and negative evaluations of the infant may be biological precursors of the cultural concepts of "good" and "bad."

If Schiller's thesis is correct in suggesting a connection between aesthetics and morality, then the infant's evaluative system may bear a relation to aesthetics. A simple test could help us to decide. Infant preferences for attractive faces appear to be largely in agreement with those of the adult, according to the developmental psychologists Curtis A. Samuels and Richard Ewy. Will infants, then, associate attractive faces with positive actions? Will they associate unattractive faces with negative actions? Will they be surprised if attractive faces hit or hinder others, while unattractive faces stroke or help others? If infants make these associations, then Schiller's thesis is present in the infant.

Aesthetics in Human Movement

At what age are children able to make aesthetic judgments about movement? Observing, as we have, our grandchild (about two and a half years of age) performing spins and pirouettes in the living room and vocally appraising his own accomplishments ("Look, look that one!" or "No, no, don't look! no good!"), we have been encouraged to ask children to judge three kinds of movement. (See Figure 3.1.)

The first such type of routine movement includes such daily activities as walking across the living room, ascending and descending stairs, sweeping, ironing, playing hopscotch, and brushing teeth. The second and third kinds, gymnastics and ballet, are both specialized forms of movement invented by humans.

Figure 3.1 Kalahari San children dancing. (From Lee and deVore, 1976)

To evaluate the child's aesthetic appreciation of movement, we filmed individuals performing ten different acts in each of the three categories, and with a good and a bad version of each act. Each act lasted about eight seconds and was repeated three times. We hired professionals—a gymnast and a ballet dancer—to perform the actions for the special categories, but performed the routine acts ourselves. Videotapes of the good and bad acts were shown to both children and chimpanzees.

We started the study with the children, showing each child three pairs of routine acts. The child was informed which acts were good and which were bad. We assumed that even a three-year-old child—the average age of children in our study group—would be able to tell a graceful from an ungainly walk, or the expert mounting of stairs from a stumbling climb, or the consistent jump in hopscotch from an unbalanced jump. But in fact, they could not. Even after being trained until they had reached a criterion of at least 10 out of 12 correct in judging three acts, three-year-old children performed at chance level when shown new acts, thus failing the transfer test. Five-and-a-half-year-old children, however, did far better. They passed the transfer tests not only on the routine acts but also on the gymnastics and ballet.

After having tested the children, we adapted the tests for the chimpanzee Sarah. Had she been tested years earlier she could have indicated her judgments of good and bad acts with the words she had been taught, but her language was no longer functional. We then considered a more iconic procedure for designating good and bad. While initially entertaining the idea of filling a jar with feces and letting it stand for "bad" and filling another jar with chocolate and letting it stand for "good," we adopted a "king's English" version, and used these icons: well- and ill-focused photographs of a TV set (for which Sarah had previously shown strongly marked preferences). These icons successfully designated good or bad acts.

Sarah was shown the twenty acts of everyday motion on a TV monitor: ten good acts, ten bad acts, in a random order. She judged each act by placing her icons for good or bad—the photos of the well- or ill-focused TV monitor—in a designated place. She agreed with our judgments in sixteen out of twenty cases—well above chance level.

Self-Improvement in the Chimpanzee

Are humans alone in seeking self-improvement? While we see few animals primping in a mirror, animals sometimes give the impression of practicing movement. Jessie, a young female chimpanzee of about two years of age, once did so.

In the outdoor compound of our laboratory Jessie performed a series of somersaults, most of them perfect in the sense that they propelled her forward in a straight line. Now and then, however, a somersault failed and she twisted to the side. When she did so she seemed to us to acknowledge her "error" by repeating the somersault immediately, with even greater alacrity than after performing her perfect somersaults.

There are two kinds of evidence needed to justify the claim that an individual is practicing. First, he must perform acts that can be judged as "good" (such as somersaults that describe a forward trajectory) or "bad" (somersaults that go awry). Second, there must be evidence that he judges his acts by placing "good" acts in one category, "bad" acts in another, and demonstrating a preference for the "good" acts. The evidence for preference can take several forms, including the form it appeared to take in Jessie when she appeared to perform the next somersault more quickly following a "bad" somersault.

When given a bowl of food pellets, male rats typically eat while standing on all fours, their heads burrowed in the bowl. The female rat, however, rests on her haunches, seizes a single pellet with her tiny forepaws, and discreetly pops the pellet into her mouth with a certain delicacy. If, after ingesting a series of food pellets, she encounters a pellet that crumbles in her paws, she will seize the next pellet with greater alacrity. So too, when an unexpected event, such as some mechanical problem, interferes with a rat's normal running in an activity wheel, the rat will launch its next bout of running with greater vigor.

Is Jessie's quick somersault after a failed attempt the equivalent of the rat's response to a crumbling pellet or a malfunctioning wheel? What looks like practice may be an example of this general rule: An event that "interrupts" an action sequence will serve to accelerate the resumption of the sequence. To claim that an animal evaluates its actions, has images of good acts, compares its performed acts with those images, finds some acts imperfect, and is driven to "correct" the imperfect act by immediately repeating the act requires evidence beyond the few hints provided to us by Jessie.

We might ask, in concluding this section, one more question: Why is a bird's intensive "practicing" of its song not equivalent to human practice or self-improvement? Simply because the bird's practice, like the cat's training of its young, is an adaptation confined to one activity and almost certainly is associated with a specific physiological state. Birds, like cats, do not make judgments; birds do not judge the quality of their singing, nor do cats judge the performance of their kittens.

Training: An Adaptation

Mother cats bring mice to the "den" for their kittens. Initially the mother cat seriously injures the mice, making them easy targets for the young kittens. Later, the mice are virtually unharmed, posing more difficult prey for the maturing kittens. Unless a kitten receives experience of this kind during a critical period of its early development, it will not stalk mice in adulthood.

Ospreys, one of several small hawks, also train their young. Their training exploits the fact that both male and female parents are caretakers. One parent, flying above the fledgling osprey, drops a prey into the air, attracting the young bird. When the fledgling "misses" the falling prey, the other parent, flying below the young osprey, retrieves it, exchanges positions with the other parent, and repeats the training.

Monkey, gorilla, and chimpanzee mothers have been observed to remove leaves from the mouths of their infants. Field observers suggest that such leaves are not part of their regular diet. Any novel food may, in fact, provoke an aversive reaction on the part of the mother. Gorilla and chimpanzee mothers have even been observed to "encourage" their young, holding the infant's hands while gently coaxing it to "walk." The mother's encouragement is sporadic, however, and ceases long before the infant actually starts "walking."

The training, in both cat and osprey, provides us with one example of an adaptation, biological machinery that has evolved to solve a specific problem. The training has one target, food. In both cat and osprey the adaptation depends on a physiological state that the parent attains after the birth of the offspring, automatically leading the parent to train its young.

The cat cannot be said to teach the kittens because she does not judge the performance of her kittens—she does not bring additional mice to the slow learners while releasing the fast learners early. Further, the stalking of mice is the only act that cats "teach"; they do not teach the kitten how to escape from predators, court a mate, construct a safe den, or the like.

Human Training

The human mother almost continually monitors her child, encouraging and correcting. In humans, training is carried out not only when the parent is in a special physiological state. Unlike the mother cat, which monitors solely the "hunting" progress of her kittens, the human mother monitors almost every act of her child. And unlike the sporadic training of the gorilla and chimpanzee mothers in coaxing their infants to walk, human training is persistent, coming to an end only when the parent judges that the child has reached a certain level of achievement.

Because it is persistent, and because it can be as repetitive as the training found in cat or osprey, human training resembles an adaptation. It has the "passion" one associates with an adaptation. Yet human training is not an adaptation, for unlike the animal training that focuses on a single target, human training has indeterminately many targets. The human is the only species that combines the persistence of an adaptation with the general flexibility of human intelligence. Indeed, human training is so unique that we shall give it a new name, pedagogy.

Pedagogy and Its Aesthetic Roots

Although all human groups appear to have pedagogy, this fact is often missed since the pedagogic goals in one culture often differ completely from those of another. Almost any activity can be a pedagogic target. The !Kung San teach their infants to sit and walk, but do not teach them to forage. And while parents in western societies teach their children how to dress themselves, and to use proper table manners, they do not teach their children how to sit or walk.

When teaching the child, the parent judges the child's appearance—how the child looks, speaks, moves—and judges what the child produces—how and what the child writes, plays, paints. When the child's appearance or performance displeases the parent, the parent will intervene and attempt to bring both appearance and performance into conformity with the parental "ideal." On what basis, though, does the parent intervene, and what is the parental "ideal"?

The root of human pedagogy lies in aesthetics, in the judgment of beauty which, like charity, begins at home in the judgment of self. Humans are as intent on improving their own performance as they are on improving the performance of others. And yet, while the aspiration for improvement starts with the self, it later reaches out and enfolds the other one.

Pedagogy inevitably begins with the attempt to bring one's own appearance and performance into conformity with an ideal. The face, being the main source of social identity, is a principal locus of aesthetic judgment. It is the face that provides the smiles and frowns one directs at others, and it is the face of others that one reads for smiles and frowns. We look at ourselves in the mirror over a lifetime, carefully examining every facial detail—hair, lips, teeth, skin—and comparing the totality with an implicit ideal. Discrepancies disturb us, prompting us to make changes in hair style, cosmetics, dentistry, even our facial expressions. If every human had a dollar for every minute he spent examining his face in the mirror, he could surely manage an early retirement!

But the face is not the only object of scrutiny. Motion is another primary candidate for judgment. Are there any who have not tried to perfect a performance—practiced batting tennis balls, shooting baskets, bowling, dancing, casting flies, playing instruments, singing? How many of us, in leaving a movie, have found our bodies inadvertently moving and acting in the style of the hero or heroine we have just seen? How we move, and how others move, inspires our aesthetic sense and leads us to critical judgments and to pedagogy.

The Techniques of Pedagogy

Punishment is undoubtedly the most popular method for modifying the behavior of others. When an infant monkey urinates while being carried, wetting its mother, the mother responds by pushing the infant away from her until the infant has completed its "toilet." The infant screams in protest at the loss of the mother's warm body but soon learns to anticipate its needs, and avoids wetting its mother. The popularity of punishment is hardly groundless. It works. Not only does it effectively eliminate the unwanted actions of another, but punishment is wonderfully cathartic. Biting, hitting, kicking, scratching, pushing are natural reactions to the offensive behavior of another individual. These require no training.

But just as there is a technique for reducing the frequency of undesired actions, so there is a technique for increasing the frequency of desired actions. Patting, smiling, praising, caressing—rewarding, in general—have as great an effect in increasing desired behavior as punishment has in reducing undesirable behavior.

Unfortunately, rewarding another individual is not as cathartic as is punishing her. The likelihood of an animal caressing another who pleases it is far less than the likelihood of an animal hitting another who displeases it. Thus, although behavior can be modified either by punishing undesired acts or by rewarding desired ones, punishment is the modification of first resort. The Hamadryas baboon, for instance, manages its harem by biting the nape of the neck of any female who wanders off; he does not reward his harem with pats or with morsels of food for remaining by his side, even though gifts of food are not unknown among animals.

Humans, too, prefer dispensing punishment to reward. In many cases the human reaction to a misbehaving child is not different from that of any another animal. Rather than respond with constructive pedagogy, explaining and reasoning, parents often seek relief from their own frustration and respond with punishment.

Passive Guidance

Passive guidance, where the body of another individual is molded into a desired form, is a primitive and effective form of training. The San mother puts her child's body into a desired sitting position, and piles sand behind the infant's back to help it to maintain that position. When the infant loses her balance, as she often does, the mother once again props the infant up, restoring the displaced pile of sand. So too, a ballet teacher may place an adult dancer's body in a desired position, or a coach may do so when an athlete's arm, head, or legs are not correctly held. Passive guidance is a tried-and-true approach to training in humans.

We were greatly surprised to observe a (weak) case of passive guidance in one of our captive chimpanzees. Within this group, the dominant chimpanzees claim the prerogative of being accompanied by another animal when changing locations. The dominant animal stations itself before a submissive one and waits until the submissive animal has joined her. A well-trained, submissive animal will either grasp the dominant animal from behind or line up beside her and place an arm around her shoulder. Once the submissive animal has complied, the two set off to a location selected by the dominant animal. What happens when the submissive animal fails to comply? In the case we observed, Sadie, the dominant animal, resorted to training the submissive animal, Jessie, as you shall see.

Sadie and Jessie were members of a group of juveniles who had been in the laboratory for over three years. Although when first placed together, in the half-acre compound, Jessie ran off whenever Sadie approached, Sadie finally succeeded in wooing Jessie to her side. She patted Jessie on the head and shoulder, reassuring her, and then stationed herself beside Jessie, taking Jessie's arm and curling it around her own neck and shoulder. This was not passive guidance, because rather than guiding Jessie into position, Sadie moved her own body into the embrace of Jessie's arm. That accomplished, the two set off.

But Jessie was too short for Sadie. Her arm slipped down Sadie's spine until her full weight lay across Sadie's back. When Sadie halted, Jessie ran off. Sadie patiently reinstated the training cycle. At the end of about two hours, Jessie was fully retrained. When Sadie approached, Jessie lined up beside Sadie, placed her own arm around Sadie, and the two set off together.

The problem caused by Jessie's stature had not been resolved, however, and after a short distance Jessie slumped across Sadie's back again. Both halted, but now Jessie righted herself, and the two trotted off once again.

Although deceptively simple, passive guidance is not a trivial competence. It is far more difficult to place another's body into a desired position than to place your own body in such a position. When you want an object, you reach for it automatically; but when you want *me* to reach for it, you cannot automatically use passive guidance in demonstrating *how* I am to reach for it. First you must "picture" the position I must take, then you must locate yourself relative to me in order to direct me into the desired position. Because true passive guidance is very likely to require simulation, it is probably not available to species other than the human; though in some limited degree, it may be open to the chimpanzee.

Sadie's training of Jessie has much of the cognitive complexity of human training. It is virtually an example of human pedagogy—except for one important consideration. The training was carried out for Sadie's benefit, not for the benefit of Jessie.

Although human training is carried out under the auspices of aesthetics, on behalf of the teacher's standards, it invariably has the effect of benefiting the individual being trained. Were a human teacher to follow Sadie's model, training students solely for her own benefit, she would undermine the evolutionary function of pedagogy. She would seek to benefit only those whose training would benefit her, and thus fail to transmit skills and knowledge to all needy parties from generation to generation. The pedagogue does not confine his instruction to only those students who will benefit the teacher. Pedagogy is directed to any individual whose performance fails to satisfy the teacher's standards.

Signs of Pedagogy in the Signing Chimpanzee

Adult chimpanzees, trained to use simple hand signs, have been said to teach these signs to a younger chimpanzee. The adult chimpanzee "molds" the hand of the young chimpanzee with the same passive guidance used originally by its human trainer. This seems to qualify as pedagogy, but is it? The fact that such guidance is found in chimpanzees reared by humans makes the claim credible. Chimpanzees reared by humans show complex behaviors never reported in the wild—Sadie's training of Jessie, for example. But having said this, claims for pedagogy in the sign-trained animal still remain inadequate.

Let us suppose that a father, while on a walk with his daughter, picks a dandelion, and tickles his daughter under the chin with it. Then the daughter picks a dandelion and repeats the act, tickling her friend under the chin. Is this pedagogy, or mere imitation? And does the behavior of the daughter toward her friend differ in any significant way from that of the adult chimpanzee toward the younger animal?

In molding the hand of a young chimpanzee, the adult animal carries out what was initially done to it by the human trainer; the child, in tickling her friend under the chin, repeats what was initially done to her by her father. From a behavioral point of view the two cases do not seem to differ, yet many are inclined to construe them differently, calling one pedagogy, the other imitation. A hand sign has a referent and therefore can be correct or incorrect, whereas tickling someone under the chin with a flower, having no referent, is neither correct nor incorrect. Consequently we dismiss tickling under the chin as imitation, and upgrade the hand sign to pedagogy.

In teaching hand signs to the chimpanzee the human trainer spent considerable time showing it how to distinguish correct from incorrect signs, continuing the training until the animal could perform both correctly. But is this the goal in the case of the chimpanzee "teacher"? Does the animal persist in training the "student" until it has produced the correct sign for the correct object? The data do not permit a clear answer. Unless the chimpanzee is not merely imitating the behavior of its trainer, unless the chimpanzee has adopted the trainer's goal, there is no reason for us to distinguish the chimpanzee from the child who simply imitates her father.

To qualify as a pedagogue the chimpanzee must do more than "teach" hand signs; she must generalize, adopting pedagogic targets different from the original ones. A true pedagogue does not confine himself to one target, that of shaping hand signs. But what if the chimpanzee, as a result of having had its hands molded into signs, branches out and begins to train its offspring in a variety of other acts? What if it teaches its infant to take its first steps, for instance, or instructs it in fishing for termites, or in hammering nuts?

We then could talk of pedagogy, for training the young in these new acts could not be written off as imitation. Pedagogy consists of persistent training—in a variety of tasks—that benefits the young. The chimpanzee's failure to teach is not the result of a cognitive deficit but is better explained by a lack of concern for whether the performance of the other one conforms to a standard. Indeed the animal does not judge its own performance relative to a standard.

The chimpanzee's style of pedagogy is nicely demonstrated by Sadie's training of Jessie, but this is not the only case of its kind. Though such cases are rare, they can be observed in captive animals. All such cases however, have the same motivational character: The pedagogue trains the novice for his own benefit. Thus the chimpanzee does not have true pedagogy.

The claim that chimpanzees practice pedagogy in the wild, and human observers just don't see it, has been refuted. The acquisition of nut cracking skills by a group of infant chimpanzees over an entire ten-year period has been recorded on hundreds of hours of film by Tetsuro Matsuzawa. The film does not show a single case of pedagogy in this most complex of chimpanzee technologies.

The failure is not owed to the infants. They observe carefully as their mothers place a nut on an "anvil" and strike it with a rock. The infants make repeated attempts to imitate. After several failures the infant will return to its mother's side and lean heavily on her body, carefully observing her procedure. It then returns to its own problem of unsuccessful nut cracking. This is a cycle the infant repeats indefinitely, the mother never interfering. The detailed film, registering hundreds of hours of nut cracking, demonstrates clearly why there is an absence of pedagogy: Although the infant chimpanzee repeatedly observes its mother cracking nuts, the chimpanzee mother never reciprocates, never observes her infant's efforts at nut cracking. Ten years of filming does not yield a single instance of a chimpanzee mother either observing or attempting to help her infant to crack nuts!

A chimpanzee mother allows her infant to take and eat the nuts she has cracked; she tolerates her infant as it leans heavily on her while she is busy with her task; but she never turns away from her own successful nut cracking to watch the efforts of her infant. Without maternal training it takes a chimpanzee infant ten years to perfect nut cracking, a task which might require about six months if the mother were to undertake to train the infant.

Although the chimpanzee mother does not assist her infant by acting as a watchful pedagogue, she does make a vital contribution: Her repeated, daily, successful cracking of nuts contributes to her infant's "motivation." In other words, by watching its mother the infant "gets hooked" on the problem of nut cracking.

The motivational significance of problem solving may also be seen in the monkey. Monkeys do not persist in working on a problem simply when given food for doing so. In their case, too, food is not the primary goal. For when a previously solvable problem is now made insoluble, the monkey stops responding. Even when it is given food at every trial! Evidently the monkey's primary goal is to solve the problem, and finding a solution to the problem is its reward.

It is this same motivation, the solving of the problem, coupled with the observation of its mother's successful example, that keeps the young chimpanzee hooked on nut cracking until it eventually manages the problem perfectly.

Chimpanzees that are not exposed to nut cracking as infants, that encounter nut cracking only as adults, never learn the technology. Probably the adults fail because only infants can be led to engage in the endless trials and errors needed for the animal to solve the problem.

The Cognitive Gap

The wild chimpanzee teaches its young very little. But does the young chimpanzee suffer? No. For everything the parent does the young chimpanzee learns to do by itself, without parental training. Even the most complex acts of the adult chimpanzee—nut cracking, termite fishing, water sponging—do not depend on parental assistance. While these acts do not occur in all chimpanzees, they are nevertheless species-specific acts for which all chimpanzees have a potential.

Human adults, however, engage in many acts that the young cannot acquire on their own. The child would suffer greatly if not trained by its parents. Indeed, even when given special training children may find it hard to acquire certain skills, such as in reading, writing, and arithmetic. There is a gap that exists among humans—between the performance of the adult and that of the child—a gap which cannot be bridged without parental assistance.

Nor is this disparity in competence between adult and child a product of recent times. It is of long standing. The child was as much in need of parental assistance during the Pleistocene as it is today. Lithic tool making, jewelry design, butchering—all ancient technologies—could not have been acquired without parental assistance.

How did this cognitive gap arise? First, the gap presupposes individuals who invented technologies. Although their names are lost to history we can be certain that these gifted individuals were responsible for the use of the wheel, cooking with fire, hunting with the bow and arrow, developing an alphabet writing system, and so on.

In addition the gap presupposes individuals who, while not themselves the inventors of the technologies, were good observers, and thus capable of acquiring the new technologies without assistance, by imitation alone. It was these individuals who probably taught the system to others. For inventors often are not ideal pedagogues. Having acquired their systems through inspiration and original insight, inventors have difficulty teaching others. Those who observe the innovation and recognize its merits make better pedagogues. They are gifted in their own way, in that they are able to acquire the system without assistance, as most individuals cannot. Having taught the system to themselves they are in a position to teach it to others.

A pedagogue has special virtues. She provides superior feedback because she knows the ideal form of a product. By explaining the purpose of an act or a device, the pedagogue relieves the student of the need to learn through blind mimicry. The pedagogue can assist the student by encouraging him not to attempt everything but to concentrate his efforts on skills for which he is talented, and to trade the products of his talents with those of others whose skills complement his own. The advantage of pedagogic instruction for the novice may be that of greater efficiency, a reduction in errors—an advantage not to be underestimated. The cost of an error in the real world often is substantial; the novice who errs may not get a second chance.

The human specialization in intelligence ensures profound individual differences in intelligence, greater differences than are to be found in any other species. The specialization results not only in highly gifted individuals but also in a considerable disparity between the gifted and the less gifted. This means that a large proportion of the population will be unable to acquire innovations without assistance, making pedagogy truly essential for humans.

Once upon a time there was a chimpanzee that invented nut cracking. Another that invented termite fishing. Are these inventions not like those of the human? Did the survival of nut cracking and termite fishing, skills still found among today's chimpanzees, depend upon inventors and pedagogues? Inventions such as these do not depend on pedagogues because the acts they require lie within the competence of most chimpanzees. In every generation most chimpanzees acquire these technologies through heightened motivation and trial-and-error learning. The small percentage that do not are left to struggle without them.

Pedagogy transforms the human. It perpetuates old technologies and launches new ones. A mother teaches her child to do the things her mother taught her, preserving tradition. She may also teach her child new technologies, creating new traditions. Nothing may contribute more to human transformability than this humble fact: Humans teach one another.

Chapter 4
The Sentence
Action and Object, Noun and Verb

The first report on animal language to appear in a professional journal was entitled "Teaching Animals to Converse." Written in 1884 by Sir John Lubbock, it described the procedure he used in teaching words to his dog Van. The claim that a dog could converse, while considered extraordinary, was not dismissed. Lubbock was a distinguished naturalist of his day and the article had appeared in the respected journal, *Nature*. The report was honored for yet another reason: The British take their dogs seriously.

Because Lubbock wrote of "conversing with animals" we thought he had done the obvious: taught his dog the names for a few objects, for a few actions, and then combined them to produce dog "sentences." A "sentence" in the dog's language then could have been any action-object combination, such as "fetch bowl," "sniff slipper," or "fetch slipper." In fact, if Van had been taught just four object names—ball, slipper, bowl, stick—and the names of just four actions—fetch, sniff, bite, push—Van could have carried out at least sixteen commands! Moreover, the dog need not have been trained in all sixteen. He might, from being trained in just four commands, have generalized to sixteen. For Van would have learned the rule: Sentence = action + object. And having done that, Van should, in addition, have been able to apply the same rule to any *new* names of objects and actions added to his lexicon.

But Lubbock's "conversing with animals" was no more than a high-spirited claim. He simply taught his dog the names of a few objects and a few actions; he had never combined them! In the limited "dialogue" that Lubbock did carry out with Van, the dog demonstrated its competence with individual words and in the production mode only.

Lubbock placed several "words" on the ground and invited the dog to select one and bring it to him. If the "word" the dog chose agreed with what

Lubbock guessed to be the dog's current interest—a particular food, a walk, a bit of play, or the like—he interpreted the word as a request for the item, and scored the dog "correct." Lubbock and Van communicated remarkably well, in part thanks to Lubbock's ability to diagnose the dog's motivation.

But Van made an even more striking contribution: He used completely arbitrary objects—little pieces of paper on which Lubbock wrote English words to make implicit requests. Van's ability to "make requests" indicates that this use of "words" is more primitive than has been appreciated. Lubbock missed his chance to make Van the first "talking" dog, for surely Van could have learned to combine the names of actions and objects and produced sentences. In missing this chance Lubbock did the entire canine species a disservice—dogs have not been given a fair shake since. The social intelligence of canines has never been vindicated by experimental study but has been palmed off on seers, poets, and pet owners. It has been left to them to extol the gifts of dogs. All of this could have been avoided if Lubbock had just taken the next step and given Van the chance to learn a simple rule.

Delphinian "Grammar"

Not dogs, but dolphins, were the first to learn the Lubbock grammar. This quintessentially simple system, mistakenly credited by us to Lubbock, was actually first taught to dolphins by the comparative psychologist Lewis Herman and his colleagues. They embroidered the system a bit, taking it beyond the simplest version, but what they taught the dolphins can still rightfully be called a Lubbock grammar.

The dolphins were taught what Van should have been taught: to combine the names of objects and actions. Though taught only three or four names for each category, those few names were sufficient to permit their combination according to the Lubbock rule: Any object can go with any action. And indeed, after being trained in just a few of the object-action combinations the dolphins successfully generalized to new combinations. For example, after being trained on "ball spit" (spit at the ball) and "hoop touch" (touch the hoop), they responded correctly to "ball touch," "hoop spit," and other such cases.

The dolphin system contained two additional elaborations. A third category, *properties*, was added and made optional. In other words, while a command had to contain both an object and an action, there was the option of adding a property to the object. For example, "ball touch" also could appear as "surface ball touch" and "bottom ball touch." And since the animal's environment is a pool, "surface" and "bottom" name the locations of objects in the dolphin's liquid environment. Therefore "surface ball touch" means "touch the ball that is on the surface of the pool."

"Fetch," another action, then was added. "Fetch" was more complicated than the original actions "spit" and "touch," since it required two arguments rather than one. For example, while "ball spit" and "ball touch" meant "spit on the ball" or "touch the ball," "fetch" in "frisbee ball fetch" meant "take the frisbee to the ball." Thus the dolphin's version of the combinatorial system could be described by these two rules:

1. Rule 1 } (property) object action
2. Rule 2 } (property) object [1]: (property) object [2]: fetch.

When a speaker uses the property option, the dolphin is instructed to "surface ball spit" (spit on the ball which is on the surface of the pool), or "bottom ball touch" (touch the ball which is on the bottom of the pool). "Fetch" is a special term. It involves two objects, instructing the animal to bring one object to the location of another object, as is seen in Rule 2. "Surface ball bottom frisbee fetch" instructs the animal to take the ball (which is on the surface of the pool) to the frisbee (which is on the bottom of the pool). This system, though more complex than the simple Lubbock grammar, is nonetheless an object-action grammar, and one the dolphins had no problem learning. They followed all specified commands, whether novel or familiar.

"Command Performances" of a Bonobo

The animal psychologist Sue Savage-Rumbaugh and her students compared a bonobo's comprehension of spoken English with that of an eighteen-month-old child. It was argued by these researchers that the bonobo, although never trained, acquired English just as a child does. Actually, however, the bonobo was "trained" in language from infancy. For the first nine years of its life the bonobo was given spoken commands and checked for accuracy in carrying them out. Its failures were corrected by the trainers.

The child, of course, had not been been given this kind (or any other kind) of language training. Because children produce speech, the child's comprehension of language could be judged from what the child said. Unlike children, language-trained animals produce very little language. Therefore there is no way to check their comprehension of language except by monitoring their accuracy in carrying out commands. The bonobo not only was taught language by being given commands, but the very test used to compare the bonobo with the child simply reinstated the bonobo's training conditions. It was based entirely on commands!

Both child and bonobo were placed in a small suite of rooms containing several objects, and given commands: to move from one room to another, to move objects from one location to another, to act on objects by cutting them, and so forth. The bonobo outperformed the child. It followed 74 percent of the commands accurately, as compared to the child's 64 percent—an outcome that nicely replicates an earlier comparison of the same kind made by the comparative psychologists Beatrice and Allen Gardner. Their chimpanzee Washoe also outperformed the child with whom it was compared.

The commands given both child and animal leave one much impressed with the complexity of the language they appear to understand. The commands include such sentences as "Go to the refrigerator and get a banana," "I want Kanzi [animal's name] to bite Rose," "Can you find the ice cubes?", "Make the doggie bite the snake," and even a sentence that includes an embedded clause: "Go get the carrot that's in the microwave." Were an eighteen-month-old child able to actually comprehend such sentences it would indeed have a remarkable grammar, one well beyond that of other eighteen-month-olds.

The sentences, however, cannot be taken at face value. They contain many words for which there is no evidence of comprehension by either animal or child. Although these words are presented as having the status of any other word, they are bogus or phony words. There is no evidence that either child or animal understands words such as *some, in, and, the, that, on, could, can* (as in "can you"). Like most closed-class words, these are acquired by children well after the age of eighteen months.

Figure 4.1 presents parallel lists of the commands given to both child and bonobo. On the left are the actual commands given, on the right the corresponding commands with the bogus words removed. For example, "Could you put the apple on the hat?" reduces to "Put apple hat." "Go to the bedroom and get the tomato" reduces to "Go bedroom, get tomato." Notice that when the bogus words are removed the impression of grammatical complexity dissolves and we arrive at a familiar level of complexity, the level found in all tests of language-trained animals.

In order to demonstrate comprehension of the otherwise bogus words, one must show that both child and animal can: understand such grammatical distinctions as that between a definite and an indefinite article between "a" boy and "the" boy; distinguish the quantifiers, "some" from "all"; understand the connectives, attending to the difference between candy "and" gum versus candy "or" gum; distinguish between prepositions ("in" versus "on" the refrigerator, and so on).

Put some pine needles in the back pack.	put pine needles backpack
Put some toothpaste on the hotdog.	put toothpaste hotdog
Put your clay in the umbrella.	put clay umbrella
Put some toothpaste in the clay.	put toothpaste clay
Get the toothpaste and put it on the Fourtrax.	get toothpaste put fourtrax
Get the hamburger (hotdog) and put it in the bowl.	get hamburger (hotdog) put bowl
Get the soap and put it in the umbrella.	get soap put umbrella
Get some clovers for Kelly.	get clovers Kelly
Get the phone and give it to Rose (Linda).	get phone give Rose (Linda)
Get the bubbles and put them on the book.	get bubbles put book
Get the bubbles. Get Kelly with the bubbles.	get bubbles get Kelly bubbles
Take your ball over to the vacuum cleaner.	take ball vacuum cleaner
Hide the doggie in the pillow.	hide doggie pillow
Hit the can opener (fork) with the rock.	hit can opener (fork) rock
Can you put the hat on Karen?	put hat Karen?
Can you ask Rose to tickle Kelly?	Rose tickle Kelly?
Do you see the rock? Can you put it in the hat?	see rock? put hat?
Could you take the pine needles outdoors?	take pine needles outdoors?
There is a new ball hiding at Sherman and Austin's play yard.	ball Sherman Austin play yard

Figure 4.1 Commands, with and without their bogus words, given to both child and bonobo.

Demonstrating that children can make these distinctions is a demanding task, with many controls being required to eliminate competing alternatives. And yet none of these demanding tests was ever given to either child or animal.

But is there really a need for such tests? Why bother with them, when the point of the test is simply to compare child and animal? And since neither child nor bonobo was tested for the comprehension of these distinctions, isn't the comparison fair and square?

Actually, the fairness of the comparison is not the point. It is highly misleading in both cases to draw conclusions on the basis of commands that contain bogus words. The sentences that the child and bonobo *actually* comprehend are those with the bogus words removed. And to comprehend these sentences the grammatical categories of noun and verb are not needed. Like the commands comprehended by the dolphin, the actual commands can be understood by means of a Lubbock "grammar." Such a grammar is based on perceptual categories like action/object, not on grammatical categories like noun/verb.

The Lubbock Grammar Revisited

Since all the instructions given the child and bonobo were formed in the imperative mode, the main rule needed to understand these commands would take the form "action-object"—a rule we remember from both dog and dolphin.

The "action-object" rule accommodates all such sentences as these: "Put dog," "Knife ball," "Hide tree," "Eat candy." To handle other instructions, we need only to amplify the basic rule with the same optional features we assigned to the dolphin grammar: action-object (location), with the parentheses indicating the optional nature of location, and action-object (object), with the parentheses indicating the optional nature of a second object. The first accommodates sentences of this kind: "Get dog (in) kitchen," "Take cat (to the) microwave,"; the second, sentences of this kind: "Give Jack dog," "Put milk (on) jam," "Put jam (in) milk." The parentheses in these latter cases indicate bogus words.

While the ability to carry out commands probably does justice to the bonobo's language competence—as it does to that of dolphin and dog—it does not do justice to that of the child. While an eighteen-month-old child lacks an adult grammar, its language knowledge is not limited solely to carrying out commands. It is inarguable that in due time the child will acquire "bogus" words along with other closed-class words and move from perceptual to grammatical rules, from rules based on object/action to rules based on noun/verb. This is not a transition the bonobo is likely to make.

Is the Bonobo Gifted?

Although field observations show some clear differences between bonobo and chimpanzee with respect to temperament and social behavior, there have been no serious comparisons of the cognitive performances of the two species. Bonobos are far less aggressive than chimpanzees, and thus are easier to work with.

The bonobo is seen as socially precocious owing to its polymorphic and promiscuous sexual practices, which exceed those of chimpanzee or human; only the dolphin (in which erection is a voluntary response) is as active sexually. Sexual activity in the bonobo is not confined to adult heterosexual pairs but is commonly engaged in between adult and child, female and female, etc. In addition, bonobos copulate in a variety of positions, whereas chimpanzees copulate only in the dorso-ventral position. This difference, though sometimes taken to indicate a lack of imagination on the part of the male chimpanzee, actually is due to an anatomical difference. The sex skin of the female chimpanzee makes ventral-ventral copulation impossible, whereas the sex skin of the bonobo can accommodate virtually all sexual connections.

But what about cognitive comparisons? Have any emerged from the field? One, which concerns tool use, favors the chimpanzee. Tool making and tool use have been widely observed in all four chimpanzee subspecies, while neither toolmaking nor the use of tools has been observed in the bonobo.

The Special Status of Function Words

How would the child or animal in Savage-Rumbaugh's study have responded to the commands if the bogus words had been removed? Or, what would be even more interesting, if the bogus words had been replaced by nonsense words?

Recent work by the psycholinguist Peter Juscyck and his students, on the human infant's sensitivity to function words, bears directly on the question, in that most of the bogus words in the commands are function words. Function words do not name anything in the real world but nonetheless are required by the grammar of the sentence. For example, the function words *and* and *or* distinguish conjunction from disjunction; that is, give the ball to Mary *and* John versus give the ball to Mary *or* John.

In her doctoral thesis Michele Shady found that, even at a remarkably early age, infants are sensitive to function words. They listen longer to speech passages that contain normal function words than to those in which nonsense words have been substituted for function words. So too, they listen longer to passages in which function words are in their normal locations than to passages in which they are not. For example, they listen longer to "A bike with three wheels is coming down the street" than to "*Is* bike with three wheels *a* coming down the street."

This test should be given to the bonobo, or to any other language-trained animal. For if an animal were to show an infant-comparable sensitivity to function words, it would be difficult to explain this peculiarity without invoking grammatical categories. It would constitute serious evidence for grammatical learning, since it could not be explained on the basis of perceptual categories. Of course, care must be taken to ensure that changes in function words do not entail changes in prosody. For although animals would be unlikely to be sensitive to function words, they easily could be sensitive to prosody.

Curiously, in virtually all habituation tests, when an infant's expectation is disconfirmed the infant increases its looking at the new item. In the case of function words, however, the infant appears to do the opposite, listening longer to normal passages than to abnormal ones.

But does an abnormal speech passage really disconfirm an infant's expectation? Is an abnormal speech passage equivalent to the disconfirmed expectancies of visual perception, as when an object passes through a barrier or does not fall despite a lack of support? Abnormal speech passages would seem to be more comparable to nonsense sequences than to unexpected ones. Presumably an infant will listen longer to a speech passage than it will to a nonsense passage.

A passage that conforms to grammatical rules should be more interesting to an infant than a passage that does not. Notice that the distinction between rule-conforming and non-rule-conforming sequences is not comparable to that between a memorized nonsense sequence and a changed nonsense sequence. An individual accustomed to the sequence 2 6 9 7 will show increased listening when given 2 6 7 9. But this is not a contrast between rule-governed and non-rule-governed sequences; rules do not apply to either of these sequences. The results suggest that sequences that are compatible with the grammar will be given closer attention than those not compatible with the grammar.

We used the child's disposition to imitate as an index of grammaticality (see Chapter 2). The present results suggest, however, that we could as easily have used the child's willingness to listen to the sequence. For both the willingness to listen to sequence and to copy it may reflect the same underlying factor, the child's recognition of grammaticality.

The Bidirectional Symbol

The pioneering French linguist Ferdinand de Saussure speaks of the "bidirectional sign," and points out that a fundamental property of normal communication is the ability of a speaker and listener to reverse roles. According to the classic tradition, production and comprehension are two sides of a single competence.

Animal language researchers, by contrast, often complain that focusing on language production rather than comprehension leads to an underestimation of the animal's achievements. Neither bonobos, chimpanzees, nor dolphins "say" much, it's true, but that should not be held against them, the investigators contend, since they comprehend far more than they say.

This argument gives the impression that comprehension and production are distinct competences. Indeed Savage-Rumbaugh, in arguing that comprehension evolved independently of production, suggests that if we were to test species that do not produce language—such as robins, gophers, and snakes—for their comprehension of language, we would find that language, far from being unique to humans, belongs to the whole animal world.

A bidirectional sign has the same meaning for the sender as for the receiver, and has a considerable advantage, as de Saussure pointed out. Interestingly, the computational linguist J. R. Hurford, using a simulation procedure, showed that individuals having this trait tend to out-reproduce those that did not. Both de Saussure's theoretical proposal and Hurford's model, however, leave open the empirical question: What is the actual case with the child? Does the child learn words bidirectionally from the very beginning?

To test this issue with children would require that the child be taught two independent lexicons, one for production and another for comprehension. The independence of the two lexicons would be maintained in a simple fashion: Adults would speak to the child using a set of words entirely different from the set the child would use in speaking to adults. In terms of production and comprehension, the child would be bilingual!

To explore de Saussure's claim, one would have to use a transfer test. The goal would be to gain answers to these two questions in particular: Is the child able to produce sentences using the words previously spoken to it only by adults? Is the child able to comprehend sentences composed of words that only the child previously produced? And yet, obviously, this is not an experiment that could be done with children! Something very similar, however, was tested in the course of our instructing three chimpanzees in a language consisting of words the animals were taught.

We taught the animals independent vocabularies for production and comprehension: The animal "wrote" sentences with one set of words while the sentences it "read" were composed of a different set of words. Although this procedure could not be used with either speech or sign it can be used with a language "written" in plastic words, because one can control the supply of words, restricting some of them to the production mode, others to the comprehension mode.

The animals were trained initially in a small set of words which were used to *produce* short "requests" such as "GIVE APPLE" and "WASH ORANGE." During the same period the animals also were trained in a different set of initial words which were used to *comprehend* short commands written by the trainer such as "TAKE KEY" and "PUT BOX." (Henceforth plastic words will appear in capital letters.)

The animals were trained until they had met the same criterion in both modes, and then they were given their first transfer tests. Words they had "read" (in instructions given them by the trainer) now were given them to be used in their own productions. Conversely, words they had used when producing requests now appeared in instructions given them by the trainer.

Did the results indicate that the words one has only produced are comprehended immediately? And are the words one comprehends, but has not yet produced, words that one can automatically produce when necessary? In other words, are initial words bidirectional symbols?

The answers from the chimpanzee test was a resounding "no"—for all three animals performed at chance level on the first transfer test. They could not understand the instructions given them even though they were composed of words they themselves had used in their own productions. Nor could they produce instructions using words they had comprehended when given them in instructions. A dramatic finding, but the next one was equally so.

After failing the first transfer test, the chimpanzees were given a minimal experience in the cross-modal use of the words; that is, a handful of words used exclusively in comprehension were now used in production, and vice versa. Following the cross-modal experience, a new test was made by first teaching the animals entirely new words—some in comprehension, others in production.

The animals then were given a second transfer test exactly like the first. Words taught them in the context of instructions *from* the trainer were now presented for use in requests *to* the trainer. And words taught them in the context of requests they had made *to* the trainer now appeared in instructions *from* the trainer. The outcome of this second transfer test was as dramatic as that of the first. Now all three animals succeeded. Words taught in comprehension were used perfectly in production, and vice versa.

To clarify: If told to INSERT, the animal demonstrated its comprehension by performing the correct action; and if the trainer performed the act of inserting, the animal demonstrated its production by selecting the word INSERT to "describe" the trainer's performance. The question remains, however: Is such an outcome peculiar to the chimpanzee and the use of an artificial language, or is it one that obtains in children as well? We are never likely to have a definitive answer for a comparable test with children is not possible.

The chimpanzee results do however lead us to contemplate a possibility we might otherwise have rejected out of hand: Initial words of children are not bidirectional symbols. In seeming defiance of the great French linguist, comprehension and production may start as separate systems. But if they do begin in this isolated fashion, then their unification requires truly minimal experience! Really, though, Saussure seems to be right: Humans (and chimpanzees as well, or so it seems) are heavily biased toward the bidirectional symbol. They do, however need a soupçon of experience to trigger the bias.

Chimpanzees Learn "Sentences"

The chimpanzee Sarah and several of her colleagues, were, like other species, taught names for objects and actions. The two kinds of words were combined, in the style of a Lubbock grammar, to form such simple sentences as CUT APPLE, WASH GRAPES, INSERT ORANGE, and GIVE BANANA. Other categories also were named; categories such as individuals, properties, quantifiers, prepositions, and these led to ever longer and more complex sentences as new words were incorporated. For example: MARY CUT APPLE; PUT APPLE DISH; MARY CUT YELLOW APPLE; PUT APPLE RED DISH; PUT RED ON YELLOW; MARY PUT APPLE RED DISH.

Originally, words were taught by associating a plastic word with its referent, which could be an object, action, or property. When lessons reached the stage in which words were combined to form sentences it was possible to teach new words, not by using the old-fashioned "association technique" but through the use of the sentence itself; that is, by placing an "unknown" in the sentence and marking it with an interrogative particle.

Questions were formed by removing a word from a sentence, marking the omission with an interrogative particle, and teaching the animal the new word to be substituted for the interrogative particle. The word had the effect of completing the sentence. For example:

APPLE? APPLE

APPLE SAME APPLE

or

APPLE ? BANANA

APPLE DIFFERENT BANANA.

The incompleteness can occur at other points in the sentence, as in APPLE SAME?, for which the answer is APPLE SAME APPLE, or APPLE DIFFERENT?, for which the answer is APPLE DIFFERENT BANANA. These WH-type questions were converted into yes/no questions by appending the interrogative particle to the head of the sentence and then offering the plastic words YES and NO as alternatives. For example:

? APPLE SAME APPLE, for which the answer is

YES APPLE SAME APPLE, or

? APPLE SAME BANANA, for which the answer is

NO APPLE DIFFERENT BANANA.

See Fig. 4.2, for examples of all four questions.

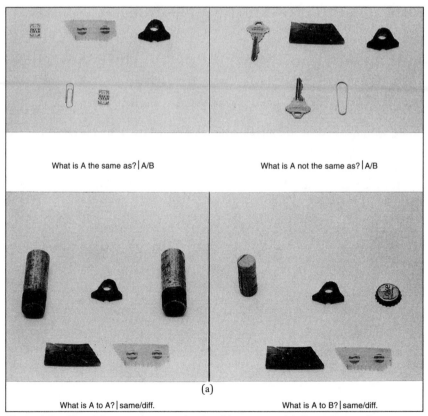

Figure 4.2   The eight questions taught the chimpanzees. (*a*) Four wh-questions.

This same method was used to teach the animal the names of properties such as *colors*, RED, GREEN, YELLOW, and so on; *shapes*, ROUND, SQUARE, TRIANGLE; and *sizes*, SMALL, LARGE. Having taught the chimpanzees these words, it then was possible to teach the names of the categories to which the words belong. For example, Sarah was taught the word COLOROF with these four questions:

RED ? APPLE

YELLOW ? BANANA

RED ? BANANA

YELLOW ? APPLE

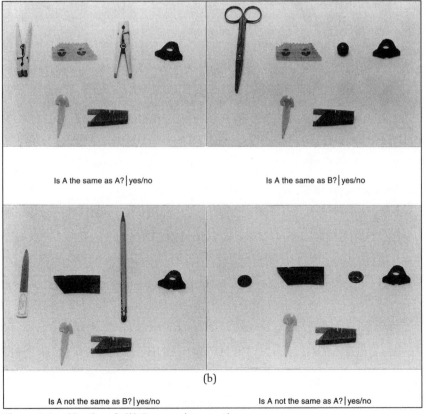

(b)

Figure 4.2 (*Continued*) (*b*) Four yes/no questions.

Only plastic words appear in the sequences. There are no objects present. Sarah was given the new word COLOROF and its negation NO-COLOROF (formed by gluing the negative particle to the word COLOROF). Sarah replaced the question mark with COLOROF in sequences one and two, and with the word NO-COLOROF in sequences three and four, producing: RED COLOROF APPLE, YELLOW COLOROF BANANA, RED NO-COLOROF BANANA, YELLOW NO-COLOROF APPLE.

To establish that she understood these new words, Sarah was given sentences composed of words already in her repertoire,

GREEN ? GRAPE

ORANGE ? ORANGE

ORANGE ? GRAPE

GREEN ? ORANGE

once again giving her the alternatives COLOROF and NO-COLOROF, along with a half-dozen other plastic words. She selected COLOROF for the first two sequences, NO-COLOROF for the last two.

The names for the categories "shape" and "size" were taught in the same way, except that in these cases actual objects were present and depicted: square and round, small and large. And in a final step, names for the three categories (and their members) were combined, with Sarah then being tested on her ability to distinguish among the category names. She was given:

ORANGE ? ORANGE

ROUND ? APPLE

SMALL ? GRAPE,

with the plastic words COLOROF, SIZEOF, SHAPEOF, NAMEOF (and other plastic words) as alternatives. Sarah was posed more than 300 questions of this general kind and she correctly answered over 80 percent of the time—thereby qualifying for a scholarship to the Ivy League!

Blue Triangle Nameof Apple

It soon became arduous to teach new words by repeated direct associations between word and object, so we developed a simpler procedure to teach new names by simply using the word NAMEOF. Unlike the category names

COLOROF, SIZEOF, and so on NAMEOF does not refer to a natural category but is the *explicit product of language training itself*. The ability of an animal to acquire the word NAMEOF indicates the effectiveness of language training; it has taught the animal the concept of *word*.

When an animal can distinguish between TAKE APPLE and TAKE NAMEOF APPLE, between PUT APPLE IN RED DISH and PUT NAMEOF APPLE IN RED DISH, as Sarah could, we can safely conclude that the animal understands the concept of word.

NAMEOF was taught Sarah using the same format used in teaching her COLOROF, and the like. She was given these sequences:

APPLE ? actual apple

ORANGE ? actual orange

APPLE ? actual orange

ORANGE ? actual apple,

once again with the alternatives NAMEOF and NO-NAMEOF (along with other plastic words), as may be seen in Figure 4.3. She chose correctly, selecting NAMEOF for the first two sequences, NO-NAMEOF for the last two.

In addition Sarah was taught the names of new objects by means of NAMEOF. For example she was told FIG NAMEOF actual fig, fig being an unnamed object, and when told to TAKE FIG in the presence of several fruit including a fig, did so.

How does the instruction "X NAMEOF Y" work? Evidently, when the appropriately trained animal is "told" X NAMEOF Y, its representation of the object Y is transferred to the word X. From that moment on the object can be evoked mentally by means of the word alone. Such an ability to talk about things that are not there is part and parcel of the competence that makes displacement possible. It is an uncanny, automatic property of the machinery of mind!

One can also teach new words to a chimpanzee nonostensively; that is, in the absence of any referent! This is how the word BROWN was taught:

BROWN COLOROF CHOCOLATE

The plastic words COLOROF and CHOCOLATE were already part of Sarah's repertoire. The plastic word BROWN was new, and it did not yet have a referent. It was the first word taught Sarah nonostensively: No objects were present when the sequence was taught. In order to associate the color brown with BROWN, Sara had to *image* chocolate, using the word CHOCOLATE

Figure 4.3   The teaching of names using (*a*) "NAMEOF" and (*b*) "NOT NAMEOF."

to do so. To further check whether Sarah understood the meaning of the plastic word BROWN, we showed her four objects, one of which was brown, and gave her the instruction TAKE BROWN. She did.

Perceptual Rules and Rules of the Sentence

We can distinguish two kinds of grammatical rules. One set governs relations within the sentence: among clauses, phrases, and between words. A classical example concerns noun-verb relations: Plural nouns require plural verbs. So too, in languages that distinguish gender, the female (or male, or neutral) form requires the female or male or neutral form of both the noun and verb. Still more elaborate agreement between word-forms is found in languages that recognize case—such as Latin, Greek, German, and Russian—and distinguish among nominative, genitive, accusative, dative, and so on, increasing noun-verb agreement to include case, gender, number, and the like.

The other kind of grammatical rule reflects distinctions that lie "outside" the sentence. These real-world relations are subject to direct perception, and are given their initial interpretation by means of the infant's modules.

But what does that mean? It means that the distinction between an action that takes an object—for example, John breaks the window—and an action that does not take an object—"John breathes"—is made initially by the infant's physical module. In other words, the grammatical distinction between transitive and intransitive verbs has its roots in early, real-world distinctions. Further, the child can distinguish between intentional and nonintentional interactions prior to the first year of age.

The infant can distinguish between individuals interacting with one another and individuals engaging in actions but not interacting. The child can distinguish between those cases in which two individuals direct their actions toward one another by caressing or hitting or helping or hindering one another, and those cases in which two individuals do not direct their actions toward one another, as when both jump rope, or scoop sand with shovels, or wave "bye-bye" in unison. In such cases of "parallel play" there is no intentional interaction between the two individuals, and infants as young as nine to eleven months of age are sensitive to this distinction.

The psycholinguist Lila Gleitman and her students argue that children need syntactic information in order to learn the difference between verbs that apply to the two kinds of actions described above. They point out that verbs which apply to intentional interactions are "marked" differently than verbs that do not. This is indisputable; for example, one says "A paints B" for the intentional action, "A and B are painting" for the nonintentional actions. Verbs that apply to the two kinds of action are distinguished from one another in English by means of -s at the end of the verb in the one case, -ing in the other.

Does the infant require a grammatical marker in order to distinguish between the two kinds of action, or will the infant's psychological module automatically distinguish between the two cases? The Gleitman test used the "nonsense" verb *glub* to answer the question. One group of children was first told "Big Bird glubs Cookie Monster," another group, that "Big Bird and Cookie Monster are glubbing." Both groups of children then were shown two videotapes. In one, Big Bird, standing beside Cookie Monster, raises and lowers Cookie Monster's arm. In the other, Big Bird and Cookie Monster, standing side by side, twirl their arms in unison.

The children who had been told "A and B are glubbing" spent more time looking at the film in which the two characters, standing side by side, twirl their arms in unison; those told that "A glubs B" spent more time looking at the film in which one character raises and lowers the other's arm. Clearly, then, these children "knew" the grammatical markers. But how did they learn them, and what kind of information did they use in learning them? Was it syntactic, as the Gleitman argument proposes, or does that argument have things turned around?

The ten-month-old infant's ability to distinguish intentional from non-intentional interactions does not depend on syntax. The distinction is drawn strictly on perceptual grounds. Indeed, it is the perceptual distinction that provides the basis for the learning of syntactic markers.

But perhaps we are missing the emphasis that Gleitman et al. wished to give to their argument. It may be their point that grammar calls the child's attention to particular distinctions. For instance, "glubs"/"glubbing" organizes the scene around the difference between the two kinds of actions, giving prominence to a distinction the child might otherwise miss. Can that really be the case, though, when the distinction between the two kinds of action is demonstrably highly salient to the infant?

It is sufficiently salient to lead the infant to react differently to the two kinds of actions, to assign value +/− to the one case but not the other. Infants attribute value +/− to appropriate interactions between objects they construe to be intentional. If Cookie Monster were to hit or caress Big Bird, the infants would assign a negative or positive value +/−, respectively, to the two interactions. They would, however, assign no value at all, if the two creatures were merely engaged in parallel play. Thus we see how a distinction, ultimately drawn by grammar, has its origins in the modular knowledge of the infant.

Whorf: Grammar and Thought

According to Benjamin Whorf, the amateur anthropologist whose influence far exceeds that of most of his professional colleagues, the language one speaks affects one's "world view," one's conception of time, space, and causality, and how one thinks and solves problems. This claim is a rather extraordinary form of "languagitis," a disease prevalent among philosophers, anthropologists, and linguists whose major symptom is the treatment of language as the unique causal or transforming factor in the cognitive world!

From this perspective the world looks like a great body of raw material waiting to be shaped into a Whorfian proof. On the one hand there appear to be endless differences in culture and cognition between different groups of people; and on the other hand we also see much linguistic nonequivalence, the well-studied profusion of lexical and syntactic devices that differentiates languages. Whorf claims that the two kinds of differences—cultural/cognitive and linguistic—not only are deeply connected, but that the one causes the other. As Whorf sees it, differences in grammar produce cognitive differences of utmost importance—conceptions of time, space, casuality, and so forth. What then is the evidence for this extraordinary claim?

The Dutch psycholinguist W. Levelt was among the first to distinguish three systems that humans use in describing the location of objects in space: deictic, absolute, and intrinsic. In the deictic system an individual describes the location of objects relative to his own position in space. The door is on his right, the window is on his left, and so on. In the absolute system the individual makes use of the compass and will say, for example, "The tree is to the north, the house is to the south." In the intrinsic system it is the referent that serves as the central location; for example, "the dog is to the left of the tree" (to the tree's left). Although certain groups favor one system over the other, humans can and do use all three systems.

The three spatial systems have an interesting effect on logical properties. The deitic and absolute systems permit the use of transitivity, whereby if aRb and bRc, then aRc, in other words, if a is bigger than b, and b bigger than c, then a is bigger than c. Transitivity does not hold for the intrinsic system, however. Does this difference imply that people who use the intrinsic system are handicapped, and cannot manage to make transitive inferences? Or might they use an alternate system, even a nonverbal one? Nonverbal systems for transitive inference have been credited to animals, mistakenly we think, since animals lack the concept of monotonic order, which is a precondition for transitive inference. But this does not mean that humans could not use a nonverbal system for transitive inference.

Even if the different systems used in describing space did affect reasoning, however, this factor would not support Whorf's claim, for the systems employed to describe space do not differ in syntax, semantics, or even lexicon. The systematic differences among the systems are conceptual, not linguistic. Therefore if differences in the systems for describing space did affect reasoning, this would just represent cognition of one kind affecting cognition of another kind.

The cognitive anthropologist John Lucy recently compared two Spanish-speaking groups, one of which distinguished count and mass nouns while the other did not. (An example of a count noun is "dog"—one dog, two dogs; an example of a mass noun is "sand"—some sand, not one sand, two sands.) When given objects to match, the group that distinguished count and mass nouns preferred to match objects on the basis of shape; the other group preferred to match them on the basis of texture or material. The developmental psycholinguist Deidre Gentner and her colleague M. Imai, a psycholinguist, have since confirmed Lucy's finding in a test using Japanese, another language that does not distinguish between count and mass nouns. In a comparison of English- and Japanese-speaking children, they found that the former prefer shape and the latter texture.

Additional support for the Whorfian position comes from a study done by the developmental psychologist Lera Boroditksy, who compared the ways of treating time as a spatial metaphor employed by Mandarin and English speakers. Time may be an ideal dimension in which to detect the effects of language, for unlike most sensory experience, time does not have a natural representation. It is an abstract domain that relies largely on metaphors for its representation.

For example, in English we represent time on the horizontal, placing earlier events to the left of later events. This spatial metaphor is one that both English and Mandarin speakers share. Mandarin speakers, however, also use vertical metaphors to talk about time. Earlier events are said to be *shang* or "up," and later events are said to be *xia* or "down." Boroditsky notes that although English speakers do speak of "handed-*down* knowledge" and say "the meeting is coming *up*," thereby using vertical spatial metaphors, this use is far less common than it is in Mandarin.

Does the difference between the English and the Mandarin ways of talking about time lead to a difference in how they think about time? Specifically, are Mandarin speakers more likely to rely on vertical metaphors when thinking about time, English speakers on horizontal metaphors? Boroditsky used a schema-consistency paradigm to answer this question. If an appropriate metaphor is primed, people should be able to more quickly understand statements made about time that employ the same metaphor. For instance, when thinking about time in absolute terms, English speakers should be faster following horizontal than vertical primes. The reverse should be true of Mandarin speakers. Indeed, Stanford college sophomores confirmed Boroditsky's predictions.

Really, though, the Lucy and Boroditsky findings confirm Whorf only in a weak sense. The use of spatial metaphors to represent time affects the speed with which one processes sentences concerning time. Although, as we have seen, speakers who distinguish between count and mass nouns prefer to match objects on the basis of shape, while those who do not make this distinction prefer to match objects on the basis of texture, these hardly constitute differences in worldview.

Rather than supporting Whorf's hypothesis, the extraordinary diversity of human language actually serves as its embarrassing refutation. All this diversity in language, and still no cognitive difference of any magnitude to show for it! Though uniquely powerful, language is not a device for producing major changes in cognition.

Whorf's attempt to explain cognitive differences in linguistic terms has diverted attention from other, more fruitful puzzles. Whorf takes language differences for granted, attempting to use them as a causal factor. He does not ask: Why do languages differ in the first place; why do they lexicalize entirely different distinctions? Although it is customary to assume that such basic cognitive factors as space and number will be analyzed in the same way by all groups, the psycholinguist Melissa Bowerman points out that there is, in fact, no core set of spatial relations. Even languages as close as Dutch, English, and German lexicalize different spatial relations.

For example, the fly that in English is "on the wall" is not, in Dutch, "aan" the wall, as a picture is "on (aan) the wall; rather, it is "op" the wall because the contact between the fly and the wall is discontinuous whereas that of the picture is continuous. By contrast, continuity/discontinuity of contact does not interest either English or German speakers. The German speaker is interested in whether contact is horizontal or vertical, and calls a band-aid on the shoulder, "auf," one on the leg "an." Neither the English nor Dutch speaker gives a hoot about that distinction.

English requires clarification as to whether an object is to be found in a flat or a raised container—*on* the plate versus *in* the cup—an issue which is ignored in both German and Dutch. More exotic differences are there for the asking; one just needs to consult more distant languages such as Korean, and the dialects of India. But somehow finding even small differences among first cousins is more surprising than finding larger differences among total strangers. Why does Dutch concern itself with continuity/discontinuity—because there are more flies in Holland?

On the other side of Whorf's would-be causal coin we find differences in cognition that are far-reaching and more profound than those related to language. Let us propose for the sake of discussion that cultural specializations—poetic language (Ireland), music (Germany), mathematics (Bengali), visual and gustatory arts (France)—are forms of cognition whose differences are unlikely to be explained by syntax or semantics. We then have two major puzzles—that of linguistic nonequivalence and that of cultural cognitive specialization—both of which have escaped attention. Now might be a propitious time for these topics to receive the attention presently being squandered on Whorf.

Chapter 5
The Word
An Information-Retrieval Device

The Speech Stream

Language is a correspondence between two streams of information. Units of the sound stream must be mapped onto units of meaning. Since neither the sound nor the meaning stream comes prepackaged, that is, cut into ready made units, one must ask: What cue or cues does an infant use when dividing the streams?

There are no pauses separating spoken words that correspond to the spaces that separate written words. Nevertheless infants at a tender age manage to divide the speech stream into words, long before they know their meanings. The system infants use for "cutting" the stream is of such subtlety that adults are having trouble figuring it out.

There are several contending views as to how the infant's system works. One is based on intrinsic cues that identify the beginnings and ends of words; another, on the computation of transitional probabilities among syllables; yet another, on prosody.

Related to the issue of segmenting the speech stream into words is that of the categorical perception of phonemes. Phonemes are the basic building blocks of speech, and words are composed of a combination of phonemes. Humans, however, are not alone in being able to discriminate phonemes.

Over twenty years ago the psycholinguist Pat Kuhl and the auditory psychologist James Miller showed that both rhesus monkeys and chinchillas perceive phonemes. In their study the animals were able to perceive the boundaries between ta/da. More recent studies have extended this finding to many avian species and other species of monkeys, and have shown that these animals can distinguish boundaries between phonemes other than ta/da.

The fundamental neural mechanism for processing acoustic events important to a species is the combination-sensitive neuron. Unlike most neurons, which are activated by a single event, this neuron is activated by a pair of events. The combination-sensitive neuron has been found to be widespread, appearing in all species for which complex acoustic events are biologically salient, including frogs, birds, mice, bats, monkeys, and, of course, humans. The neuron is active in bat sonar, in the barn owl's localization of sound, and in human speech. The neuron produces an unusual output, apparently by plotting one event as a function of the other.

In the bat the combination-sensitive neuron is activated by paired events: the pulse emitted by the bat and its returning echo. In the human the neuron is activated by specific formants typical of certain phonemes. The comparison that the bat makes between pulse and echo is equivalent to the comparison humans make when they maintain a given consonant but modify the following vowel in creating a word; for example, by maintaining the consonant d and changing the sound of the vowel so as to say, "d(ough) / d(ay) / d(o) / d(ie)."

Were it not for the problem of biochemical rejection, one could probably replace the combination-sensitive neuron of the bat with that of the human, and vice versa. Currently we do have evidence of an overlap between humans and nonhumans at two levels of auditory processing: Bats, humans, and other species have auditory neurons in common; birds, monkeys, humans, and other species discriminate phonemes.

Most recently there has emerged evidence of an overlap at a third level: A bonobo appears to segment the speech stream into words, just as the human infant does. While the animal does not demonstrate any evidence of grammar (no more than is shown by any other language-trained animal), this does not pose a problem, since dividing the speech stream into words does not depend on grammar. Children divide the speech stream at a tender age, long before they have grammar.

The grammatical analysis of speech is specific to humans. The auditory analysis of speech apparently is not. Many species communicate by means of audition—through mating calls, predator calls, food calls, and so forth. The mechanisms that permit the analysis on which the communication depends are not specific to speech, but are its evolutionary precursors.

This reasonable conclusion is further strengthened by another dramatic finding. Four-day-old infants have been found to discriminate among languages they have never before heard! French infants, for instance, played tapes of Dutch speech until they had habituated (or lost their interest in listening) dishabituated (or regained their interest) when played tapes of Japanese speech. Further, the infants did not show this effect when the tapes were played backward, that is, when the sounds did not sound like speech from any language.

These remarkable findings might incline one to conclude that this result is due to the infant's modular competence in speech. But when the identical procedure was repeated with the tamarin, a small South American monkey, in a study done by the cognitive biologist Mark Hauser, the tamarins responded exactly as did the human infants: They habituated on Dutch, dishabituated on Japanese, and showed no such effect when the tapes were played backward!

The ability to segment the speech stream into words may draw on a sensitivity to prosody, and we suggest that such sensitivity can in fact be found in many domestic animals. Dairy farmers recommend "talking" to the cow during milking. Speech calms the animal, they say, and has a beneficial effect on milk production. So prosody might make dairy farmers wealthy!

It may be that infants, and perhaps animals as well, possess a hidden statistical talent that enables them to discover the boundaries of words, for ends and middles of words do have different statistical properties. Ends of words permit the free use of any syllable in the language, whereas the "middle" of a word limits syllable choice. An infant, recording the transitional probabilities among syllables, could use this information to discover word boundaries.

Are infants really sensitive, though, to the transitional probabilities between syllables? Once again, nonsense words have been called into service to find out! The psycholinguist Lissa Newport and her colleagues presented eight-month-old infants with short sequences of a continuous speech stream consisting of four three-syllable nonsense words. The only cues to word boundaries were the transitional probabilities between the syllable pairs. In the case of "words," the three syllables making up a word followed one another perfectly, whereas in nonwords they followed one another only a third of the time.

The infants were limited to just two minutes of experience of the speech stream; the nonsense words were repeated in a random order for this extremely short duration. Subsequently the infants were presented with two kinds of sound: the "words" presented during familiarization and the "nonwords" containing the syllables heard during familiarization but not in the same order. The infants discriminated the "words" from the "nonwords," listening longer to "nonwords." A striking finding! And one which establishes the fact that infants *could* use this mechanism to identify spoken words, but of course leaves open whether or not they actually do so.

The Sharing of Mechanisms

The sharing of neurons and mechanisms is not unique to language. Humans share mechanisms with other species in other domains as well; in perception and learning, for instance.

Shared mechanisms raise such interesting questions as these: What is the depth of the sharing of these mechanisms? Do the mechanisms involved play the same role in all species? The latter question takes an unexpected turn when it is applied to short-term memory, a mechanism recently found to be shared by humans and chimpanzees.

Both species have approximately the same limitations with respect to short-term memory, for when given a brief exposure to information, both remember no more than about five or six items. This limitation could seriously interfere with the ability to solve problems, thereby reducing overall mental efficiency. But does the shared limitation of memory affect humans and chimpanzees equally?

Short-term memory limits the *number* of units one can remember. It does not, however, limit the *content* of the units. Thus, despite sharing identical short-term memories, different species may well remember different amounts of information. A chimpanzee exposed to the numbers from 1 to 9, for instance, might remember, for example: 2, 6, 4, 3, 7. But while a human too can remember any five single digits, he or she also can remember 21, 43, 19, . . . ; 214, 109, 618, . . . ; 1012, 3456, 6680, . . . ; and so on. In other words, although humans and chimpanzees have the same limits on the number of units that can be remembered, the content of the unit for the human is not limited to a single digit.

In the case of language the content of a unit is even more open to expansion. While a chimpanzee may remember five words, a human can remember five sentences. Or five poems. Or five prayers. And so on. The human can make and the chimpanzee cannot make these expansions because the former is capable, the latter incapable, of acquiring the number series and language. Thus at least in this case, claims made for the sharing of the mechanism of short-term memory are misleading. The acquisition of language and number clearly enables one species to overcome the limitations of short-term memory.[1]

Chimpanzee Kindergarten

The "sophisticated" chimpanzee learns words in a single trial, whereas a naive chimpanzee often requires 300 to 400 trials before it learns its first words. Initially the animal does not learn the specific "name" for a specific kind of fruit; that is, it does not associate a particular plastic word with a kind of fruit. Or vice versa. Rather, the animal first learns to identify the properties of both words and objects; that is, it learns the generic sensory properties both of word "names" and of the objects to be named.

The "names" for objects consist of plastic shapes of different forms and colors. In early lessons, pieces of fruit are the objects to be named. After some early lessons the animal, when offered objects (other than plastic shapes) to be associated with the pieces of fruit, rejected them, as they did those objects not resembling fruit. They even rejected candy, which they far preferred to fruit. When working in the presence of plastic words and the writing board the animal rejected chocolate (a great favorite), taking the fruit instead.

The early training appears to have taught the animal this: If I want fruit, I must place a plastic word on the writing board—any plastic word for any type of fruit. This rule clearly is inadequate. It is formulated at the level of the two categories, word and fruit. The correct rule must be formulated at the level of the individual members of each category: A particular word will obtain a particular fruit. Some animals went through 200 trials (others 400!) bound to the early false rule before they finally abandoned it. Once they had made the transition to the new rule, however, the animals came to learn new words quickly—ultimately in a single trial.

The Retrieval Power of Words

In human language, words play a far more important role than has been found to be true of animal "languages." Words undergo changes in their shape in most human languages, and these changes mark such meaning changes as plurality and tense—as in, for example, "boy–boys" and "work–worked." The morphological rules that govern changes of this kind are almost certainly part of the language module; attempts to construct learning "devices" capable of acquiring rules of this kind have been unsuccessful to date.

Human words have a second property not found in those of the chimpanzee: duality of patterning. Human words are composed of pieces, bits of sound that have no meaning called *phonemes*. Only when these pieces are combined according to the word-formation rules of the language do they become words and acquire meaning. By contrast chimpanzee words— whether composed of hand signs, computer figures, or pieces of plastic— cannot be divided into meaningless pieces, have no duality of patterning, and are indivisible meaning entireties.

The main task of words, however, is to retrieve information. Words make it possible for people to sit in their living rooms and talk of kangaroos, pyramids, and the weather in the Sahara desert. The names of these objects or places can lead the individual to retrieve mental representations that have the effect of bringing the object or place right into the living room! This ability of people to talk about things that are not present, known as *the displacement of language,* rests on the information-retrieval power of words.

Words have this capacity in the first place because individuals are able to both perceive the world and to remember what they perceive. If a species were faulty either in perception or in memory, words would be of little use to it. The power of a word is limited only by the amount of information the individual is able to store. Humans are known to be well endowed in terms of the ability to perceive the world accurately, and to represent or store much of what they perceive.

How does chimpanzee perception compare with human perception? Textbooks assure us that chimpanzees have an acute perception of the world, but far less is known of chimpanzee storage and retrieval. To help fill this gap, we designed a test to find out just how accurately chimpanzees are perceiving, remembering, and retrieving.

The animals were tested not on objects for which they were paid or rewarded for remembering, but on objects that are a normal part of their daily life. Fruit, an important ingredient of the chimpanzee diet, seemed a natural for "bringing out the best" in chimpanzee memory. We tested chimpanzee memory for eight different types of fruit, all part of chimpanzee daily diet: apple, banana, cherry, grape, lemon, orange, pear, and peach.

We divided each of these into eight features: shape, color, peel, taste, wedge, stem, and seed, and then gave the animal one feature (at a time) of each fruit, requiring the animal to match this feature with other features of the same fruit. For example we gave the animal a taste of, say, apple, and then required it to choose between a red swatch and a yellow swatch, between an apple seed and an orange seed, an apple stem and a cherry stem, the white outline of an apple and that of a grape, and so on.

Cutting a piece of fruit up into features and testing the animal by means of a "dissection" procedure of this kind can be compared to cutting family photographs into sections and asking family members to match Aunt Becky's nose to the color of her hair, Uncle Horace's mouth to his eyes, Jane's face to her voice. About seventy tests of this kind—a total of twenty-six different match-to-sample tests!—were given to each of four chimpanzees.

Sarah (approximately eight years old at the time) used every cue correctly, reaching the features of every fruit from every other feature. Given a stem of any one of the eight fruits, she used it to identify: the flesh, shape, color, peel, seed, and the whole fruit (of course). She could do the same when given a taste of a fruit, and when given the seed of a fruit. (See Figure 5.1.)

The three younger animals (four to six years of age) did not have Sarah's encyclopedic grasp of the fruit but they still performed well, far above chance. Indeed, their results were more informative. For since they did not have Sarah's ceiling effect—that is, they performed less well with some features than with others—we were able to rank-order the informativeness of the features.

The whole fruit, naturally, was the most informative cue. But color and peel were almost as effective: 79 percent correct for color or peel versus about 85 percent correct for the whole fruit. Taste, somewhat less informative than color or peel, was followed in informativeness by a virtual tie among shape, wedge, and stem. Trailing behind—the least informative

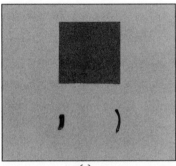

(a)

(b)

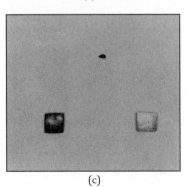

(c)

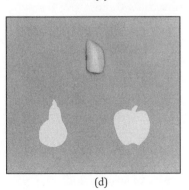

(d)

Figure 5.1   The match-to-sample test of the features of fruit: (*a*) color to stem; (*b*) seed to whole fruit; (*c*) seed to peel; (*d*) morsel to shape.

cue—was seed. These differences in the informativeness of the several cues do not, however, diminish the main finding: Chimpanzees (Sarah especially, the younger animals to a lesser degree) are able to store detailed representations of objects such as fruit.

These results place us in an ideal position to ask the fundamental question: How much of the information that chimpanzees store concerning fruit are they able to retrieve with their words?

Retrieving Information with Words

To answer the question we repeated the match-to-sample tests, but this time using the *names* of the fruits as alternatives. We gave the animal, say, a taste of each fruit, and offered as alternatives a small blue triangle or word APPLE and a small red square or word BANANA. In order to shorten this test (the original one took five months to complete), we reduced the original set of features from seven to four, testing only taste, color, shape, and seed.

The three younger animals did far better when given words rather than features as alternatives. When required to match features to features, the three failed a total of twelve tests; when, however, the test required them to match features to words, they passed eleven of the twelve tests! The improvement was not due to practice, for when the original test was repeated the animals made virtually the same number of errors again. While Sarah could not have done better on the words than she had done on the features, she could have performed less well. But she did not. She passed the word tests as handily as she had managed the features tests. (See Figure 5.2.)

The plastic words clearly are extraordinarily effective mnemonic devices for chimpanzees; indeed, they are more effective than the actual features of the fruits themselves! But why is the plastic word so effective as a retrieval cue? The answer must lie in its use.

If, as the cognitive psychologists Endel Tulving and D. M. Thompson have proposed, a retrieval cue is successful only if it has been specifically encoded with the item to be remembered, the words should have greater retrieval power than the features. While the features of the fruit are, of course, physically linked with the fruit—far more so than are the words—they were never used as symbols of fruit. The animal never asked for a banana with a piece of peel, or for an apple by offering a stem. Plastic words alone were used in this way—to request fruits, to describe actions applied to fruits, to answer questions about them.

What is the source of this essential property, the retrieval of information, which clearly is the most vital property of words, the property that

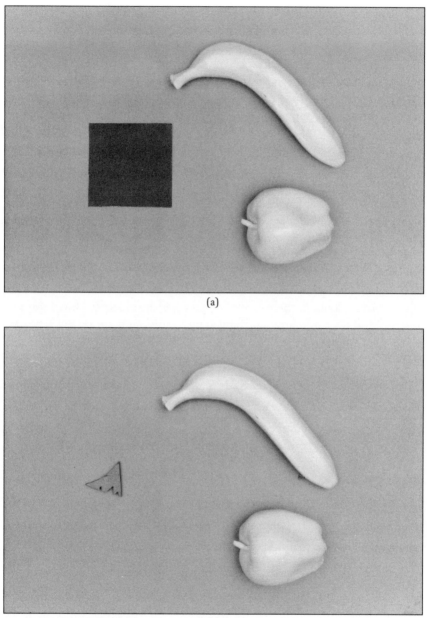

Figure 5.2 Matching both the actual color and the "name" of the color to a piece of fruit painted white: (*a*) the color red; (*b*) the word RED.

gives language its distinctive character? Is the source the language module, or is it domain-general learning? The answer is crystal clear. The source of information retrieval is domain-general learning.

In conditioning experiments, animals form mental representations of the unconditioned stimulus, typically food or water. As extensive studies have shown, they retrieve their representations of food or water by means of the conditioned stimulus of light or sound that was previously associated with the food or water. We owe these findings primarily to the learning theorist Robert Rescorla, who has filled in the previously neglected cognitive side of conditioning.

Although a word's ability to retrieve information comes from domain-general learning, this general mechanism can be coupled with a device highly specific to language. When this coupling occurs it confers a power and elegance on information retrieval that is never seen in conditioning, nor anywhere outside of language.

When a language-trained animal is told "X NAMEOF y," it can immediately retrieve a representation of the object y by using its new word X. In other words, it looks at the word X and pictures the object y. Thus, information retrieval that ordinarily is achieved by conditioning (or by the repeated association of the word and the object) can be brought about in one stroke through the instruction "X NAMEOF y." (See Chapter 4, for a more detailed discussion of this.)

Can Chimpanzees Think with Plastic Words?

In the human, words serve not only to retrieve information; they are part of the very information that is stored, and can therefore be incorporated into thinking! But while humans can think in words, is this also true for the chimpanzee? Do the plastic words leave the writing board and make their way into the ape's mind? Let us divide this question into two parts: (1) Does the animal have mental representations of the plastic words? (2) Can the animal use these mental representations in its thinking or problem solving?

The first question is answered easily. Chimpanzees definitely have mental representations of the plastic words. As we have seen, not only can they use words to retrieve the features of objects, they can do the opposite as well: use objects to retrieve the features of words. (See Figure 5.3.)

In one of several match-to-sample tests, Sarah was given an apple as the sample and plastic words that described the name of apple in the following alternative ways:

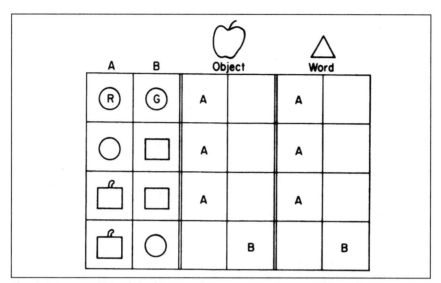

Figure 5.3   Matching of the features of the object apple to the word *apple*.

BLUE versus YELLOW

ROUND versus TRIANGULAR

LARGE versus SMALL

RED versus BLUE

All the plastic words Sarah chose—BLUE, TRIANGLE, SMALL, and so forth—"describe" the NAME of apple (a small blue plastic triangle), indicating that she has mental representations of the words. One of her choices was a surprise. In a choice between RED and BLUE she chose BLUE, the color of the NAME of the apple, rather than RED, the color of the apple itself. Probably she did so because the test leads off with alternatives appropriate to the word, biasing her in that direction.

The second question—Can a chimpanzee use mental representations of plastic words to solve problems?—has proved to be more difficult to answer. One is tempted to accept the idea that we need neural data; that the question cannot be answered with behavioral data alone. But before we abandon ship, let's take a stab with behavioral data.

We give the chimpanzees two problems: one in which the objects to be discriminated are highly similar (although their names are highly dissimilar), another in which the objects to be discriminated are again highly similar and their names, too, are similar. If objects with dissimilar names are discriminated more rapidly, then chimpanzees must be using the names to discriminate the objects. We then can conclude that names do play a role in chimpanzee thinking.

Liz Spelke and her students have found that while young children and rats solve spatial problems through the use of geometric relations alone, older children and adults use "landmarks" as well—and they attribute this difference to the influence of language. Let us suppose we find that, in solving spatial problems, language- and nonlanguage-trained chimpanzees show a comparable difference; that is, we find that chimpanzees not trained in language use geometry alone, whereas language-trained chimpanzees use landmarks as well as geometry. Would this demonstration answer our original question?

It would not answer the question, but it would suggest that chimpanzees that acquire words can use them to "rehearse." Rehearsal, presumably, is the basis of the ability to use landmarks, for when Spelke et al. interfered with their human subjects' ability to rehearse (for example, by having them recite digits backward) those subjects lost their ability to use landmarks.

Human Word Acquisition

Young children satisfy the brain's keen "appetite" for words by learning an average of ten new words each day. Although they start slowly, picking up relatively few words in their first year, by the second year they are hitting their stride, emitting a new word every ninety waking minutes. High school graduates boast a vocabulary of about 60,000 words, while college graduates manage more than twice that number.

Is the extraordinary acquisition of words the work of the language module, or can we credit their acquisition to domain-general learning? At its most superficial level a word is an association—in the chimpanzee, an association between one visual event and another, in the human, between an auditory and a visual event.

But associations are not limited to words; they come in many flavors. There is the association between a lock and its key, a wife and her mate, a car and its owner, and so on. Can we say that the associations in these cases are the same as those one finds in words? For example, is the association between a key and its lock the same as that between the spoken word "apple" and the object apple? Between the plastic word APPLE and an apple?

The Role of Shape

Child developmentalists claim that words are not ordinary associations, but rather are constrained or selective in their association. Indeed, according to the developmental psychologists Barbara Landau and Susan Smith and their colleagues the name of an object is associated only with the object's *shape!* Objects have all sorts of physical properties—color, shape, size, and the like—and functional properties—balls can be rolled, balloons inflated, bells rung, apples bitten, and so on. Nevertheless, Landau and Smith claim that initially words are associated neither with the functional properties of objects nor with most of their physical properties. Words are associated only with *shape.*

A child may be well acquainted with toy cars, having played with them on numerous occasions, rolling them on the floor, bumping them into furniture. Nevertheless when the child learns the word car he will completely ignore all his experiences with the car (the rolling and the bumping) and forget the car's color, how it felt in his hand, the noise it produced, and how it smelled. He will associate the new word car only with the shape of the car.

This hypothesis, known as a *constraint theory of word learning,* is troublesome, because we have no fundamental data concerning associations in general. Is it words alone that are selective in their association, or could associations formed between objects also be selective? Do we associate a key just with the shape of the lock, or also with such other properties as the metal of which the lock is made, the lock's location on the door, and its color? Perhaps the common, ordinary associations we make between one object and another are just as restrictive as are associations between words and objects.

Here are two main alternatives. Ordinary associations may be no less restrictive than words (although here the restrictions may differ from one type of object to another); or the Landau-Smith restriction may be special, peculiar to the language module, so that when the child regards a word as the name of an object that object automatically falls under the shape restriction.

The Diagnostic Value of Reaction Time

Constraint theory strikes us as being counterintuitive, in part because humans can so easily retrieve, simply by hearing associated names, functional experiences we have had with objects. We remember the pleasure we had driving the family "Ford" for the first time, the displeasure we had playing the hated clarinet. Do we recall such experiences directly from hearing the words "clarinet" and "Ford"? Or are these experiences recalled indirectly, the words first recalling the visualized objects and the visualized objects then retrieving the associated experiences?

To put it simply, is the recall of functional experience a one-step or a two-step process? Constraint theory says it is two step: first, name to object, and, then, object to functional experience. Intuition says it is one step: name to both object and functional experience. An ideal way to decide which is in fact the case: the reaction-time experiment.

In this test we measure the amount of time it takes the child to "go from" the name of an object to its correct static property versus to its correct functional property. For example, when we say "ball" the child must choose between "round" and "square" or between "bounce" and "cut." Common sense predicts that when a child is given the name of an object there will be no difference in the time it takes her to choose either the correct shape or the correct function of the object.

Constraint theory predicts otherwise. It says that when given the name of an object the child will choose the correct shape most quickly; in other words, "round" will be chosen before "bounce." The grounds for this prediction are illustrated in Figure 5.4. In the commonsense model, two arrows lead from the word "ball": one to the object, the other to function. In the constraint model, there is only one arrow, leading from "ball" to shape, with no arrow leading to function. To reach function in the constraint model, first "ball" must lead to shape, shape to object, and object to function. This path clearly takes more time than is required by the commonsense model.

The Indexical Power of Shape

If it turns out to be supported by the reaction-time experiment, constraint theory will be able to give us an entirely new perspective on word acquisition. If the commonsense model is right, each object name carries a heavy memory burden of past associations. If constraint theory is right, the mnemonic burden carried by each object name is light.

Consider the educated adult who has stored 100,000 words. According to the commonsense model every object name will associate with the numerous previous associations already stored in the brain. In the constraint model each object "name" will associate with one item only: shape. All additional information associated with the object will be carried by

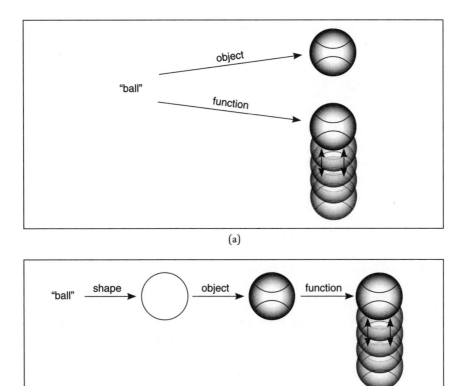

(a)

(b)

Figure 5.4   Word learning, contrasting (*a*) the commonsense model and (*b*) the constraint model.

shape. Such a mental organization certainly would greatly reduce the burden of learning.

The commonsense model requires the duplication of the many thousands of associations carried by the object and their transfer to the name of the object. Names in this case will end up "furry," as furry as objects are themselves, in the sense of covered with a patchwork of associations. If, however, constraint theory is correct, such duplication and transfer will not take place. Words will remain simple, as streamlined as their one association: shape.

But can shape carry this heavy burden? Is it sufficiently distinctive as a cue? Obviously shape does not have the indexical power of fingerprints, yet it can identify categories of objects and that may be sufficient. The identification of object names refers not to individual objects, of course, but to categories of objects. The perceptual theorist Donald D. Hoffman and his

colleagues have shown that, at the categorical level, shape is quite effective
as an index.[2]

The Shift Effect

When you hear the word "dog," which association comes into your mind,
cat or bone? According to the literature, if you are four or five years old
you'll think cat, the "categorical alternative"; if, on the other hand you are a
child of two or three, you will opt for bone, the "thematic alternative." Why?
There is no clear answer, and adding to the puzzle is the further suggestion
that as people age they revert to the choice of the very young child, the thematic alternative.

"The shift effect" refers to the fact that the two-year-old can, in a particular circumstance, behave like the four-year-old. Simply introduce a nonsense word into the body of the test. Using for instance a French poodle
stuffed animal as the sample and a stuffed fox terrier and a bone as the alternatives, we tell the child that the Glaplanders (a fictitious people) call the
French poodle a "dax." We then ask the child "to find another dax." The
young child now behaves like an older child, forsaking the bone (the thematic alternative), and selecting the fox terrier (the categorical alternative).

This shift effect, made popular by the developmental psychologist
Ellen Markman and her students, has been taken as proving that children,
even very young ones, "know what a word is." They know that words name
objects, not the specific object associated with the word, but the category to
which the object belongs. Where could knowledge of this kind, knowledge
that refers specifically to words and their distinctive properties, have
emerged from, if not from the language module?

If this reasonable-sounding hypothesis is accepted, then one also must
tolerate a hypothesis that seems less reasonable: Chimpanzees have a language module, for language-trained chimpanzees, when tested with nonsense words, behave exactly like children. They too show the shift effect.
Young chimpanzees, like younger children, prefer the thematic alternative.
And when given a nonsense word in association with the test, young chimpanzees too shift to the categorical alternative.

What is a nonsense word for a chimpanzee? Exactly what a nonsense
word is for a child: an object that could be a word but has never been used
as a word; in other words, a plastic shape that conforms perfectly to the
properties of a plastic word but that has never been "used" as a word. These
potential words must be distinguished from ordinary objects such as screws,
bolts, and hairpins, because when those objects were used in the test they

did not produce a shift effect. The young animals continued to choose the thematic alternative. Only when in the presence of chimpanzee "nonsense words" did the animals shift to the categorical alternative.[3]

Evidently the shift effect does not depend on the language module, and the shift effect is not the only characteristic of words to be shared by young children and language-trained chimpanzees. When taught the name for, say, an apple, neither takes the name to mean red, or round, or sweet. Both child and chimpanzee take the word to be the name of apple. And not the specific apple used in training, but apples in general, the category apple.

Both chimpanzee and child assign the word "apple" to the object itself (rather than to its color or other properties), because objects have a special perceptual status for both species and this status takes priority over other alternatives. As behavioral psychologist B. F. Skinner showed in 1930, all learning is an association between the classes to which items belong, as opposed to an association between the items themselves. Therefore both chimpanzee and child will assign the word "apple" to the category apple, not to the specific object itself. Many properties that have been discovered in the context of the study of words are not specific to either words or humans. Rather, they reflect general properties of learning and perception and will be found in all learning, of words and nonwords alike.

Shared Attention

Shared attention plays a role in word learning. If the child pays attention to its mother and looks at the same object or toward the same spot as she does, the child is more likely to learn words. But shared attention is not specific to the learning of words. Infants of eight or nine months of age, hugging a doll while riding in their stroller, will, when they spot a smiling stranger, glance repeatedly from the doll to the stranger, implicitly asking, "Do you see what I've got?" and thereby inviting shared attention.

Chimpanzees participate in shared attention as well. Sarah often searched my skin closely, checking carefully for cuts from which to draw blood. Because she lacks an opposable thumb, she would place her index fingers on opposite sides of a cut, pressing gently until a thin red line appeared. She would then look into my eyes, back at the oozing red line, and back yet again to my eyes, asking implicitly "Do you find this as interesting as I do?" Shared attention is not a language-specific event. The shift effect, like the forming of associations by means of objects rather than of their properties, and like information retrieval itself, is not a language-specific event.

Shared attention, however, like other domain-general mechanisms, can combine with language to produce unique acts. All three of our children used their first words in a way that was vitally dependent on shared attention. Each child was captivated by a moving object—the daughter by a fish swimming in a bowl, the older son by a yellow school bus, the younger by trucks. Upon seeing the object they would point at it excitedly, shouting its name, insistently seeking out a parent for eye contact. No child was ever content merely to point. Pointing, in fact, was secondary, a supplement to the spoken word.

"Shared attention" starts with gaze, the only mechanism available to the eight- or nine-month-old infant. Pointing develops in the next month or two, then words appear, and at last gaze, pointing, and words combine. When the young child, having barely a handful of words to her credit, no longer is content to share attention by pointing alone but repeatedly calls out the name of an object, we see a harbinger of things to come. This tells us that language, once it begins in the human, quickly takes over the mind.

Where does the chimpanzee stand in this developmental sequence? Gaze is the animal's sole mechanism of shared attention. Social pointing does not develop spontaneously in the chimpanzee, and the spontaneous production of words is hardly a characteristic of language-trained chimpanzees.

A Mistaken Word Model

Recent interest in call systems has been greatly stimulated by a convincing confirmation of Thomas Struhsaker's original finding. Cognitive biologist Peter Marler and his former students, the psychobiologists Dorothy Cheney and Robert Seyfarth, have verified Struhsaker's findings: The calls of the vervet monkey are not simple reactions to the inner state of the animal but rather signal differences in the world—between eagles and leopards and pythons.

Because vervet calls reflect these differences they have been proposed as homologues of words. But is a word like a vervet call? Do humans, or even chimpanzees, use words in the same way as vervets use their calls? Sure, the shout "Fire!" is emitted in the presence of smoke or fire just as a vervet call is emitted in the presence of a predator. But the word "fire" (as opposed to the shout "Fire!") also is spoken in the absence of fire, as are all words. Words are not spoken only in the presence of the object or event they name. The word "fire" appears in sentences; for example, "Fire is used for cooking" and "A cold day calls for a fire." It is only the shout "Fire!" that never appears in sentences.

Are vervet calls even voluntary? Doubtful, for a vervet with voluntary control of its calls could, upon finding food, use a leopard call to disperse its rivals, thereby preserving the food for itself!

An act can be considered to be voluntary on two grounds: either because the animal produces the act in the absence of the normal stimulus, or because the animal fails to produce the act despite the presence of the normal stimulus. Producing a call in the absence of food is far stronger evidence for volition than is inhibiting the call in the presence of food. Hauser and Marler have shown that monkeys can inhibit food calls in the presence of food but not the reverse: produce the call in the absence of food.

An example of the difficulty of outright "lying," as opposed to inhibiting the "truth," can be seen in a study of four young chimpanzees trained to "tell the truth" to a good trainer and "to lie" to a bad one. Woodruff and Premack found that although all four animals benefited from the training, and could manage *not* to inform the "bad" trainer by inhibiting their pointing, only the oldest animal of the four could actually deceive the bad trainer by pointing him in the direction of the wrong container.

More recent fieldwork by Hauser and his students has added a twist to the vervet word story. They found that the vervets of Uganda are the victims of the traditional predators—pythons, leopards, and eagles—and make the same calls, but in this environment in conjunction with a seemingly emotional reaction to a predator (M. Hauser, personal correspondence, 1999). When a dog approached at a distance the vervets uttered snake calls; when the dog moved closer they uttered eagle calls; and when the dog was immediately below them, leopard calls! Rather than being linked to a specific predator the calls were linked to the proximity of the predator and the intensity of their fear. Although these data are preliminary they suggest the possibility of a second communication system, one based on emotion rather than semantic cues.

Which is the better system, communicating on the basis of specific predators or on the basis of fear? Basing communication on emotion, or on any other internal state, has an enormous drawback. Unless all parties feel the same way about the predators, assigning them the same rank order of fearfulness, they will never understand one another. If for instance one individual gives the call for snake (the predator it fears most), another may anticipate leopard (the predator *it* fears most), and rather than adopt a defense appropriate to the snake prepare itself inappropriately for a leopard. By contrast, communication based on actual objects rather than on emotions permits individuals with very different likes and dislikes to communicate accurately. Such is the wonder of words!

Did You Understand My Call?

Human speech is an intentional system. The vervet's use of its call system may appear intentional because vervets are influenced by the presence of others; that is, they are more inclined to call when in the presence of others than when alone. Biologists have treated this "audience" effect as evidence that the call is intentional and thus that calls are similar to words. The claim is premature.

To prove that a call is intentional one must show that the caller takes into account the listener's reaction to his call. When a vervet sender makes a python call intentionally, its goal is to protect its audience from the python. If, upon observing its audience, it finds they have responded inappropriately, by taking the countermeasures appropriate for a leopard for instance, it will not have achieved its goal and will therefore take immediate corrective measures. It will repeat the python call or call more loudly, despite the fact that this directs the predator's attention to it and thereby increases its risk of being located. If a receiver responds appropriately the intentional sender will take no corrective measures, because in that case he will have achieved his goal. But there is no evidence that vervets make this distinction, that is, respond differently to listeners that do and do not respond appropriately to their calls. Therefore there are no grounds on which to say that vervet calls are intentional.

Are vervets capable of storing and retrieving information about those predators for which they have species-specific calls? Taking the correct countermeasures is not itself informative. Taking cover under a bush, in response to the eagle call, may be no more than an association, one that could be either learned or innate. Does the vervet "picture" an eagle when hearing the eagle call, and then use this "picture" when "asked questions" about the eagle? In order to answer these questions we would need to test the vervet by means of the same plastic-word experiments that were used with the chimpanzees.

Reconstructing the Past

The !Kung San, a group of hunter-gatherers who inhabited the Kalahari desert, lived amidst scarcity. Their hunting was planned, not opportunistic.

Often the animals they hunted were far larger than themselves; they made use of weapons, and in the course of the hunt, they communicated with one another. But the most unusual part of the hunt took place *after* the hunt was over.

As may be seen in Figure 5.5, upon their return the hunters describe the experience of the hunt to those who have remained at home. The hunters recount, with enormous pleasure, the details of the hunt: the towering giraffe slowed down by a poisoned arrow, arduously tracked for two days; the finality of its end, when brought down with their simple spears.

Chimpanzees hunt once. Hunter-gatherers hunt twice: once in the field and a second time around the campfire. Whereas humans, having brought meat home to be shared, hunt again through their descriptions for those who stayed home, chimpanzees, having caught a monkey and eaten it, simply digest their meal.

The San do not wonder at their own uncanny ability to describe, to mentally reconstruct, the past. They do not wonder at their ability to describe

Figure 5.5 San hunters "telling" the hunt. (*From R. B. Lee and I. DeVore, Kalahari Hunter-Gatherer, Harvard University Press, 1976*)

tracks that are no longer visible, arrows that no longer fly, the once living and fighting giraffe that they are even then eating. That this small epic can be resurrected by means of words, with arbitrary sounds, is not something they puzzle. Neither do their listeners marvel at the storytellers' curious ability to share the adventure of the original hunt through "mere words."

Owing to certain trivial laws of physics, we cannot literally reconstruct the past by picking up the stones of our birthplace and reassembling them at the feet of a listener. Like the San we cannot reconstruct the towering giraffe as it directs its dangerous hooves at a hunter defended by nothing more than a spear. We can however reassemble the past mentally, with the use of language. Indeed, as humans, we mentally reconstruct the past routinely, never once taking special pleasure in the accomplishment or asking, how am I able to tell this story? Why is it that can I relive my past through words? The answer to that question has been the main topic of this chapter. The word is the principal instrument of the accomplishment.

The ability of a word to recapture the major elements of the past rides piggyback on two simple faculties.

First, in order for words to perform their magic an individual's representations must do justice to the acuity of perception. Both the hunter who brought down the giraffe and those who observed him do so must form an accurate representation of the event. Second, they must be able to retrieve their representations and, more mysterious still, execute this retrieval with respect to completely arbitrary events. The words "giraffe," "kill," and "track" must serve to recapture vivid representations of events to which they bear absolutely no resemblance. Only in this way can a speaker recapture the event for a listener.

The word is the major device by which we recapture the past, whether that means yesterday's apple pie or the Shetland pony of childhood. It is the major "invention" for restoring missing items of every kind: persons, places, objects, and actions. The sentence assembles all the recovered parts—is the structure that knits words into *story*—a sequence that takes the listener from one event to another. But it is the representational power of the word, the magic of the retrieval of images, that infuses the story with such power.

Notes

1. The ability to expand the content of the memory unit, even with all its strengths, nevertheless is a weak device for overcoming the limitations of short-term memory. There is a far more powerful device to work around this limitation: writing. Humans can write down what they cannot remember. The invention of writing

virtually eliminated the detrimental effects of short-term memory in the case of the human.

The discovery of mechanisms shared among species is important, for it helps to establish the evolutionary origins of human mechanisms. But we also must not fail to recognize the elaborations that such mechanisms have undergone in the case of the human. Short-term memory, for example, has undergone not only dramatic biological changes, but also elaborations that are uniquely cultural.

2. But manufactured objects in particular have multiple shapes: Clocks and irons and desks do not come in one shape. Isn't this a problem? Not necessarily, for even if the word "chair" were associated not with one shape but with twenty, this would still require fewer associations than if chair were associated with all the diverse experiences one has with chairs.

A more serious problem may stem from the fact that while shape is a dominant cue in object identification for speakers of English, it is not so for many non-English speakers. The developmental psychologist Deidre Gentner and her colleagues and the anthropologist John Lucy find that texture supplants shape for people whose grammar does not distinguish count and mass nouns. This includes the Japanese, whose children reveal their preference for texture over shape by their second year. Perhaps, however, texture plays the same role in these languages as shape plays in English. And if texture is the dominant feature associated with object names, then the only question is this: Does texture have the indexical power of shape?

Consider the names of people rather than those of inanimate objects. For people, face is the dominant feature, not shape; and face, we know, is a superb indexical cue, far superior to shape. Moreover, if the names of people were associated with their faces, the economic advantage would be far greater than that of associating names of objects with their shape; for one has many more experiences with people than with chairs or other artifacts.

3. The Landau-Smith hypothesis, in calling attention to the importance that names of objects confer on shape, provides a possible explanation of the shift effect. Even a nonsense word, when doubling as the name of an object, may confer importance on shape. This fact would lead both the child and chimpanzee to select the fox terrier over the bone. The shapes of a fox terrier and a poodle are more alike than are the shapes of a bone and a poodle. Note the interesting implication of this argument. It says that plastic words, like human words, confer importance on shape and thereby grants constraint theory to the chimpanzee!

Chapter 6
Belief
A Concept Mired in Common Sense

Seeing, wanting, and *believing,* the three most widely attributed mental states, are borrowed from our common sense, our everyday language. They are not scientific discoveries. While seeing and wanting have become legitimate topics of experimental study, belief remains mired in common sense. Nevertheless psychologists and other social scientists, in formulating explanations of mind, use the term "belief" as though it were a legitimate scientific concept.

Certain key scientific questions—What causes an individual to have a belief? Is there a part of the brain that is active when one has a belief?—cannot be answered. Critical biological questions—How did belief evolve? What are its animal antecedents?—are equally unanswerable. If belief were a legitimate scientific subject, these questions could all be answered. In the case of both "see" and "want," they can be.

The causes and neural events of seeing are well known, as they are for audition, olfaction, and the other modes of perception. The evolution of vision is in fact both fascinating and surprising. Vision evolved independently, perhaps as many as seven or eight times, with human vision being one of the last to appear. Olfaction, by contrast, evolved only once. Consequently human olfaction, unlike human vision, was inherited directly from our animal ancestors and remains primitive—not much different from that of the bee. The work that has been done on wanting or motivation is far less elegant than that on perception (wanting is a "messier" state than seeing). There are, however, both causal and neural accounts, as well as an evolutionary history of motivation.

Language and Pseudo-Concepts

We suspect that believing and knowing are pseudo-concepts that the grammar of everyday language has duped us into accepting as real. When an individual perceives that a clock is on the shelf, we might say of that individual "He knows the clock is on the shelf"; or if the individual merely hears the sound of the ticking clock, we might say: "He believes the clock is on the shelf." In these cases "knowledge" and "belief" are treated as mental states in their own right, as caused by perception.

But are "belief" and "knowing" really mental states caused by perception? Or is perception alone the mental state, while "belief" and "knowing" are merely ways of speaking? As a rule perception will cause the individual to act immediately on the environment, and not lead to further mental states. Or as in the present case, it will prompt him to speak.

How might we find out whether "belief" and "knowing" are mental states? Brain imaging certainly could be helpful. Many studies have identified the neural events that accompany visual perception. Will we find separate neural events corresponding to "belief/knowing"? Specific neural events are known to correspond to our perception of the clock on the shelf; will tests reveal a further neural state corresponding to "knowing" that the clock is on the shelf?

On the other hand we can speak of what we "believe" on the basis of what we are "told." For although we may not have seen or heard the clock on the shelf, if we are told a clock is there we can say, "I believe there is a clock on the shelf." Does this mean that our acceptance of information given us by a second party *caused* a state of "belief"?

Perhaps it would be best to divide "accepting the information of a second party" into two states, the first being the comprehension of the statement and the second, the acceptance of the statement. Comprehension is as genuine a mental state as is perception, inference, or memory. It is the result and final state of the successful processing of a language utterance.

Comprehension alone does not lead the individual to say "I believe . . ." Rather, it is the fact that the individual finds the speaker reliable, and therefore accepts what he or she comprehends. Acceptance (of verbal information) is specific to communication, and is itself a unique mental state.

An exchange of information between two or more individuals is required to set the stage for belief. A listener, even though comprehending an informant perfectly well, will reject (that is, not "believe") what she is told if she lacks confidence in her informant. The kind of "belief" that refers to the acceptance of verbal information is, we suggest, a legitimate mental state; we surmise that ultimately it will be found to be represented by unique neural events in brain-imaging studies.

In one kind of "belief" we essentially grant to the information given us by another individual the same status as we grant to our own perception or inference. This mental state we will refer to as *little b*. We distinguish little b from *big B*, a state of belief distantly related to the former and discussed a bit later on.

According to commonsense usage, belief plays a role in all intentional action; it is not restricted to the acceptance of verbal information given us by a second party—the case we singled out. Any and all inputs that can be experienced by an individual—for example, perception, inference, and memory—lead to belief, but only belief can culminate in action. This view is depicted in Figure 6.1, as the commonsense model. Is there evidence to support this view?

The view is based on an implicit "theory" of how the "mind works" that is embedded in everyday speech. It is not a view that has been tested; nor has it ever been formulated as a scientific theory that *could* be tested. There is, however, experimental evidence on hand that contradicts it.

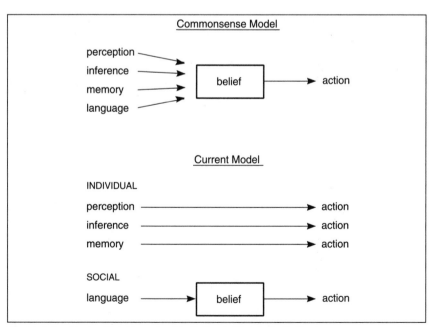

Figure 6.1 Contrasting the role of belief on action in both the commonsense and the current model.

Recent neural evidence shows us cases of motor action—of a kind that qualify as intentional action—that are caused directly by perception. There is no evidence of an intervening or mediating cognitive state between the perception and the action. On the basis of recent evidence we do possess, we have constructed the contrasting model of action seen in Figure 6.1. In this model, all inputs experienced by an individual—such as perception, inference, and memory—lead directly to action. Only social inputs, which include language, lead first to belief and then, in turn, to action.

Philosophers of mind have formalized the commonsense view into what is termed *propositional attitude theory*, a model which appeals to three factors: *rationality*, *belief*, and *want*. It says: Should you want x and believe you can get x by doing y, then if you are rational, you will do y. In short the theory says that a rational individual does whatever he believes will get him what he wants. The philosopher's formula accords with the commonsense view of belief we have seen in Figure 6.1. Every intentional act requires "belief."

Let us look at a classic example of intentional action in which one goal-directed party pursues another: The goal of the first party is to eat the second party, while the goal of the second party is to avoid being eaten. The action here clearly is intentional, each party certainly having a representation of the other's intention.

The pursued party, in its effort to escape, makes frequent changes in location. It turns right, left, and so forth. The pursuing party immediately accommodates those changes, moving left when its target moves left, right when it moves right, and so on. Every change it makes is automatic—that is, involves action that maps directly onto the perceptual representation—as we saw in the neural evidence cited above. But where then is the intervening "I believe that if I move left I can catch my target," "I believe that if I move right I can escape," and so on. "Beliefs" of the kind presupposed by propositional attitude theory, in its formula for intentional action, could only impede the actions of the two participants, leaving one in greater danger and the other farther from his prey!

That "belief" plays no causal role in the conduct of intentional action is not a conclusion dependent upon a special kind of agent, one in whom reflexes have replaced cognition. While the participants could be a lioness in pursuit of food and a zebra fleeing for its life, they could equally well be two children playing tag, or teenagers on ice skates, the boy skating deftly in pursuit of his girlfriend. Action in all three cases will map directly onto the perceptual representation; "belief" will play no causal role.

Belief is not the only troubled concept on which propositional attitude theory stands; the other is "rationality." Here the problem is of a different kind. Some of the philosophers' accounts of rationality/irrationality are immensely lucid; to appreciate their lucidity, however, one must treat them as completely hypothetical accounts, for they bear no relation to this world.

Consider Hume's superbly simple account of irrationality: An irrational individual is one who fails to maximize his preferences. Unfortunately clarity is the only virtue of this account, for the logical possibility that Hume describes is not one that any living creature instantiates. How long has it been since you saw an individual "fail to maximize his preferences"? For example when was the last time you saw a thirsty individual operate a drinking fountain and then turn his head to the side so that the water could not enter his mouth? Or how many people have you observed who, after having waited patiently in long lines, finally purchase their tickets only to tear them to shreds? Or a client who, having waited endlessly for his appointment with the barber, doctor, or dentist, walks out the minute his name is called? In short, who has seen an irrational individual à la Hume?

Not every philospher accepts Hume's account, of course. An irrational individual, some say, would be irrational even if she did maximize her preferences, for her very preferences are what make her irrational (when offered a choice between a nicely done steak and a manure sandwich, she rejects the steak). We cannot condemn this account on grounds that "bizarre preferences" do not appear in this world. In Houston Family Court on February 8, 1993, the state of Texas convicted a woman for having just such a preference. During the course of the trial the accused woman did not deny the charge brought against her. She in fact admitted that she preferred the sexual attention of the family German shepherd to that of her husband.

Is a preference of this kind equivalent to irrationality? If part of a general condition, it is. But suppose it is an isolated aberration, as it apparently was in the case of the woman from Texas. Aside from her "criminal" preference she appeared to be quite normal.

In this world it is neither the isolated bizarre preference nor the unmaximized preference that constitutes irrationality. The closest approximation to irrationality in this world can be found in social behavior that lacks normal inhibition. An individual who smiles at perfect strangers and enters into immediate conversation with them, broaching intimate topics reserved for friends, and who then stops talking as abruptly as he began, is this world's approximation of irrational.

Even children are wary of social deviants of this kind, and do not need to be told to avoid them. Ironically, while the philosopher's theory is intended as an account of folk psychology, or an explanation of the lay theory of intentionality, the lay populace have no use for the concept of rationality. For the layman, the precondition for intentionality is "normal." Normal is his default value. People act reasonably, he assumes, because they are normal—where "normal" means social behavior that conforms to the norms of the community.

Conviction: Zealous Beliefs

It is important to distinguish ordinary beliefs, or little b, from what will henceforth be called conviction, or belief with a big B. Although both kinds of belief concern the social case—information in the form of language provided by a second party—they differ with respect to the kind of information that is provided. The information provided in little b concerns conditions in the world that can be confirmed by perception. The informant claims to have perceived them himself, or to have been told of them by a party whose testimony he believes.

In big B, rather than being told about conditions that can be verified by perception, the individual is trained, purely on the basis of words, to hold a conviction about a state of affairs for which there is no perceptual evidence.

Although accepting information that *can* be verified has no special motivational consequences, accepting information that *cannot* be verified may have dramatic motivational consequences. In a sense humans accept unverifiable information at great risk, for once an individual accepts such information he is unlikely to ever be the same. Not only will he hold the conviction stubbornly, spurning all attempts to change it, but he is likely to strive to persuade others to join in accepting the same conviction, substituting social consensus for perceptual verification.

The Prelanguage Child

Religious conviction is taught the young child when its mind is in a special state. Virtually all the representations in the mind of a young child are based on perception; even when the child begins to speak, mother and child talk about events they both perceive. Mothers do not at first talk about past events or "imaginary" events the child has never seen.

At this stage the child has no representations based purely on words, though in a year or two the composition of the child's mind/brain will undergo a great shift. She then will enter the classroom and hear of things she has never seen, such as the pyramids, Abraham Lincoln, and the Pacific Ocean. Representations based on words will then join those based on perception. It is, however, through serious religious instruction that the child first encounters a whole world based purely on language.

Religious figures—God, angels, and the like—cannot be introduced perceptually, of course. One can only speak of them. Pictures and statues provide the closest approximation, but since these lack motion they do not have the impact of first-order perception.

Good teachers of religious belief probably make their stories graphic because they have recognized the child's craving for perceptual experience. Religious training for five-to-six-year-olds, for instance, may concern instruction in how to recognize legitimate saintly visions. The child must be taught to distinguish the saint from the devil masquerading as a saint. This can be done, the child is taught, by lifting the skirt of the apparition. If the feet are hoofed, it is not a saint but the devil in masquerade. In seeking to do justice to the human need for perceptual experience, hell and purgatory are taught not as abstractions, but in the most graphic terms. Pictures and stories depict "souls" entering purgatory to expiate their sins through burning. Real burning! Just how real can be seen when an occasional witness appears on Earth, presses his hand against a door, and leaves a scorched imprint, perceptual proof.

While pictures, statues, and graphic images are used as props, the basic ideas are implanted in the child's mind through speech. In accepting those ideas that lack perceptual content the child will become the innocent victim of convictions that grip her with a peculiar force. A few children will resist, and others will escape their convictions upon reaching adulthood; most, however, will overcome whatever doubts they might have had and return with renewed vigor to hold these early views for life.

Why do religious convictions frequently have peculiar characteristics? Why do they grip the individual with a unique force, so that the surrendering of one's faith, or the conversion to another, is experienced as a major upheaval? Is it simply that everything one learns as a child has this character? Actually not. Most of what one learns as a child—such as how to spell "Mississippi," how to identify breeds of dogs, and how to recite the multiplication tables—does not have a special character.

Our hypothesis is this: The mind/brain reacts differently to conditions that are actually perceived than to conditions that are merely described (even if quite vividly!) but cannot be confirmed by perception. Perception, the original source of information, leads automatically to stable representations, whereas verbal accounts of conditions that lack perceptual confirmation lead to representations that are unstable. And unstable representations are continually in search of confirmation.

While people with stable representations have had them confirmed by perception, those with unstable representations cannot achieve stability through perception. So people whose representations have been instilled by language alone seek continual shoring up. They find a kind of stability in social consensus. People who share religious conviction seek one another out. Many of them proselytize, hoping to spread the seed of their convictions, widening the circle of believers and their social influence.

Brain imaging may make it possible to test the hypothesis that systematic stories lacking in perceptual content produce an unstable brain state. But we need to make a distinction. Is it really the lack of perceptual confirmation, or is it the peculiar content of religious material per se? To test the issue we need to find stories that, though lacking perceptual confirmation, do not have a religious content.

Such stories, according to our hypothesis, should also acquire the motivational character of a religious conviction. They should lead to instability, a quest for social support, even to proselytizing. Unfortunately, test cases are hard to find. But consider the following example which, though not exactly what we are looking for, is close. People find deep satisfaction in visiting countries they have learned about as children but never seen. An American child may hear about England from the lectures of a gifted teacher who is enamored of the country and a frequent visitor. Such a teacher may instill vivid representations of the Lake District, the Dover cliffs, the home of Shakespeare. Students who subsequently walk through these regions as adults will experience a special thrill, one they will excitedly communicate to others.

The pleasure a student finds in the perceptual confirmation of representations instilled with the gifted words of a teacher suggests that there is a state of disequilibrium inherent to language-based representations. Actually seeing events and places about which one has only read, or about which one has only been told, brings unusual fulfillment—suggesting that a longstanding disequilibrium has been laid to rest. Can we compare this experience to the satisfaction one might have were one to experience the perceptual confirmation of a religious belief?

Even as the lack of perceptual support produces religious convictions in the first place, so, we speculate, will their confirmations by perception lead to their demise. If God were actually to appear, He would in due time end up no better off than Santa Claus (who has been virtually "done in" by repeated perceptual confirmation). In other words, were religious conviction given perceptual confirmation, it would lose its original character. It would cease to be religious belief and, in losing its fervor, become like any other belief.

Suppose God were to appear. He might raise the dead and turn the Sun blue to confirm His status. Let us assume that all believers found His proof convincing, that they accepted His credentials. At first, His appearance would fill the churches; He would be pursued by the press, and everyone, especially the laity, would want His autograph. But in the long run?

In the long run, and we have no idea of how long "long" would be, the churches would empty. In order for them to fill again God would have to disappear and become a memory, eventually to become a perceptually unconfirmed story. For only as such a story can God maintain His powerful hold. Provided, of course, the story is told to the child in the form of religious instruction.

Are All Representations Equal?

Representations are not all equal. They differ not only in stability but also in their strength. Representations that emerge from different sources have different strengths. We can measure them by placing them in competition, and observing which one wins out.

Perception, the original source of all information, produces representations that are not only stable, but strong. Representations based on perception always trump those from other sources.

Language, a decidedly more recent source of information, is not entirely successful as a substitute for perception. Language is not the only source of "weak" representations; another weak source is that of *inference*. Both language and inference appear to be incomplete substitutes for perception.

Perception Overcomes Inference

Let us define inference by means of an example. We see Roger put milk in the refrigerator. Well, we don't actually "see" him place the milk in the refrigerator, but we see him head in the direction of the refrigerator with milk in his hand, then return empty handed a moment later. We infer that Roger has placed the milk in the refrigerator, and if we later want some milk, it is there we go to find it. What do young children do in a similar situation? What do young children do when asked to place inference in competition with perception?

In a test room a small group of children were shown two containers: A whole cookie was placed in one container, a piece of a broken cookie in the other. Each child then was asked to indicate which container he or she preferred. Naturally, every child preferred the container with the whole cookie.

Each child was asked not to take the cookie he preferred, but first to defer to a classmate. The classmate would make the first choice and then the child could make his. The child could observe when the classmate had completed her selection, but could not actually see which container she chose because his view was occluded by a screen. The child could only "infer" that his classmate had taken the whole cookie. After she left the room, the child made his choice.

Many children chose the empty container. Almost 60 percent of the nearly-four-year-olds, and 50 percent of the slightly-over-five-year-olds, chose the container that had held the whole cookie. Naturally they found the container empty, for the classmate always chose the container with the whole cookie.

To make this mistake once is not unthinkable. The children did not actually *see* the classmate take the whole cookie. But many children who made this mistake on the first test continued to choose the empty container over the course of ten trials. Even though they ended up with an empty container, every single time! Why?

Our hypothesis is this: The children correctly inferred that the classmate took the intact cookie but the inference could not displace the perceptual representation. For at the start of each new trial every child saw an intact and a broken cookie placed in the containers. Despite the fact that the child correctly inferred that the classmate had taken the whole cookie, the inference could not "budge" the perception. The motor behavior of the child was controlled not by inference, but by perception.

Why such a fancy hypothesis? Why not simply assume that the children who responded correctly made the correct inference, while those who erred did not? Because the assumption is inadequate. Why should those who make a mistaken inference on the first trial continue to make the same mistake ten trials in a row? And why does finding an empty container teach the child nothing? Are these children incapable of learning?

Why they cannot learn is not explained by an initial failure to make the correct inference. Their failure is best explained by our hypothesis: They cannot learn because the perception of an empty container in their final choice trial is replaced, at each new trial, with the perception of a whole cookie in one container and a broken one in another. The "old" inference cannot dislodge the "new" perception. The next experiment can best decide the issue.

In this second study we shifted to pretzels and began, not by *showing* the child where the pretzels were, but by telling her: "In this container there's a big pretzel. In the other container there's a small pretzel." After confirming the child's understanding by having her tell us the location of each pretzel, we introduced a classmate as before and then advised the child that the classmate would make the first choice, after which she could make *her* choice. Once again an occluding screen prevented the child from seeing her classmate's choice.

Children who were *told* of the contents of the containers behaved very differently from those who had been *shown* the contents. "Told" children selected the container with the small pretzel. They correctly inferred that the classmate took the larger pretzel, and their motor behavior was guided by the inference. These children ended up with the smaller pretzel rather than no pretzel at all.

Such results confirm the original hypothesis, and indicate that inference is not necessarily an unreliable process in young children. The inference of these young children was completely successful in overcoming a representation based on *language*. By combining the two studies we can order the strengths of the representations.

If we assume that strength is a transitive property, as seems reasonable, then, since perception resisted inference in the one test and language did not, we predict that perception will resist language. The strength of representations will order as follows: perception strongest, inference intermediate, and language weakest.

What makes representations "strong" or "weak"? Are some better formed than others, more three-dimensional, more complete in detail—printed in capital letters, as it were? Perhaps none of these. It may be simpler to assume that rather than differing in their composition, representations differ in their access to the motor system.

Perceptual representations appear to have privileged access to motor behavior. The alliance between perception and action is, after all, an ancient one. As children mature, representations produced by inference are somewhat better able to cope with those produced by perception, which is why the nearly-five-year-olds did better with the cookie test than the nearly-four-year-olds. Still, the fact that half of the nearly-five-year-olds continued to make repeated errors indicates that representation based on perception does not easily relinquish its hold on the motor system.

In adults, inference obviously can hold its own against perception. An adult, shown an object in a container, and then given reason to infer that the object has been removed, will amend his earlier perceptual representation and respond appropriately. But does this mean that inference is as effective as perception, even in an adult? Perhaps it would be worthwhile to make this comparison: Give some adults the opportunity to actually observe the object being removed, while giving other adults simply evidence on which to make the inference that the object has been removed. In each case, measure the latency of the adult choice of container. One might be in for a small surprise! Although an adult certainly will not make the child's error, he may make his selection more quickly after actual observation than after making an inference.

Inference in a Chimpanzee

Using Sarah as our subject, we now placed inference in competition with perception just as we did with children, but our procedure was slightly different. Rather than tell Sarah about a classmate who would choose before she did, we used Sarah's knowledge of the "preferences" of two of her trainers as the basis of an inference.

Our first step was to give Sarah evidence from which to draw conclusions about preferences. Whether chimpanzees understood preference was not known at the time, and we were as interested in this topic as in the other. We combined both questions in the same experiment.

Sarah was shown two trainers, Henry and John, each of whom was offered a plate containing cabbage and peanuts. These foods were chosen not by chance, but because previous tests had shown that Sarah enjoyed both foods about equally well. Each trainer chose carefully from the plate, ate with great relish, and selected one food consistently. Henry always selected the portion of cabbage (rejecting the nuts), while John always selected the peanuts (rejecting the cabbage).

The flourishes of the trainers, including lip smacking and belly rubbing, were highly successful in capturing Sarah's attention. Clinging to the front of the cage, Sarah participated vicariously, trembling as she watched. After being shown four demonstrations of the trainers' preferences, we were ready for the next step. Two opaque containers were placed on the outer edge of her cage and Sarah was given an opportunity to demonstrate her knowledge of the trainers' preferences.

A small piece of cabbage was placed in one container, and a peanut in the other. The trainers then entered Sarah's room one at a time and chose one of the two containers. Each trainer entered four times a day in an irregular order. Sarah watched the trainer as he approached the containers, apparently made a choice, and then left the room visibly chewing and smiling. She could not actually see the trainer's selection, since a small screen blocked her view of the containers. Like the children in the previous study she could merely infer what each trainer had taken.

Once the trainer had left the room, Sarah was allowed to select a container. Knowing where each food had been placed, and which food was preferred by each trainer, Sarah was in a good position to avoid selecting an empty container. After Henry made his choice, Sarah should have avoided selecting the cabbage container; likewise after John made his choice, she should have avoided selecting the peanut container. By combining two key pieces of information—the location of the food and the trainer's prefer-ence—Sarah should have been able to enjoy a favored food on every trial.

But she didn't. She failed completely, performing at chance level. She failed not only in her early choices but, like the children, in trial after trial. After having been given four trials each day for ten days she showed no improvement. The same argument that explained the children's failure will, we suggest, explain Sarah's. Although Sarah too made the correct inference about the trainers' preferences, as we'll demonstrate below, her inference was unable to override her perceptual representation.

In order to sustain this claim in Sarah's case, however, we must first demonstrate that Sarah understood preference. To find out if Sarah really understood preference, we turned to the "causality test." Normally this test was used in the context of physical action. Causal action brings about a transformation; it changes the state of an object, its location, or both. Typi-cal examples of causal actions are cutting an apple, moving a cup, or water-ing a plant.

A causal change consists of a three-item sequence. In the case of cutting an apple we have the intact apple, a knife, and then a cut apple. Suppose we remove one of the items from the sequence. Can the individual choose an alternative that will complete the sequence? For example, when we elimi-nate the knife from the sequence, and offer instead these alternatives—a knife, a pencil, and a container of water—the individual who understands the test will select the knife, reconstructing the sequence as apple, knife, cut apple (see Chapter 8 for details). Preference can also be expressed by means of a physical action that brings about a transformation, and hence as a three-item sequence. Henry expressed his preference by removing cabbage from the food tray, John his preference by removing peanuts. To exploit this fact and use it as the basis of a test, we presented Sarah with this sequence: a photograph of the tray holding cabbage and peanuts; a blank space; a photo-graph of the tray that held only peanuts on some trials, only cabbage on others. Sarah's task was to fill in the blank space.

Her alternatives were two photographs, one of Henry, the other of John. Sarah chose correctly from the start. When the content of the tray changed from cabbage and peanuts to peanuts alone, Sarah chose Henry's photo. And when the content changed from cabbage and peanuts to cab-bage alone, Sarah chose the photo of John. This already suggests that Sarah understood preference. To strengthen the conclusion, however, we gave her another test, one that was more demanding because it involved sequences she had never seen before.

Sarah was shown a photo of a tray laden with cabbage in some trials and with peanuts in others, a blank space, and a photo consisting of an empty tray. In this test, when shown a change from cabbage to an empty tray Sarah chose Henry's photo, and for the change from peanuts to an empty tray, John's photo.

In effect Sarah used the photos of her human trainers exactly as she had used the knives, pencils, and containers of liquid in the standard version of the causality tests—as instruments of transformation. Just as a knife changes an intact apple into a cut one, so does Henry change a tray of cabbage and peanuts into a tray of peanuts alone.

These results suggest that Sarah understood preference, and could correctly infer which container each trainer would choose. Her failure to solve the problem, therefore, cannot be explained by an inability to understand preference. Sarah's predicament was the same as that of the children: Her inferential representation could not compete with her perceptual representation. And Sarah was in this predicament despite the fact that she was an adult animal. In humans, by contrast, as children develop into adults inference (and undoubtedly language) come increasingly to hold their own in a competition with perception for control of motor behavior.

Chapter 7
Theory of Mind
The Attribution of States of Mind

The ability of chimpanzees to "take into account" the looking behavior of another individual was established many years ago in a painstaking field study conducted by the Dutch ethologist F.X. Plooij. In a study of the genesis and development of grooming, Plooij found that infant chimpanzees of two to four months of age "request" grooming from the mother without first "checking to see" whether she is "looking" at them. At that age they simply extend an arm or leg toward the mother. At about ten and a half months, however, the infant looks into the mother's eyes, establishes that she is looking at it, and only then extend an arm or leg toward her. In other words Plooij established that making eye contact is an early precondition for social interaction among chimpanzees.

Do animals have a theory of mind? Do animals understand that they must see or hear events in order to act appropriately? Do they understand that the same holds true for other animals? Is there evidence that animals attribute mental states to themselves as well as to others? Or, as has long been thought, is the attribution of mental states confined solely to humans?

In humans, the evidence for attribution almost always comes back to language. Therefore in order to answer the question of whether animals attribute mental states, a method for testing must be found that does not involve language.

I Look, I See, I Know

In the course of teaching object names to four chimpanzees, we came upon a useful method for testing attribution that bypassed language. Chimpanzees between five and six years of age were first trained to associate a plastic word with each of a number of different objects. The plastic words being backed with metal adhered to a magnetized slate that was held before the animal. The actual objects were placed in the corners of a small room and changed from trial to trial. In each trial the animal was shown a plastic word, and required to retrieve the object named by the word. In due time all four animals learned to select (80 percent correctly) the object that corresponded to the plastic word.

Now that the animals "knew" the names of the objects, the main question arose: Did the animals understand that their ability to select the correct object depended on their ability to "see" the plastic word? To answer this question we degraded the visibility of the word, in some trials by rotating the magnetic slate away from the animal's normal viewing angle and in others by turning the slate completely around so that the words were no longer visible at all. What did the chimpanzees do?

One of the four animals did nothing. She responded exactly as she had before, going obediently into one of the four corners and choosing an object. She chose at chance level, naturally. The disparity between being correct 80 percent of the time (when the words were visible) and only 25 percent of the time (when they were not) did not lead the animal to adopt any remedial steps. Clearly, this chimpanzee had no understanding of the need to "see" the word in order to make a correct choice.

A second animal differed from the first in one respect but not in another. Right from the first trial she whined and whimpered, but she did not act to improve her viewing conditions. Though reluctant and "complaining" she, like the previous animal, automatically "chose" an object in each trial, responding at chance level of course. Her discomfort with the test conditions may have indicated she understood that something was amiss, but the problem was not one she could resolve.

Two of the four chimpanzees, however, redeemed the species. When shown the inverted board they immediately seized it and turned it around so that the word was visible to them. And when the board was set at a bad viewing angle they changed their original viewing position to a location that afforded a better view. Both animals made the changes immediately, on the first trial. Actions and adaptations of this kind demonstrate an understanding of the conditions on which *seeing* depends.

Tests of the kind described above clearly demonstrate that language is not necessary for discovering whether or not an individual understands what is necessary for successful seeing. Only when we undermine the normal conditions on which seeing depends and the individual acts to restore them can we say that the individual recognizes the necessity of seeing.

You Look, You See, You Know

The next issue of interest is this: If an animal recognizes that it cannot see, can it also recognize that another animal cannot see? This question, being a bit more complex, required a slightly more complicated test.

Four young chimpanzees were shown that a cache of bananas was to be found at the far end of the compound; the cache was hidden in a locked box. The trainer, who accompanied each animal to the cache, wore a key around his neck, and unlocked the box upon their arrival. All the animals soon learned to "lead" the trainer across the half-acre compound to the box of bananas. The animals enjoyed the problem and the food. They set out briskly, the trainer five or six paces behind, each animal looking back repeatedly for reassurance that the trainer still was following.

Once all four animals had adapted to this routine, a change was made. When brought into the compound, the animal now found the trainer seated on the ground with a cloth tied securely about his eyes. Jessie, the youngest but also known from other problems to be the smartest, solved the problem immediately. She went to the seated trainer, removed the blindfold, and then led him to the cache in the normal way (Figure 7.1). Moreover, she continued to remove the cloth on subsequent trials, provided it was placed around the trainer's eyes. When it was placed over his head or around his nose, she did not remove it.

The three and a-half-year-old Jessie can be said to attribute seeing to the trainer on the same grounds that she attributes seeing to herself. She eliminates conditions that impair the seeing of the other one as promptly as she rectifies conditions that impair her own seeing, as she did in the first experiment.

The other three animals appeared not to notice the cloth around the trainer's eyes. They set off into the compound as usual, but when they looked back, the trainer was not there. Since he was literally unable to see, the trainer remained seated on the ground. The animals returned, waited, and then resumed their outward trip. But the trainer did not budge. Finally, the animals approached the trainer, grabbed the key attached to the chain around the trainer's neck, and tugged, forcing the trainer to follow.

Which he did, but very slowly, scrambling mainly on his knees. After three or four trials of this kind—the weather sultry Pennsylvania in the summer and the piece of banana a poor return for an arduous trip—two of the animals quit. They declined to participate in further trips, finding solace in the shade rather than in the experiment.

The animal that did not quit, Sadie, the oldest of the group, repeated the behavior of the other two unsuccessful animals. On her third trial, how-

Figure 7.1   Jessie removes Keith's blindfold. (*Courtesy of Paul Fusco*)

ever, she accidentally brushed off the trainer's blindfold; thereupon the trainer stood up and followed her to the cache in the normal way. But this sequence of events did not teach Sadie much, for the next day she failed again. On the following day, she once again displaced the blindfold accidently (in the course of reaching for the key around the trainer's neck). And this appeared to have taught her something, for on the next trial, she went immediately to the seated trainer and removed his blindfold, continuing to do so on all subsequent trials.

In removing the blindfold accidentally, Sadie cannot, of course, be said to have attributed seeing to the trainer. But later, when deliberately removing the blindfold at the start of each session, what can we say? Did Sadie learn merely that removing the blindfold is "helpful" in getting food, or did she learn that the blindfold prevented the trainer from "seeing"? Only a series of additional tests can decide this. Can Sadie apply her "new knowledge" broadly or succeed only in situations that repeat the present test?

A Consequence of Seeing: Knowing

In removing the blindfold from the trainer, what can we claim for Jessie? Did she demonstrate simply this: seeing depends on an unobstructed view—or did she recognize the benefit that would accrue to her of the trainer's being able to see? In the tests we have looked at, the trainer's being able to see had this consequence for Jessie: She could now lead the trainer directly to the cache as she had done before. But seeing has a more general consequence: It permits an observer to perceive his surroundings and be a source of information about them. Does the animal understand that seeing has this general consequence, and that it too can benefit by entering the informed state of the observer?

This question was so intriguing that it was tested immediately. In a preliminary step the chimpanzee watched while a trainer baited one of two opaque containers. When offered a choice, the animal consistently chose the baited container. The animal's view of the containers was then blocked with a screen. Unable to see the baiting, the animal now selected at chance level.

Two screens now were introduced, and two trainers stood, one *inside* a screen, the other *outside* a screen, as shown in Figure 7.2. The trainer standing inside the screen could see the baiting of the containers. The view of the trainer who stood outside the screen was the same as that of the animals—blocked.

A string was attached to each trainer, and before each trial we gave the animal an opportunity to choose one trainer or the other by pulling the attached string. The trainer chosen by the animal stepped forward, and if it

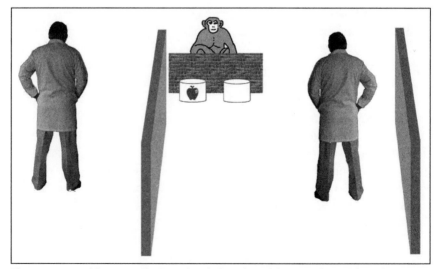

Figure 7.2 A chimpanzee is given the choice of receiving help from either of two trainers—one who can see the baiting of food, the other who cannot.

was the seeing trainer he pointed to the container that was baited. The "unseeing" trainer should of course have pointed at chance level, but to dramatize his ignorance for the animal's sake he always pointed to the unbaited container.

All three young chimpanzees chose correctly from the beginning; a fourth animal, with impaired vision, failed. Of the animals that chose correctly, however, one ignored the trainer's pointing, choosing at chance level! Her behavior awakened us to the fact that this problem actually has two components, one of which we had taken for granted.

For us what was paramount was the distinction between the seeing and the unseeing trainers. We had never once doubted that an animal would take advantage of the trainer's pointing. Thus it took the behavior of this one animal to teach us that recognizing the significance of pointing is in fact part of the problem. Though chimpanzees do not themselves point, ordinarily they do follow the pointing of humans. This was our first encounter with an animal for which this was not the case.

The above three tests leave little doubt that some chimpanzees are capable of attributing seeing to themselves and to the other one; they thus confirm Plooij's original field observations. The test results also point up the range of intelligence which, though negligible in most animals, is appreciable in chimpanzees.

How are we to reconcile our positive results in the attribution of seeing in chimpanzees, with the consistently negative results recently reported by a former anthropologist turned psychologist, M. Povinelli, and his associates? The chimpanzees in the Povinelli laboratory apparently showed no understanding of seeing. The luck of the draw, a draw from the "bad" end of the bell curve? Or were experimental procedures at the root of the problem? Perhaps a description of a recent Povinelli experiment will answer that question.

The experiment started with the trainer being separated from the chimpanzee by a large plastic shield. Two large "portholes" then were cut in the shield. The animals are trained to place their arms through the portholes, and are consistently rewarded with food by the trainer when they do so. After extensive pretraining in this task the animals, upon entering the experimental space, immediately place their arms through the portholes. The official experiment then begins.

Two trainers sit facing the plastic shield; one looks at the chimpanzee, the other does not. The position of the trainer who looks at the chimpanzee is varied "randomly" from trial to trial. If the animal is going to demonstrate that it takes seeing into account, it will have to put an arm through the port-hole in front of the trainer who is looking at it. And yet Povinelli et al. report that the animals failed at this task, responding at chance level. They contrast this failure with the success of four-year-old children. The children did what the chimpanzees failed to do: reached for food in the direction of the "look-ing" trainer.

But were these two experiments really comparable? Although the authors assure us they were, in fact they were not: The pretraining given the chimpanzees was different from that given to the children. In hundreds of trials the chimpanzees were rewarded with food simply for extending their arms though a porthole, whereas the children were not pretrained in this way.

Pretraining essentially disqualified the chimpanzee for the experiment, since it can only have taught the animal *not* to pay attention to "looking." How so? Simply because the animal received food whenever it reached through the porthole, regardless of whether the trainer was looking at it or not! Oddly enough, though, the experimenters set great store by their pre-training procedure, considering it a "guarantee" of the scientific status of their study. Of course, by the end of the pretraining there was no point in continuing the experiment. Any chimpanzee worth its salt had learned to pay no attention at all to whether the trainer was looking at it.

It is doubtful that two species are required to produce the contrast the experimenters obtained. The same contrast could almost certainly be pro-duced with one species, be it human children or chimpanzees. Children could be successfully pretrained to pay no attention to the looking behavior of the experimenter, in which case they would behave just like chim-panzees. Or one could resist pretraining the chimpanzees, in which case they would behave like children.

Chimpanzees Attribute Goals

Seeing is only one of the several mental states that chimpanzees attribute to the "other one." Chimpanzees also attribute goal-directedness and inten-tion, mental states that human infants attribute as early as the tenth or eleventh month. (See our earlier discussion of infant's modules, in Chapter 1.) That chimpanzees read the goals and intentions of others has been demonstrated in a series of studies.

Chimpanzees, when shown videotapes of an actor struggling to solve various kinds of problems, were required to choose the appropriate alternatives that would solve the problems. In the first series of tests an actor encountered inaccessible food. Bananas were out of reach overhead, or lay outside the cage; or access to bananas was blocked by a large movable box or by a large immovable box filled with bricks.

In the second series of problems an actor encountered malfunctioning equipment: a disconnected hose, a phonograph whose cord was unplugged, a gas heater that was unlit, and so on. Sarah was shown videotapes of all these problems, one at a time, and the terminal image of each sequence was put on hold. She then was given a manila envelope containing two or three large photographs, one of which depicted the solution to the actor's problem while the other photos depicted solutions to problems shown in other videotapes.

For example, in the case of bananas out of reach overhead, the correct photo showed the actor stepping onto a chair; the incorrect alternatives depicted solutions such as reaching out with a stick, pushing aside a box, and so on. In the case of malfunctioning equipment—for example, a hose that was not connected to the faucet—the correct photo showed a hose connected to a faucet; the incorrect alternatives included a hose which, though connected, was too short to be useful, and a hose connected to the wrong faucet.

In the first trial, Sarah withdrew the photos from the manila envelope, laid them out on the floor, and chose the correct solutions in eighteen of twenty cases. And of her two mistakes only one was genuine, the other resulting from an unclear photo. The mistake occurred when she was shown the problem in which access to bananas was blocked by an immovable box filled with bricks. She selected the photo of the actor simply pushing the box aside rather than the photo of the actor removing bricks from the box, as she should have. Almost certainly this error reflected her ignorance of the difference between chimpanzee and human strength; she mistakenly attributed to the actor a strength equal to her own.

In order to consistently choose photos depicting the proper "solutions" to particular problems, as Sarah did, one must first see a "problem." But what is a "problem"? A videotape depicts merely a sequence of events, not a problem. A "problem" is produced by a reader who interprets a videotape. The reader must see the actor as being goal-directed, as *trying* to reach inaccessible food or *trying* to rectify malfunctioning equipment. Sarah's consistent choice of solutions to the actor's problems demonstrates that she did interpret the videotapes, attributing mental states to the actor.

Nor is interpreting a videotape a simple matter. Almost 50 percent of three-and-a-half-year-old children failed the test given Sarah! Upon first encountering this high percentage of failures we placed the blame on the test materials, which had been designed for Sarah. The scene in the videotapes—a caged environment in which trainers hosed cement floors and lit the gas heater in cold weather—was not familiar territory to three-and-a-half-year-old children. So we adjusted the material to the lifestyle of suburban children.

An enthusiastic seven-year-old girl served as an actor in the videotapes, jumping for cookies out of reach on the top of a refrigerator and so on. And yet as it turned out this change in the test materials had no effect: The same percentage of children failed these tests. Moreover, the children who failed continued to make the same kinds of errors they had made originally.

Children who fail this test do so because they revert to a primitive cognitive disposition. They see the videotape as a simple sequence of events. At this age children often make the same kind of error on causality tests. Shown an illustration of a causal transformation such as an apple, a blank, and a cut apple, and offered water, knife, and pencil as alternatives, the children select the pencil rather than the knife because the pencil happens to be red and matches the color of the apple. This is a demonstration of the power of *similarity* to intrude when the disposition to interpret is weak or nonexistent.

The ability to go beyond the sensory level and interpret test materials is evidently not well developed in three- to three-and-a-half-year-old children. The same kind of error appeared in our theory-of-mind tests, when irrelevant photos were added to the alternatives. Rather than selecting photos that solved the actor's problems children chose such irrelevant items as the photos of birds and flowers. A yellow bird was popular, as its color matched that of the bananas.[1]

Interpretation: A Unitary Competence?

Both tests, that of theory of mind and that of causality, make essentially the same demand on the test-taker: The test material must be interpreted. The videotapes in the theory-of-mind tests must lead the viewer to ask: "What is the actor's goal? Why is he pushing the box? Why is he jumping up and down? Why is he trying to connect the hose? And so forth. The three-item sequence in the causality tests are designed to lead the viewer to ask: "What object turns a whole apple into a cut apple?" "What object turns a dry cloth into a wet one?" And so on.

Although the contents of the two tests clearly differ, both require the child to pass beyond the sensory level and place an interpretation on the test material. Only if we find an overlap among the children who pass the two tests—that is, find that children who pass the causality test pass the other test as well, and vice versa—can we seriously consider the process of interpretation to be a domain-general, or unitary, competence.

The Notion of False Belief

The publication of our study "Does the Chimpanzee Have a Theory of Mind?," which summarized much of the above research, led to lively commentary from philosophers in particular. A small group of leading philosophers of mind—Jonathan Bennett, Dan Dennett, Pat Churchland, and Gil Harman—were agreed on this point: False belief is pivotal to the claim that an individual is attributing states of mind. In fact they insisted that only a demonstration of false belief can provide unequivocal evidence for the attribution of states of mind.

Let us backtrack to observe that the very notion of false belief was introduced by yet another distinguished philosopher, David Lewis. It was he who proposed that only an individual who is able to distinguish her own knowledge of a (true) condition from another individual's (false) belief concerning the same condition has the capacity for "false belief."

Lewis's idea, translated into an experiment by the developmental psychologists Heinz Wimmer and Joseph Perner, clarifies the concept of false belief. In the latter's experiment, a child is shown that Georgie watches his mom place a package of chocolate in the cupboard after baking cookies. Georgie leaves and his sister enters, finds the chocolate, eats some, and places the rest in a green container.

The viewing child is asked: When Georgie returns, where will he go to find the chocolate? Children below the age of about four fail the test; they send Georgie to the green container, where they know the chocolate to be. Older children pass the test, sending Georgie to the cupboard, for they know that Georgie did not see his sister move the chocolate.

Older children are credited with having representations both of where the chocolate actually is and of where Georgie believes it to be. Their representation of Georgie's representation is considered to be a metarepresentation. And the ability of the older child to distinguish Georgie's metarepresentation from their representation is what enables them to pass the test. The younger child, by contrast, is considered *not* to have a representation of Georgie's belief, being incapable of metarepresentation, and therefore fails the test.

A capacity for metarepresentation is considered by some to be unique to humans and to be the "real" basis of theory of mind. In due time false belief became the Rubicon, the auto-da-fé, for claiming that a species has a theory of mind. Unfortunately, this position has led to false negatives, to the refusal to grant a theory of mind to individuals who do attribute states of mind, though none as complex as those of false belief.

The reader will notice that the terms *belief* and *false belief* are used incorrectly, for neither is a case of either little b or big B, information told to a listener by a trusted speaker or a conviction instilled through purely verbal training. False belief in these tests refers simply to a representation of a perception that is out of date. In using the term *false belief* we are simply adhering to our earlier advice: Use vernacular terms whenever they facilitate discussion.

Metarepresentation in the Chimpanzee?

The fundamental issue of false belief concerns metarepresentation, the ability to form a representation of the representation of the other one. Goals, intentions, seeing—the attributions so far credited to the chimpanzee—require only attributing a representation to the other one.

When Sarah attributes a goal to John she forms a representation of his goal, selecting the photograph that satisfies her representation. But can she take the next step and attribute to John the attribution of a goal, for example, a goal that John attributes to Henry? In other words, can she select a photograph that will satisfy her representation of the representation of the goal that John attributes to Henry?

In testing Sarah's capacity for metarepresentation, it would be ill advised to test her on the "attribution of a belief," for as we noted above, creatures without language cannot attribute belief. She does, however, attribute goals, and therefore we could properly test her ability to attribute the "attribution of a goal." Moreover, attributing an attribution of goal makes the same demands vis-à-vis metarepresentation, requiring the representation of a representation.

So what is the answer? Can Sarah attribute attribution? To find out we showed her a videotape in which, at first, two trainers appear in the cage. John and Henry are in the cage together but Henry alone jumps up and down, trying to reach the bananas overhead, while John simply watches Henry.

In the next scene, John is in the cage alone and is being offered a choice of photographs. One photo depicts Henry stepping on a chair, while in another he is engaged in an act (such as reaching out with a stick) that will not solve the problem of reaching the bananas. At this point we hit PAUSE, and Sarah is given two photographs. One shows John selecting the photo of Henry stepping on a chair, the other shows John selecting the photo of Henry reaching out with a stick.

Suppose Sarah selects the photo showing John choosing the photo of Henry stepping onto the chair. We then can say, "Sarah thinks: John thinks that Henry's goal is to get the bananas." In other words Sarah has made this attribution: John attributes a goal to Henry. She has made an attribution of an attribution, and thus has formed a representation of a representation.

All this sounds very complicated, but humans do this sort of thing all the time. We are always talking about what Mary thinks of John or about what Henry thinks Mary thinks of John, and so on. We take such recursive representation for granted, and are not at all confused by it. Only when we are required to arrange nonverbal tests does metarepresentation become unwieldy. In testing a nonverbal animal, our objective is simply to illustrate what attribution of attribution, or representation of representation, might look like to it.

Is Metarepresentation Special?

Does the attribution of attribution make cognitive demands that are not made by simple, first-order attribution? In other words, is second-order attribution special? Given its profligate use among humans, it probably is not. Some psycholinguists claim, in fact, that seventh-order attribution is a routine feature of a normal human conversation! (See, for example, Sperber and his coauthor, the linguist Deidre Wilson.) Probably the cognitive demands made by seventh-order attribution are no greater than those made by sixth, sixth no greater than those made by fifth, and so on. What is essential for higher-order attribution is not special cognitive power but the special kind of social observation that sets the stage for higher-order attribution. And social observation of this kind is found in the human but not in other species.

Consider the infant chimpanzee that checks its mother's attentiveness—"Is she looking at me?"—before extending her leg and requesting that the mother groom her. Will this infant ever observe another infant for attentiveness—"Is that infant looking at *its* mother to see if she is looking at it"? In all likelihood, not. Yet it is precisely such second-order social observation that is at the root of second-order attribution. An animal that does not observe the observations made by other animals will have no occasion to attribute attributions to others.

We noted earlier (in Chapter 3) that the lack of social observation in the chimpanzee plays a decisive role in its failure to engage in pedagogy. Chimpanzee mothers do not engage in first-order social observation; that is, they do not even observe their own youngsters' attempts to crack nuts, let alone engage in second-order social observation: observe another mother observe her infant's attempts to crack nuts; or third order, observe a mother observe yet another mother observe her infant. The chimpanzee would be hard put to observe such cases even if it were disposed to do so; cases of this kind do not even exist in chimpanzee groups. But one may well ask, then, what is cause and what is effect?

If chimpanzees were placed in human social groups, where such cases do exist, would they comprehend the higher-order social behavior in which humans engage? "Say" to themselves: "Jane is watching Janet watch Betty watch her kids"? Or is it the original incapacity for higher-order representation which debars any higher-order social behavior from emerging among chimpanzees?

We may, however, be able to induce a greater degree of social observation in the chimpanzee in the laboratory. Just as Povinelli taught his chimpanzees *not* to pay attention to the other one, so we might do the opposite; make it profitable for the chimpanzee to pay attention to the other one. It might even be possible to go further and induce second-order observation in the chimpanzee, thus setting the stage for second-order attribution or metarepresentation.

Solving the Problems of Others

Sarah made an error when the actor encountered a box laden with bricks: She did not choose the photograph showing the actor removing the bricks. Is the error innocent, meaning simply that she doesn't know the difference between chimpanzee and human strength? Or not so innocent, meaning that rather than solving the actor's problem she is instead solving her own problem? And if she did select the alternative that solved her problem rather than the actor's problem, can we really speak of her as possessing theory of mind?

What we require is an unequivocal test showing that Sarah does indeed take the actor into account, that the photographs she selects represent solutions to *his* problems, not hers. One such test consists of showing Sarah a videotape in which several actors confront the same problem. If she selects a different alternative for each of the actors, she then cannot be said to be solving her own problem; she must be taking the actors into account.

We gave her a test of this kind using two actors, toward each of whom Sarah had a special attitude. One was a preferred companion, the other not. The difference in her attitude toward the two trainers could not be explained by any known factor; she liked one and disliked the other, more or less from first acquaintance.

Using essentially the original test materials, we filmed two videotapes in which each trainer was shown attempting to reach inaccessible food. We modified the alternatives, however, using now two sets of photographs for each trainer, one positive and the other negative. In the positive set each trainer was shown carrying out an action that solved the problem, whereas in the negative set the actor was shown carrying out an action that failed to solve the problem.

As may be seen in Figure 7.3, failures included an actor using a stick too short to reach the food, an actor falling while stepping onto a chair, and an actor lying on his back with bricks on his stomach. Sarah was shown the videotapes of the preferred and nonpreferred actors in random order. Once again, after each videotape she was given the alternatives in the usual manila envelope. This time there were three alternatives.

One photo showed the actor carrying out a proper solution, a second an improper solution. A third showed an actor carrying out a proper but irrelevant action—irrelevant because it did not solve the problem shown in the videotape. Sarah made different choices for her preferred and nonpreferred actors. When looking at photos of the actor she liked, Sarah chose exclusively proper solutions; of the actor she did not like, eight improper solutions, two proper ones, and one that was irrelevant.

It is interesting to ask if Sarah would actually have inflicted such outcomes on the individuals in the videotapes. In other words, if she had been given a button to push that would actually have brought about these outcomes, would she have used it? She might indeed cause the preferred actor to obtain the inaccessible food; but would she have caused the nonpreferred actor to fall, to end up supine and with bricks on his stomach?

The actual alternatives Sarah chose clearly reflected her attitude toward the actor; they were not alternatives she would have chosen for herself. Moreover, while the alternatives she chose would make no sense if applied to herself, they made perfect sense in terms of satisfying the goals or intentions she attributed to the actors she likes and dislikes.

In passing this test, what was Sarah's real accomplishment? The recognition of goal-directed action and the attribution of intention to the goal-seeker can be found in the repertoire of every normal ten-to-twelve-month-old human infant. Sarah differs from the infant in this way: Whereas the infant makes these attributions automatically, Sarah does so thoughtfully by examining the alternatives given to her and deciding which would satisfy the actor's goal and which would not. (See Chapter 9 for a further discussion of this important distinction.)

In Sarah's case, there is no requirement for higher-order representation; no requirement that she attribute to the actor a representation different from her own. Sarah's accomplishment may represent an upper limit of chimpanzee social competence; in the human, it represents the point at which human social competence starts.

Selecting What's Next

The philosopher Jonathan Bennett has proposed the most intriguing objection to the interpretation given of the Sarah data. Bennett argues that, as opposed to attributing states of mind, Sarah simply selected the photograph that depicted the *next* step in the sequence. And Sarah knew what came next in the sequence, says Bennett, simply because she either had solved similar problems herself or had watched others solve them.

The concept of "next," on which Bennett's interpretation hinges, seems a perfectly simple notion, but it is not. When we examine this concept we find that it comes in at least two varieties: literal next and appropriate next.

Literal next, clearly the kind of next Bennett has in mind, is not strong enough to enable Sarah to choose the right photographs. It is the stronger variety of next, appropriate next, that is needed to enable Sarah to select the right photographs. Moreover, "appropriate next" presupposes exactly what Bennett wishes to exclude: attribution of states of mind. The distinction between the two kinds of next can be clarified through the following Gedanken experiment.

An actor again jumps up in a repeated but failed attempt to reach inaccessible food, but now stops jumping occasionally so as to hitch up his pants. We familiarize chimpanzees and/or children with the videotape, then give them the usual test. In this case, though, we pit "literal" next against "appropriate" next.

In showing the children the videotape of the actor jumping, we stop the film exactly at the point where the actor's next act will be to hitch up his pants. We then offer the children three photos: one of the actor stepping onto a chair, another of the actor reaching out with a stick, and a third of the actor hitching up his pants. Which will the chimpanzees and/or the children select?

If Bennett is correct and it is a knowledge of what comes next that guides Sarah's choice, the children will choose the actor hitching up his

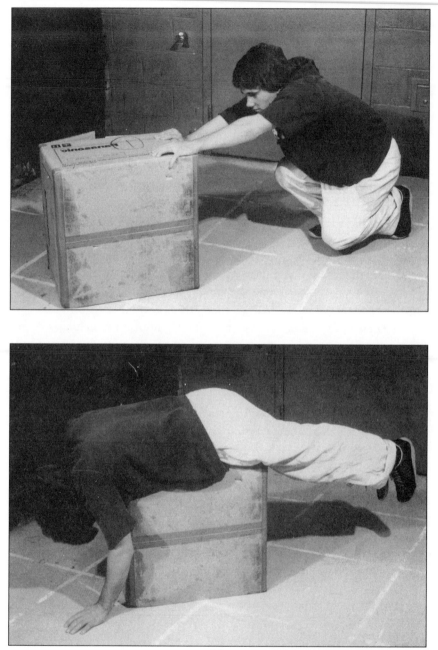

(a)

Figure 7.3   Corresponding photographs showing (*a*) "good" and (*b*) "bad" solutions to problems.

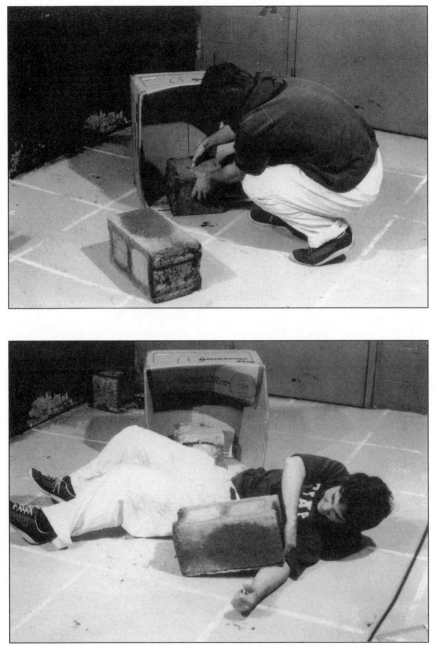

(b)

Figure 7.3   (*Continued*)

pants because that is what literally comes next. If however the children have attributed a goal to the actor and are interested in having him solve his problem, they will choose "appropriate next"—the actor stepping onto the chair.

Satisfied that the Gedanken experiment revealed the hidden weakness in Bennett's objection, we were content to leave the issue alone. But a "thought" experiment never fully convinces everyone. "Real" proof came twenty years later—long after the chimpanzee lab had been closed—with the arrival of Verena Dasser, a postdoctoral fellow from Zurich. She turned the Gedanken experiment into a real experiment, an experiment for children.

Dasser prepared six different videotapes, each showing a problem analogous to "hitching up your pants." Here are two examples:

1. An actor tries to drive a nail into a wall using his bare hand; he stops, looks at his wristwatch, then resumes pounding the nail.
2. An actor tries to obtain music from a record player; he shakes the player, but cannot obtain music because there is no record on the turntable. Whereupon he picks up some Kleenex from the floor, blows his nose, and resumes shaking the player.

After she had familiarized the children with each videotape, Dasser tested them. She showed each child the videotape again, stopping the film exactly at the point at which the actor's next act was analogous to "hitching up his pants." In one case the actor looked at his wristwatch, in the other case, picked up a Kleenex and blew his nose.

After being shown each videotape the children were given three photographs: a relevant solution, an irrelevant act, and the "literal next" act. For example, in the videotape where the actor pounded a nail with his bare hand, the photographs given the children were these three:

Relevant act: an actor grasping a hammer

Irrelevant act: the actor holding a pair of scissors

Literal next act: the actor looking at his watch.

Most of the twenty-four children selected the photo depicting the "relevant act," the act that would solve the actor's problem (in our example here, the actor grasping a hammer), thus confirming the Gedanken experiment.

The only exception to this trend came from a procedural error in which Verena, when showing the children the alternatives, said "Choose what comes next in the movie"—an instruction that would of course bias the children toward "literal next." To make the test comparable to that used with the animals the proper procedure was to have said nothing; but while it is easy to say nothing to a chimpanzee, even highly competent experimenters have a hard time saying nothing to children!

Despite the error, even the older children did not favor the literal next alternative; they made fifty-eight choices of the relevant alternative as compared to only twenty-eight choices of the literal next act. So it seems that even when told to "choose what comes next," children have difficulty doing so!

A robot could be programmed to choose "literal next" acts, and children can be influenced to select such acts by being given biased instructions. Human adults, and chimpanzees, however, cannot be programmed to chose "literal next" acts because they are innately programmed to attribute goals and intentions. They therefore choose "appropriate next" acts, acts that satisfy goals.

Note

1. Why did Sarah not revert to the use of similarity? Very likely because, as noted earlier, the predilection to match objects on the basis of similarity is far weaker in the chimpanzee than in the child.

Chapter 8
Causality
Apple? Cut Apple

Although humans appear to have only one idea of cause, they can be led to this idea in at least three different ways: the "natural," the "learned," and the "coincidental."

We have an immediate sense of cause when we see a moving object hit a resting object and move it forward. This is an example of *natural cause*, whose principal characteristic is its immediacy. One viewing of the event is sufficient—there is no need to repeat the sequence. We have the same immediate sense of cause when one intentional object bristles or scowls at another, and the other object cowers or pales. Thus "natural" cause is not confined to the physical domain but is found in the psychological domain as well.

The mechanisms of "natural" cause are those derived from the infant's physical and psychological modules. *Force* is the causal mechanism the infant inherits from his physical module; *intention*, the causal mechanism the infant inherits from his psychological module. Although both mechanisms depend on temporal contiguity, they part company almost immediately. Force requires a spatial contiguity between events, intention does not. The efficacy of a smile/scowl does not depend on spatial contiguity. Intention requires a causal agent, an intentional object who initiates the action.

By contrast, neither an infant nor an adult will have a sense of cause when he sees, for example, a wisp of smoke emerge after hearing a bell ring. Nevertheless if this quite arbitrary pair of events is paired repeatedly, both infant and adult will grasp the relation between the two events and interpret the ring of the bell as causing the wisp of smoke. In other words the repetition of any pair of events, provided they are contiguous in time, will lead a human (and perhaps an animal) to interpret the first event as the cause of the second.

"Learned" cause has been studied in a variety of species over a period of years. Animals (and some humans) in several laboratories have been trained to operate an instrument that automatically delivers some desired item; the rat presses a lever for food pellets, pigeons peck a key for grain, and humans push a button to obtain "points." Studies done by the learning theorist Tony Dickinson and his associates suggest that rats, pigeons, and humans all place a causal construal on the goal-directed acts of pressing a lever or pecking a key, and respond to this simple device in the same way.

All seem to calculate the profit to be gained by responding correctly by using intuitive statistics, probably the same statistics the infant uses in his detection of word boundaries. As we noted in Chapter 5, the end of every word allows for the free use of any "next" syllable, whereas the middle of a word does not. Infants can "keep a record" of the transitional probabilities among syllables and could use this information to detect word boundaries, though whether they actually do so is not known.

While lever presses and pellets do not of course resemble syllables, from the point of view of statistics they are events that occur in time and give rise to the same question implicitly posed by the syllables: If one event occurs, what is the probability of a particular "next" event occurring? This type of intuitive use of statistics seems to be available to all vertebrates.

Individuals operate instruments in the laboratory because they find it profitable to do so. But we can make responding unprofitable. This can be done in two ways, one direct and the other roundabout. In the direct way we disrupt the connection between the apparatus and the desired item, so that the operation of the device no longer produces the "goody." The round-about way is managed like this: We make the desired goody more or less *constantly* available, such that the individual does not need to operate the device at all. This approach is referred to as "free lunch"!

When the device is disrupted so as to no longer produce the desired item, humans and animals gradually decrease their responding, then stop operating the device altogether. But both groups promptly resume responding once the original contingency has been reinstated. Free lunch has a different effect, one that is peculiarly disruptive. Individuals that find that food or points are free for the "taking" abandon the device completely. And even after the original contingency has been reinstated they are slow to resume responding.

When "free lunch" is applied to natural cause, it has the same strong effect as when applied to "learned" cause. A human observer, shown a scene in which an object strikes and launches another, has an immediate sense of causality; when however this scene is followed by a second scene, in which an object is launched *without* having been struck (the equivalent of free lunch), he abandons his causal interpretation of the first scene! The influence of seeing an object move on its own, without having been struck, has eliminated the observer's sense of causality.

The third way to produce a sense of cause, which we call "coincidental" cause, is best illustrated by a household example. If, when an individual turns on the faucet of a kitchen sink, his act is followed by a loud noise in the street, he will have the immediate sense that he caused the noise by turning on the faucet. Is there anything special about the act of turning on a faucet, though?

In one sense, no. The individual could just as well have reached for a towel or dipped a spoon into the sugar bowl. These acts too, if followed by a noise in the street, may lead to a sense of cause. But these acts are all special. They are intentional, which is to say, goal directed. If the individual had sneezed, slipped on a rug, or upset the sugar bowl, and these acts were followed by a noise in the street, he would not have had a sense of cause. Coincidental cause has two requirements: an intentional act and an event that is paired in time with the act.

A human adult understands that his act of turning on a faucet and hearing a noise in the street is a coincidence. The next time he turns on the faucet he does not expect to hear a noise in the street. The effect is transitory. And yet the effect of the repetition of merely observed events is permanent; in other words, as long as an individual observes repeated scenes of one arbitrary event being followed by another, he senses that the first event causes the second.

Is the sense of cause that one experiences in the "natural," "learned," and "coincidental" cases the same? We speculate that they are—that humans have only one sense of cause.

But we can test the question by using habituation/dishabituation to compare the effect that each of the three cases has on the other. Just as we can habituate an individual's interest in "learned" cause by showing him one case of "learned" cause after another, and habituate his interest in "coincidental" cause by showing him one case of "coincidental" cause after another, so too perhaps we can habituate his interest in either "learned" or "coincidental" cause just by showing him cases of "natural" cause, and vice versa. If so—that is, if we can show that the habituative effect of one kind of cause on the other is the same as the habituative effect of one kind upon itself— then clearly the three kinds of cause are equivalent.

Cause in the Doll House

A three-and-a-half-year old child once surprised us by revealing that she saw not only a representational relation between a room and its dollhouse replica, but a *causal* relation as well. The child, having observed a trainer place candy in a tiny container in a room of the dollhouse, then went to the actual room and chose the corresponding container. This in itself is not an unusual act for most three- to four-year-old children, for unlike young chimpanzees, all children pass this test of representational competence. (See Figure 8.1.)

On one of the test trials, however, the child found her way back to the dollhouse before the trainer had returned to it, and reached inside the dollhouse. She lifted the tiny container under which the trainer had placed the candy and expressed great surprise: The candy was still there! How could it be? She had herself removed it from the real room!

Clearly, the child's surprise suggests that she expected that her having taken the candy from the actual room would cause the candy to disappear from the dollhouse. That in turn suggests that she expected that the trainer's having placed candy in the miniature room would cause candy to

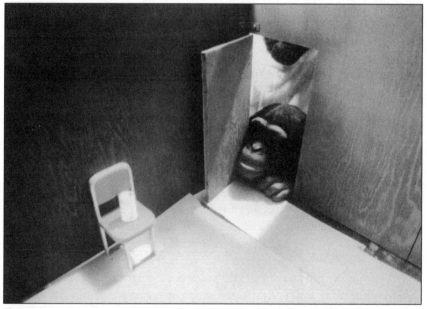

Figure 8.1 Chimpanzee observing placement of food in dollhouse. (*Courtesy of Paul Fusco*)

appear in the actual room. The child seems to have placed a causal construal on the relation between the actual room and the miniature room.

Is this reaction characteristic of a developmental stage in the child, or rather a characteristic of this child? The experiment did not make a provision for even entertaining such a question; but later, when testing the chimpanzees, we had an opportunity to answer the question. Although our attempts to train chimpanzees to use maps, miniature rooms, photographs, and other representations failed, there was an exception. The chimpanzees were able to use one room as a "guide" for finding objects in another room.

Both rooms were located off the same hall and were similar but hardly identical; tests showed that all three animals could readily distinguish the two rooms. In the test, an animal observed us place food in one of four containers in room A; the animal was then released into the hall. The animal promptly went down the hall to room B and chose the corresponding container more than 80 percent of the time, giving us the impression that it was treating room A as a representation of room B. The results, however, also are compatible with the interpretation suggested earlier: Like the child, the animal construed the connection between the two rooms as causal—placing candy in room A caused it to appear in room B.

Which alternative was it? To decide, a small change was made in the test. We placed food in *three* of the four containers in room A and again allowed the animals to enter the hall. This time, however, they were allowed to make only one choice in room B. Once they had made that choice, they were interrupted and returned to room A. Back in room A the animal resumed its choices, but it avoided two containers: one in which food had *never* been placed and one that corresponded to the container from which it had taken food in room B. All three animals avoided both these containers in over 86 percent of the trials.

The avoidance of one container was easily explained, since food had never been placed there. But the avoidance of the other container suggests that the animal interpreted the relation between the two rooms as causal. The idea of a causal relation between the two rooms clearly violates the constraints on causality of the physical module. The interpretation of a causal relation by both chimpanzee and child in this case is reminiscent of voodooism, in which actions perpetrated on a doll are intended to have a causal effect on the person the doll represents.

Origins

How might the concept of cause have evolved? It may have evolved in the context of personal action. If so, a purely reflexive creature, one that could react to the actions of others but not initiate its own actions, could not have had a concept of causality. It could have had a sensitivity to temporal contiguity, however, storing in memory events whose co-occurrence had important consequences for its personal well-being. Such a sensitivity could be beneficial to the individual and the species, and may have been a precursor of the concept of cause. A purely reflexive creature, however, must first evolve a capacity for voluntary action before it can make the transition from sensitivity to temporal contiguity to actual sense of cause.

When we humans think of primitive examples of cause, we are drawn to "natural" cause in the physical domain: one object launching another by striking it. But what set the first object into motion? Very likely the voluntary action of an individual.

This scenario for the origin of cause has only one problem associated with it. As the primatologist Hans Kummer has pointed out, most species cannot cause one object to collide with another. Causing physical changes in the world by voluntary action is not half as widespread as humans suppose. Basically only humans, chimpanzees, and Cebus monkeys manipulate objects freely, and of the three only humans make large-scale permanent changes in the world: buildings, tunnels, dams. The changes made by most species are modest—a periodic nest, dam, hive, etc.

A better scenario for the origin of cause deserts the physical domain and turns to the psychological. All species, at least all species that live in groups, interact socially, causing both psychological and physical changes in one another. Even nonsocial species interact socially with their young, causing psychological and physical changes in them. Although all species forage for food, which requires acting causally in the physical domain, probably social species cause more events in the social domain than the physical; perhaps only humans and chimpanzees cause about equally many events in both domains.

Humans, both children and adults, build on the mechanisms provided by their modules in learning about sources of force that postdate their evolutionary history; mechanisms such as electricity, gas engines, and electronics which do *not* require spatial contiguity in the intuitive sense. Although three-year-old children are still bound by the need for spatial contiguity, studies by the developmental psychologists Merry Bullock and R. Gelman show that by five or six years of age children already recognize that the efficacy of electricity does not depend on spatial contiguity. Curiously, there are no comparable postevolutionary mechanisms in the case of intention; that is, there are no sources of intention that go beyond actual and observed personal action.

Hume: Repeated Co-occurrence

The British philosopher David Hume claimed that one cannot find any such "thing" as cause in the world. Cause, he stated, is an unwarranted assumption we draw when we experience two events that co-occur with a certain frequency. According to Hume it is simply one's experience of the repeated co-occurrence of the same two events that leads us to believe that co-occurrence is inevitable, that the preceding event "caused" the following one. Hume's logic is sound; we surely cannot demonstrate causal claims. Hume's psychology, however, is not.

The idea of cause, as we have seen, can be induced by a single experience of the right kind. Repeated co-occurrence is essential only in *learned* cause; it is not essential in either natural or coincidental cause. Further, one can be exposed to the repeated co-occurrence of two events without ever having a sense of cause. If a moving ball stops a fraction short of striking a resting ball which nevertheless moves forward, no matter how often this scene is repeated we will not register a sense of cause.

Moreover, adults do not start out tied to Hume's constraint of repeated association and then gradually learn to overcome this constraint. To the contrary, studies by the developmental psychologist Alan Leslie and his associates suggest that the infant's sense of cause is like that of the adult, and that infants recognize the "right perceptual experience."

Depictions of Causality

Although actual causal sequences are, of course, dynamic—an individual acts on an object using an instrument, for example, and changes the state, location, color, and so forth of the object—we can depict causal process by means of "still" pictures. In fact, a sequence of just three pictures will do.

Picture a sequence in which the first "still" shows an object in its initial state, a second shows an instrument, and a third shows the initial object in a transformed state. An apple, a knife, and a cut apple can constitute a causal process, as Figure 8.2 shows. Picturing the "idea" as a sequence dramatizes cause as a process.

As we noted in Chapter 6, we can test a child or an animal by showing such a sequence with one of the pictures missing—for example, apple, blank, cut apple—and then offering the child several alternatives—knife, pencil, container of water—from which to complete the sequence. The child who recognizes the idea depicted by the incomplete sequence will select the correct alternative and complete the illustration by filling in the

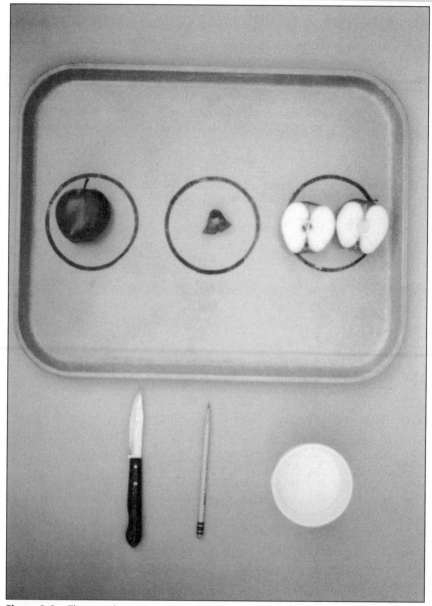

Figure 8.2   The causal process.

missing "blank." Children of about three and a half years of age complete these tests successfully. So do "educated" chimpanzees.

For example, if shown

(dry sponge) (?) (wet sponge)

and offered as alternatives

knife, container of water, pencil,

both child and chimpanzee will choose the container of water.
If shown

(intact apple) (?) (cut apple)

and offered as alternatives

knife, container of water, pencil,

both will choose the knife.

We can also modify the test, removing the third rather than the middle item so that the sequence lacks a terminal (transformed) state rather than an operator. For example, if shown

(intact apple) (knife) (?)

and offered as alternatives

cut apple, cut orange, wet apple,

the child and chimpanzee will choose the cut apple. If shown

(blank paper) (pencil) (?)

and offered as alternatives

scribbled paper, scribbled sponge, cut paper,

they will choose the scribbled paper.

We must point out immediately that children and chimpanzees do not pass or fail these tests owing to a reliance on learned associations. They both perform correctly on entirely anomalous cases.

When shown paper that has been soaked in water (rather than written on), apples that contain writing (rather than having been cut), pingpong balls that have been cut, etc., children and chimpanzees perform equally well, indicating that "reliance on associations" cannot be invoked to explain their performance. Success in anomalous cases indicates further that both young children and chimpanzees have abstract representations of actions.

They have the capacity to recognize highly unfamiliar examples of the actions—cutting, marking, and wetting—on which the early tests concentrated, as well as of other actions tested later.

The real bugaboo that arises when testing children and chimpanzees on causality is not a reliance on associations but interference from physical similarity. Children below three and a half years of age, and uneducated chimpanzees, both of whom fail these tests, fail in exactly the same way: They match objects based on physical similarity.

When shown a sequence which requires completion—say, an intact apple, an empty space, and a cut apple—and offered three instruments to choose from—a knife, a pencil, and a container of water—they choose the pencil. Why? Because in the test the pencil, like the apple, is red. Moreover we can shift their choice from one alternative to another, simply by dissolving a red dye in the container of water and using a black pencil instead of the red one. This will lead both child and chimpanzee to select the water, which now, like the apple, is red.

Reading Cause before Effect

Does the ability to pass the test indicate that the child/chimpanzee is taking order into account and reading the sequence in the "right" direction? For example, in observing "apple ? cut apple," does Sarah map the temporal order of the action (the cause before the effect) onto the spatial order of the depicted sequence? Or does she simply select the alternative, "knife," because it is "associated" with the action?

To answer these questions we exploited the fact that certain actions can be "reversed." For example, a clear piece of paper can be marked with a pencil, or a marked piece of paper can be cleared with an eraser; a dry object can be wetted, or a wet object dried; an intact object can be cut with a knife, or a cut object restored with tape; and so on. Before testing Sarah we familiarized her with all of these cases.

She observed her trainer connect "broken" pieces of an object with scotch tape, erase pencil marks on the surface of a sheet of paper with a gum eraser, and wipe a wet object dry with a towel. The trainer then relinquished the task to Sarah, who engaged enthusiastically in all three activities.

Sarah was then trained to read the test sequences as an English reader would, from left to right. We restricted her training to the case of mark-erase, showing test pairs of this kind:

sheet of white paper/"?"/marked paper

marked paper/"?"/sheet of white paper

The alternatives given were pencil, container of water, eraser. Pencil was the correct choice for the first order, eraser correct for the second (see Figure 8.3). Sarah quickly learned to make the appropriate choices, indicating that she read the transformations in the correct order, from left to right. We then gave her a transfer test involving entirely new cases: cut-mend and wet-dry. She chose as accurately on the new cases as on the old, performing at her usual 80 percent correct level on all cases.

The basic consequence of a causal action is that of transformation—a change from an initial state to a final one. Does Sarah understand causal actions at this level? Can she observe the initial state of an object, compare it with its terminal state, and then select the instrument responsible for the transformation?

We can add to the interest of this question by removing the restrictions that were applied to the examples Sarah had been given. In most of Sarah's tests, objects were presented in their pristine state: an intact apple, white paper, a dry cloth. In addition the final state of the object never included

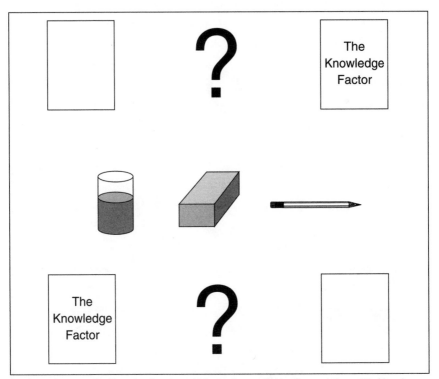

Figure 8.3   A causality test for the reversal of one of the above actions. Marking is shown on the top panel, erasing on the bottom panel.

more than a single transformation; that is, paper was marked but never both marked *and* wet, etc. In the real world, however, objects are not always encountered in their pristine state. Some are already partially transformed, and they may undergo further transformations.

In the new test series, transformations sometimes involved more than a single action; for example, paper could be both cut and marked. In addition the initial state could be an already transformed object rather than one in an intact or pristine state. Finally, we not only lifted restrictions on initial state and number of transformations but required Sarah to separate relevant operators from irrelevent.

We gave her two containers, a relevant container and a "trash" bin, and required her to compare the initial state with the final state and to place instruments that participated in the transformation into the relevant container, those that did not participate, into the trash bin. For example, if a piece of paper that began in a marked state ended up marked, wet, and cut, she was to place scissors and container of water in the relevant container, pencil in the trash bin. (See Figure 8.4.)

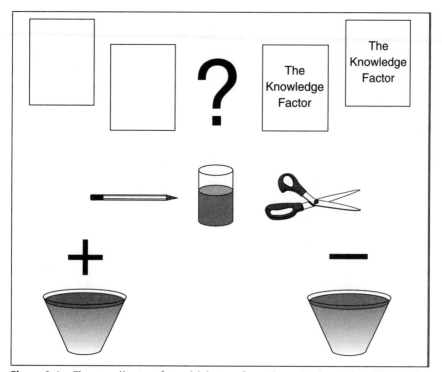

Figure 8.4 The causality test for multiple transformations: Cutting and marking, with separate receptacles for relevant and irrelevant operators.

The tests given Sarah were based on the familiar actions of wetting, cutting, and marking, and involved both single-action and double-action transformations in equal number, counterbalanced over the session. She performed equally well on single- and double-action transformations, though the test was of unusual difficulty and her performance reflected the difficulty. Her customary 80 percent correct declined to about 70 percent correct, which however is still well above chance level.

Understanding Social Causality

Although, owing to technical difficulties, Sarah was not tested for an understanding of social cause, it is interesting to see that social causality can be tested by means of the same format that we used for physical causality. This one, for example: Peony is eating a banana in the presence of Liz, who extends her hand palm-up and makes food grunts—the content of Scene 1. Scene 2 is blank. In Scene 3, Liz and Peony stroll with their arms around one another. The alternatives offered Sarah consist of three scenes:

1. Liz steals food from Peony
2. Peony gives food to Liz
3. Peony ignores Liz and keeps the food for herself.

Only Scene 2, in which Peony gives food to Liz, is compatible with the harmonious terminal scene of Liz and Peony strolling with arms around one another. Given Sarah's success with respect to "theory of mind" (see Chapter 7), it seems safe to say that chimpanzees understand social cause as well as physical cause.

Stories as Causal Sequences

An animal that can understand one causal sequence, as the chimpanzee can, may be able to understand several causal sequences. It may even understand the causal connections between sequences such as the following.

John tries to cut a melon with his knife, but the knife breaks. Mary arrives just in time to see John's problem, and lets him use her knife. John cuts the melon with Mary's knife and shares the melon with Mary. These three causal actions—cutting, lending, and sharing—consist of physical and social actions, all of which chimpanzees comprehend in some degree. By presenting the actions in the form of causality tests, the three-item sequences referred to above, we provide a test to prove this claim.

Gratitude, an important element in the story, may be too complex a state of mind for either a child or chimpanzee to handle; but both could probably cope nicely with a simpler state relating to gratitude, reciproca-tion. Reciprocation is a basic component of the infant's psychological mod-ule, leading the infant to expect an intentional object which receives a positive act to return a positive act. Since "Mary gives John her knife" would probably qualify as a positive act, "John shares his melon with Mary" would qualify as reciprocation.

The sequence provides the minimal elements of a story: a beginning, a problem, and a resolution or end. In this case, a happy end! But consider a different sequence: John fails to cut the melon; Mary happens to drop by with nothing to offer John except advice; she departs, leaving John with a melon he cannot cut. Does that make a story? Or how about this sequence: John successfully cuts the melon and begins to eat it; Mary drops by and asks for some, but John refuses; Mary leaves in a huff. Is that a story? In other words, does one of these sequences come closer to being a story, and if so, why?

The first sequence, simple as it is, is best. It both poses and resolves a problem. And while problem resolution is not the only thematic material to constitute a story it is a kind that young children and even chimpanzees are likely to understand. Is there a way to prove that the young child or chim-panzee can differentiate among the several causal sequences, accepting some as stories while rejecting others?

Suppose we translate the story into four or five pictures, handing them to the child or animal in a scrambled order, and require them to place them in the correct, the story order. If they learn to do this more quickly for some sequences, and in particular for sequences that contain both a problem and its resolution, this would corroborate the view that problem resolution is one of the basic forms of the story.

Sherlock Holmes and the Perplexing Case of Causal Reasoning

Causal reasoning, Sherlock Holmes' specialty, has two components. First, the individual must have a keen sense of normality so that he can recognize when things are *not* normal. Holmes was especially adept at ferreting this out: He could pick up small deflections from normality to which others were blind. Second, the individual must have a particularly well-stocked fund of knowledge, permitting him to make astute inferences about what caused the deflections. Holmes was expert at both: quick to recognize the abnormal, quick to infer its cause.

The causality tests given the chimpanzees are not tests of causal rea-soning. They required no more than the ability of the animal to recognize the representational character of the test items—for example, to recognize that the apple and knife were not simply arbitrary objects but stood for "cutting." The success of the chimpanzees on the causality test does not tell us whether they could go further, and do causal reasoning.

So we tested four young chimpanzees on two different kinds of causal reasoning. In the more difficult test, we placed the animals in a quandary. We introduced them to a runway that consistently led to food, then occasionally replaced the food with a rubber snake. The unpredictable snake "ruined" their quick dash down the runway. While they continued with their initial quick starts, they now hesitated midway, and approached the goal box with extreme caution. In fact the one male stood upright, hair bristling, and walked forward throwing sticks at the goal box.

At this point we gave the animals a chance to use causal reasoning in order to escape from their quandary. Before each animal was introduced to the runway it was placed in the company of an "informant," another animal that had just completed a run and was still excited by the food it had found in the goal box, or still agitated by the snake it had found there. Could the animal that was about to run benefit from the state of the informant, using the informant's state to infer what it would find in the goal box?

It could not. Not one of the four young animals was influenced by the emotional state of the informant. If they found the informant in a negative state, they neither hesitated nor refused to run. If they found the informant in a positive state they did not set forth promptly, but continued instead to run in the same hesitant way.

Is it possible that the informant "failed" to convey its emotional states? We can eliminate that alternative. Uninformed or "blind" human observers, when shown videotapes of the informant, could tell with 99 percent accuracy whether the animal had encountered a snake or food. But perhaps the problem was more subtle. Perhaps the naive chimpanzees were not affected by the informant's states. We can eliminate this alternative, too. Uninformed or "blind" human observers, when now shown videotapes not of the informant but of the waiting animal, judged with about 75 percent accuracy when the waiting animal had encountered an informant in either a positive or negative state!

This suggests an interesting possibility. An emotional state has no intrinsic informational value: It can be used informatively only if one knows what *caused* the state. Evidently, the animals did not understand what caused the informant's emotion. They did not relate it to the goal box and therefore could not use it to anticipate what they would find in the goal box.

What makes this outcome puzzling is that the informant was not a stranger to the chimpanzees for, in fact, every chimpanzee was itself an informant in one trial or another. On the average, each animal played the role of "informant" in every fourth trial!

The animal's failure to infer the cause of the informant's state suggests that the young chimpanzees cannot solve this problem by inference, but need direct perceptual experience. They need to "see" the entire causal sequence: the informant going down the runway, finding either food or snake, suffering one or another emotional state, and then being taken to the small room where it encounters another animal. Such experience eliminates the need for inference.

After an animal has been given such experiences, it may be possible to show it no more than it was shown in the original test: the informant's emotional state. It may now understand the cause of the informant's emotion and be able to use the emotion as an index of what will be found in the goal box.

Causal Reasoning in a Psychological Setting

Both children and chimpanzees were tested on a second problem in causal reasoning—the chimpanzees in an outdoor compound, the children in a classroom.

For the chimpanzees, two opaque containers were placed thirty feet apart, at the base of a triangle. The chimpanzee stood at the apex of the triangle, midway between the containers, thirty feet distant from the base. Restrained by an accompanying trainer, the chimpanzee watched as a second trainer placed an apple in the one container and a banana in the other (the two fruit were chosen because they are about equally preferred by chimpanzees). The accompanying trainer then obscured the animal's view of the container by using a "blind." He distracted the animal for two minutes, then removed the blind. The chimpanzee now saw that the second trainer was standing midway between the containers, eating an apple (or a banana). The trainer left after eating the fruit. The chimpanzee now was free to enter the compound.

Children of about three and a half to five years of age were tested with a comparable procedure adjusted to a classroom and to their food preferences, a doughnut and a cookie being substituted for the apple and the banana. The twenty children and four chimpanzees tested on this problem were both given ten trials, with an interval of thirty minutes or more between trials.

Eighteen of the twenty children responded in the same way: They consistently chose the container associated with the food *different* from the one the trainer was eating. If the trainer had been eating a cookie the children chose the container in which the doughnut had been placed, and vice versa. One of the four chimpanzees, Sadie, the oldest animal, responded in the same way as the children, always choosing the container associated with a fruit different from the one eaten by the trainer. The three younger chimpanzees were inconsistent. One tended to choose the container that held the same fruit as the trainer had eaten, while the other two tended to do the opposite.

The children (eighteen out of twenty of them) and Sadie seem to have made the same inference: The food eaten by the trainer was the food he had placed in the container; therefore go to the *other* container. Obviously, this is not an obligatory inference. The food could have come from elsewhere—the trainer's pocket, for example, or somewhere in the vicinity. However, nearly all the children and the one chimpanzee evidently rejected these possibilities, clinging tenaciously to their inference of identity. The food eaten by the trainer was the *same* as the food he had placed in the container.

Could we have convinced them otherwise? We tried the following stratagem. The children and chimpanzees were shown that the fruit was now wrapped in elaborate packages before being placed in the containers. The trainer, however, still appeared a minute and a half later, midway between the two containers, eating food. Children of four years and older were immediately affected by this change. They no longer consistently chose the container holding food different from the one eaten by the trainer but chose randomly between the two containers. However, younger children and all four chimpanzees were unaffected by the change. Children of at least four years of age evidently understand that physical acts take time. If there is insufficient time for the trainer to go to the container, unwrap the food, and carry it to a point midway between the two containers, then the food he is eating cannot be the food he placed in the container. The causal reasoning of the four-year-old child includes the fact that acts take time (a fact that plays a critical role in hunting among the San, as we shall see). It is a fact not understood by chimpanzees.

Causal Reasoning and Technology

The chimpanzee's limited competence in causal reasoning is reflected in its technology. The hunting engaged in by chimpanzees consists of the opportunistic trapping of small prey in trees. The prey are smaller than the chimpanzee, and there is no use of weapons. Hunter-gatherers, by contrast, hunt prey far larger than themselves, using weapons, dogs, and tracking. Their astute tracking relies heavily on causal reasoning.

After having tracked an eland for more than a day, a group of San hunters came upon an area where the eland's track was visibly crossed by mouse tracks. Right then and there the San terminated the hunt. Since mice are nocturnal, and the mouse tracks lay on top of the eland's tracks, the hunters knew that the eland had reached this point before evening fell. This example of causal reasoning was followed by another, in which the San converted time (the duration from night to dawn) and the speed at which they know the eland travels into distance. Recognizing that the eland could be miles away by now, they abandoned the hunt.

Chimpanzees obtain termites by scratching holes in termite mounds, inserting straws or twigs into the holes, and pulling out the termites that cling to the straws. The San, who also enjoy termites, have observed that rain leads termites to emerge from their mound to make the nuptial flight. Humans exploit this information. They combine theory of mind with causal reasoning to devise a technology for obtaining termites with truly minimal effort. While crouching over the termite mound they produce clucking noises which apparently, inside the mound, sound like falling rain. This brings the termites out of the mound, where they are gathered by the waiting humans. This technology for obtaining termites is only one of many reported to be used by humans.

The fundamental relation between seeds and growth has been understood by humans for generations. They did not, however, actively engage in planting seeds until forced to do so by population density, which led to a shortage of game and of foraging material. By using causal reasoning humans developed not just planting and gathering but agriculture, the first of many technologies that transformed the human.

Causal reasoning enabled the human to develop a suite of technologies—fire, dried food, clothing, shelter, weapons—that made it possible for him to leave Africa, his ancestral home, and migrate across the face of Eurasia. Some of his most important later technologies—math and science, which go beyond the causal reasoning of the hunter-gatherer and depend on writing—have produced technologies that have already carried him to the moon. His next migration will be to other planets. (In the long run this migration is necessary, for in ten thousand million years the sun will burn out!) The limited causal reasoning of the chimpanzee has made it impossible for it to develop technologies upon which migration depends, and thus has confined it to a small corner of Africa for over five million years.

Chapter 9
Analogies
Teaching Analogies to Chimpanzees

When we look out at the world, the sensory properties of shape, color, and size, and the like form a kind of background blur. They do not occupy center stage. Our world is object-centered, centered on grapefruit, chairs, and birds. We act on objects—on the grapefruit, the chair, the birds—not on the sensory properties of yellow, white, round. Language reflects our actions; we cut grapefruit, not yellow. And while birds fly, leaves rustle, and worms crawl, greens neither fly nor rustle, nor do squares crawl. Sensory properties do not act. Nevertheless sensory properties are our simplest perceptual category, the only category in which evolution has designed specific perceptual equipment for us.

Sensation is divided into major categories by its receptors, such as the eyes, ears, nose, mouth. Each sense is subdivided into smaller categories. For example vision is divided into shape, color, size; and these subcategories are further divided into, for example, height, width, red, and green. An innate circuit in the brain is dedicated to each of these "dimensions" and registers an automatic reading when stimulated. In other words, the assessment of brightness, sweetness, temperature, and so forth is automatic, involving neither judgment nor deliberation. By contrast no special circuits have evolved for the perception of objects, actions, or relations; that is, for the perception of elephants, or flying, or "to the left of."

The Complexity of Objects

Despite the actual priority of sensations, our world is object-centered. We perceive objects as solid, simple, indivisible—as a kind of primitive. But they are not. Only recently have neuroscientists disclosed the true complexity of objects.

When an individual perceives an object his brain is activated at many sites—for color at one site, at another site for shape, yet another for size, and another for location. These are the sites that process sensory properties, the *real* primitives into which objects can be divided.

Although in the laboratory we can show objects one at a time, in the real world we perceive *many* objects at the *same* time. Our brain is activated, therefore, not by the sensory properties of just one object but by the sensory properties of several objects simultaneously.

How does the brain separate the sensory properties of the several objects? And how does it unify diverse sensory properties into a single object? The brain has a massive "binding" problem to solve: It must cull out the activations arriving from one particular object, bind these into a separate unit, and perform the same operation for every other object it encounters.

The problem of binding is solved by the brain in two different ways, depending on whether the object is in motion or is stationary. When we observe an object in motion, velocity-detecting neurons are called into action and register the velocity of the object. When an object moves across the field of vision at essentially a constant speed, the neurons report the same value in one adjacent location after another. This succession of like values, if maintained for some minimum duration, leads automatically to the message of "Object"! If in the course of its movement the object were to undergo featural changes, the neurons would not register the change. They specialize in detecting velocity only.

For objects that are *not* in motion the brain solves the binding problem by means of an entirely different system. A natural scene usually is composed of many objects, and as we view such a scene the brain receives inputs from many features—color, shape, location—all of which come from different objects at largely the same time. The neuroscientist Wolf Singer and his associates discovered a mechanism that enables the brain to separate inputs that come from one object from those that come from another. When activated, a neuron has both a main pulse and a smaller, faster pulse called the *microrate*. Singer and his colleagues found that all the features belonging to the same object—color, shape, location, and the like—have the same microrate. They suggest that the brain uses the microrate as a signature, one that identifies the object to which the features belong. The brain identifies a single object by binding together all the sensory inputs that have the same microrate.

Faces, Speech Sounds, and Human Movement

While it is true that evolution did not provide special circuits for ordinary objects and events, there are a few special cases in which evolution *did* provide special equipment.

Special circuits could not have easily evolved for the perception of ordinary objects, for individual objects come and go and do not persevere for the hundreds of generations that would be required for special circuits to have evolved. There are, however, a handful of privileged objects and events for which special circuitry *has* evolved. One of these happens to be the human face, clearly a persevering part of human experience.

Interestingly, the first discovery of unique circuits for perceiving the face came from finding a disadvantage (rather than an advantage) that these circuits confer on the human viewer. Although our discrimination of the human face is extraordinary and acute, this holds only for the face seen in its normal orientation, that is, for the upright face. People have a great deal of difficulty in distinguishing one inverted face from another. People do have some difficulty recognizing inverted objects, such as tables, chairs, and cups, but the disparity between recognizing these ordinary objects when inverted and when upright is far less than for recognizing faces. The inverted face is peculiarly difficult for humans to recognize.

True, a distinctive area in the brain is activated by the face. But in people who are experts in discriminating varieties of cars, this same area is also activated. And the same distinctive area is activated by birds (in people who are experts in discriminating various species of birds).

Six-month-old infants do not have the adult reaction to an inverted face. Furthermore, the neural events activated when the infant processes a face are different from those of the adult. If there is an adaptation for processing the face, it is apparently heavily influenced by learning.

Speech sounds, like human faces, are another persevering facet of human experience, and also are well known to have special processing equipment discussed at length in Chapter 5. Curiously enough, reversed speech sounds have some of the character of inverted faces. Not only are they difficult to discriminate, they are not even processed in the same way as normal speech.

There also is evidence for special circuitry for discriminating human movement, which of course is another persevering feature of human experience. The Swedish perception theorist G. Johansson attached lights to major points of body articulation—the elbow, knee, shoulder, and so on—and photographed people as they moved about in the dark. When shown no more than these moving patterns of light observers could distinguish actions of different kinds, such as walking versus running, and identify both the age and sex of the people photographed.

On Relations

Relations were once given an elevated status. They were seen as special, not in a league with the simplicity of humdrum objects and sensory properties. Thirty years ago, the issue of whether such "lowly" creatures as rats could perceive relations was hotly contested. Many insisted that rats could learn only *absolute* values. They could learn to respond to a brightness value of 4, or a brightness value of 10, but would certainly fail to learn to respond to the *relation* between 4 and 10. The debate led the comparative psychologist D. H. Lawrence and his student J. De Rivera to design a clever study that provided evidence of the rat's ability to learn relations. The evidence was so definitive that it largely ended the debate.

Lawrence and De Rivera trained rats to jump to the left when the top half of a figure was brighter than the bottom half, and to jump to the right when the top half was darker than the bottom half. (See Figure 9.1.) They used brightness values ranging from 1 to 10 in a descending order, value 1 being the brightest, 10 the darkest. The rats not only learned to jump left with a figure brightness of 2/4 (top brighter), and to jump right with a figure of 8/6 (top darker), they also transferred their response to other relative values. They jumped to the left when shown a 3/5 figure (top brighter) and to the right for a 7/2 figure (top darker).

The rats did not, however, demonstrate transfer to all new figures. Here was the curious exception: Although trained to jump left to 3/5 (top brighter), they also jumped left to 5/3 (top darker). The error was not confined to 3/5. Trained to jump right to the figure 8/6 (top darker), they also

Figure 9.1   The Lawrence-De Rivera test.

jumped right to the figure 6/8 (top brighter)! In other words the rats responded incorrectly to precisely reversed figures, jumping in the same direction to the reversed values as they had to the original values they had learned. Why?

Their error can be explained by recognizing that the rat, like any other vertebrate, learns a problem at the absolute level and the relational level *at the same time*. When trained to jump right in the presence of 8/6, the rat learns

Absolute Level: jump right when shown the brightness values 8 or 6.

Relational Level: jump right when the top is darker than the bottom.

The absolute and relational levels do not send the rat the same message. After a rat has been trained to jump right to 8/6, and then is shown the figure 6/8, the absolute level bids the rat to jump right, the relational level to jump left. How shall the rat resolve this conflict? In the rat the absolute level takes priority over the relational level, so in this case the rat will almost certainly jump right. The rat obeys the relational level only when there is no interference from the absolute level.

Fortunately, the interference can easily be eliminated by using entirely new brightness values. If the rat has not been trained in say, 2 or 6, it will have no tendency to jump in either direction to these values. Therefore when it is given either 2/6 or 6/2 there will be no message from the absolute level to conflict with the message from the relational level and the rat will obey the relational message. Alternatively, we can train the rat so that it has an equal tendency to jump both right and left. In other words one must make sure, when training the rat to jump left to 6/8, that it is given an equal amount of training to jump right to 8/6. The rat's tendency to jump right or left in the presence of 6 or 8 will then be equal, and the rat will follow the relational rule. This, essentially, is what Lawrence and De Rivera have found to be the case.

Undoubtedly the capacity to form associations with the absolute level evolved first. Even a species as primitive as a worm can discriminate a rough from a smooth path, and learn to choose the path that leads to food. But evolution went beyond simply giving creatures the capacity to form associations with specific stimuli. Most species acquired, in addition, the ability to *compare* specific stimuli, and to form associations with the relation between them. When learning to form such associations, the individual continues as well to form associations with the specific stimuli that make up the relation. In other words most species learn to form associations on both the relational and the absolute levels at the same time.

Notice that there are no species that are able to form associations on the relational level only. While there are invertebrates that have not progressed beyond the absolute level, there are no species that skipped the absolute level—no species built the second floor without building the first! Although all vertebrates have evolved the capacity to respond to both the absolute and relational levels, individual species nonetheless differ greatly with respect to how they divide up their resources between these two levels.

So much of the learning in the pigeon is controlled by the absolute level that it is quite difficult to demonstrate relational learning in this bird. The pigeon is not, however, one of our typical birds. Jackdaws, bluejays, and the like—the entire corvid family—invest enough in the relational level so that they can readily solve match-to-sample problems, which require responding to the relation between the sample and a correct alternative. Although chimpanzees have a larger investment in the relational level than most species, tests are able to reveal their susceptibility to the absolute level, as is shown in the following example.

Young chimpanzees were trained in the laboratory on match-to-sample problems with toys, then taken outdoors where the test material was changed from toys to plants. In their first outdoor trial the four young animals were given a clover leaf as the sample, and another clover leaf and a toy car as the alternatives. All four animals chose the toy car, failing to match one clover leaf with the other. Their choice of the toy car was a carryover from learning on the absolute level: Take objects that have the properties of toys. On all subsequent trials, however, they rejected the toys. Their investment in the relational level asserted itself and the chimpanzees selected the plants.

While humans, like other vertebrates, learn on both the absolute and the relational levels, they are unique in being able to flexibly divide their resources between levels. When solving some problems humans can choose to concentrate on details (absolute level); when solving others, they can ignore details and shift to broad principles (relational level). Nonhuman species appear to lack this flexibility. They make the same division of resources for all problems, a division that is characteristic of the species rather than of the problem.

Same and Different

How do we decide that two objects are alike? When comparing sensory properties, this decision is made automatically by equipment specific to each sensory property, as we mentioned earlier. But we do not have comparable equipment for comparing objects.

We might decide whether objects are alike by placing one object on top of another. If we superimpose books, plates, shirts, etc., we can tell immediately whether two objects are alike. The chimpanzee Peony, in her judgments of same/different, did something of this kind; she placed like objects on top of one another and then topped them off with the plastic word SAME! But this seemingly simple approach has two severe drawbacks. First, although superimposition will work for tennis racquets and other flat objects, it will not work for tennis balls and other curved objects. And since most of the objects in the world have curved surfaces, this is an obvious drawback.

The second, and less obvious, drawback to this approach is more serious, for it affects not only curved objects, but flat objects as well. Placing one object on another would suit the humans, chimpanzees, and *one* species of monkey, the cebus, since all freely manipulate objects and would be at home with this approach. But it would not suit most species. Ninety-nine percent of species in the world probably could not place one object on another, for they do no more with objects than eat them, and, in a few cases, use them to build a nest or shelter.

Could it be that animals that lack hands, and therefore cannot easily superimpose objects, are incapable of deciding whether objects are alike? Not a chance! There is probably no vertebrate alive that could not judge when two dishes of food are alike, choosing indifferently when they are the same and selectively when one is larger than the other.

Because the ability to judge the likeness of objects is not confined to animals with hands, we are led to the conclusion that the procedure used to judge the likeness of objects must be mental, not physical or manual. Rather than comparing objects, the individual compares mental representations of objects.

This shift from hands to mind, from physical to mental superimposition, will solve the other problem, the original limitation of curved objects. Though curved objects are a problem for physical comparison, they are not for mental comparison. We regularly form two-dimensional representations of three-dimensional objects. Two-dimensional representations can be superimposed, allowing the individual to get around the problem of three-dimensional objects.

Relations between Relations

The success that rats have in discriminating "top brighter" from "top darker" shows us that singling out relations as something special is a mistake. Relations are not a special perceptual category; they belong to the category of sensory properties and objects, a category that every vertebrate species can perceive.

This is true only for ordinary relations, however; for relations that apply to objects or sensory properties. It is not true for relations between relations. In Figure 9.2 we give an example of both an ordinary and a "not so ordinary" relation in the context of a match-to-sample problem. In the top figure the sample and the alternatives consist of objects, and the individual, in matching one alternative to the sample, forms an ordinary relation, a relation between two objects. But in the bottom figure the sample and the alternatives consist of relations, and the individual is again required to match one alternative to the sample, forming in this case a "not so ordinary" relation, a relation between relations.

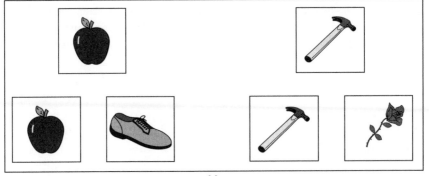

(a)

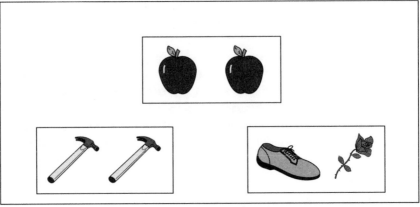

(b)

Figure 9.2   Match-to-sample tests (*a*) of objects and (*b*) of relations. (*From Holyoak and Thagard, 1995*)

In the familiar or ordinary problem of matching to sample, the individual compares physical likenesses and can see immediately that there is a match between the apples and a match between the hammers. But how shall he solve the unfamiliar problem? Nevertheless, an adult human will quickly solve the problem, matching apples with hammers and bell and bottle with shoe and flower. How does he do it?

Since the criterion of physical resemblance is of no use, perhaps she tries an approach that has worked well for her in the past: Form mental representations of the sample and the alternatives, and check to see what matches what. That approach too will fail, however, for while superimposing the images of objects can be highly informative, superimposing the images of relations is not. Unlike superimposed objects (or images of objects) that match when they are alike, and do not match when they are not alike, superimposed relations never match!

Place a mental image of the sample, two apples, onto a mental image of the incorrect alternative, a bottle and a bell. They will not match; nor of course should they. Now place the mental image of the sample, two apples, onto a mental image of the *correct* alternative, the two hammers. They too will not match! Clearly, in the matching of relations the individual must abandon mental superimposition, just as he abandoned physical superimposition, and find an entirely different approach.

The individual must abandon matching altogether and move to a different level of problem solving. He must direct the same question at each pair of objects, asking, "what is the relation between the members of each pair?" Are they "alike," or "not alike"? In other words, he labels each pair. In asking himself this question, he will find that the apples and the hammers match because they are both cases of "alike." Directing this same question to the bottle and bell, and the shoe and flowers, he will find that they too match *because both are cases of not alike!*

In other words, solving the unfamiliar problem requires giving labels to the pairs and then matching the labels rather than the pairs themselves. In adopting this approach, the individual must abandon a strategy that has served him well since infancy. From about eleven months of age, infants spontaneously place objects together on the basis of their similarity and humans, no matter what their age, never entirely abandon the strategy. The objects we group into categories are chosen, in large measure, on the basis of their similarity. And similarity plays a large role in aesthetic judgment, in matching furniture with curtains, rugs with drapes, shoes and purses with dresses, and so forth. Given the human predilection for similarity, it is striking that people can abandon this strategy and compute equivalence on an entirely different basis. Nevertheless they can abandon similarity and compute equivalence using a different strategy.

No other species makes this transition from physical to conceptual equivalence in the normal course of development. If animals observe equivalence naturally at all, it is the equivalence of physical similarity, the equivalence that appears in the primitive devices we will discuss in the next chapter: stimulus generalization, categorical perception, etc. Children and chimpanzees can readily match alike objects (A and A, B and B). Children do so spontaneously at the age of about eleven months; chimpanzees do so only when given special training. Children can match relations (AA and BB, EF and CD) at about four years of age. Chimpanzees, as we shall see, can also learn to match relations, but again, only when given special training.

Habituation/Dishabituation

There is a simpler test than match-to-sample that can be used to establish whether an individual can match relations. Habituation/dishabituation tests help us to determine whether the individual is able to recognize the sameness/difference of relations. Such tests makes weak demands, requiring nothing more than that the individual look at stimuli. It is therefore a sensitive test, and an ideal one to use with young creatures. Being sensitive, the test often registers a positive outcome when a more demanding test such as a match-to-sample registers a negative one.

Although we knew that chimpanzees could not match relations, we thought that the more sensitive test of habituation/dishabituation might provide a measure of the ability of four eighteen-month-old chimpanzees to at least recognize the sameness/difference of relations. Two kinds of "toys," consisting of pairs of objects, were mounted on a board. The pairs of objects were alike in two of the toys, not alike in two of the others. As may be seen in Figure 9.3, the like pairs consisted of a pair of bolts fixed to a board (AA) and a pair of erasers fixed to a board (BB). The unlike pairs consisted of a doll and a spoon fixed to a board (CD) and a cup and a marble fixed to a board (EF).

We allowed each animal to play with AA for fifteen minutes, then removed AA and gave it either BB or CD. Similarly, we allowed each animal to play with EF for fifteen minutes, then removed EF and gave it either BB or CD. How long the animal chose to play with the new toy, BB or CD, depended on which toy it had just played with. If an animal had just played with AA, it then spent much more time playing with CD than with BB; whereas if the animal had just played with EF, it then spent more time with BB than with CD.

Figure 9.3 Like and unlike pairs of objects used in habituation/dishabituation test for sameness/difference.

In other words, after playing with the toy whose parts were alike, the animal preferred a toy whose parts were not alike. And vice versa. These results tell us that although the animal cannot *match* relations, it can nonetheless *recognize* when relations are and are not the same. When playing with AA or EF, let us assume, the animal habituates not only on the physical features of the pairs of objects—their color, shape, size, and so on—but also on their alikeness or unlikeness. This assumption will help us to understand the results. For if, when playing with AA, the animal habituates on likeness per se, it will then play less with BB, another case of likeness. And it will do the same with the unlike pairs. After playing with EF and habituating on unlikeness, it will then play less with CD, another case of unlikeness.

This assumption will also help us to explain why, although the animal provides positive results on the habituation/dishabituation test, it cannot match relations. In order to match like and unlike relations, the animal must *judge* AA and BB to be the same, and *judge* EF and CD to be the same. The habituation/dishabituation test does *not* require any judgment. An animal that is habituated on the likeness of AA will automatically respond less to BB, just as an animal habituated on the unlikeness of EF will automatically respond less to CD. In the habituation/dishabituation test, the differences in responding are completely automatic.

If the successful matching of relations depends on giving them names and then matching the names, we should be able to extend a helping hand to the chimpanzee. Why wait for the animal to develop its own names? Although we suspect that animals probably can do this, there is no known method for inducing them to do so! Why not actually teach them names for the relations and try the test again?

We answered this question ourselves by teaching three chimpanzees plastic words for the relations of *same* and *different*. Here is a brief account of how the words *same* and *different* were taught to the chimpanzee Peony, a mediocre language student.

Peony was shown two objects on a horizontal line and taught to place plastic words between them, the word SAME when the objects were alike, the word DIFFERENT when they were not alike.

Apple_____Apple
Banana_____Orange

are examples of frequently used sequences, the former requiring SAME, the latter, DIFFERENT.

Once the animal had inserted the correct word in the space it was given a transfer test—new pairs of objects, along with the words SAME and DIFFERENT. Most of the chimpanzees were quick to learn the problem. But not Peony. She was slow, skittish, and easily derailed. Consequently we used a rigidly consistent format in training her.

Although Peony eventually performed correctly on the training material, when she was given simple transfer tests she barely passed them and showed no improvement from one test to the next. What conclusion could we draw from Peony's mediocre performance? What had she learned? It is difficult to characterize "weak" learning, and there was no point, we felt, in simply running through another round of training. Discouraged, we gave Peony "shock therapy"—a do-or-die test.

We placed three objects (two of them alike) along with the plastic words SAME and DIFFERENT in a paper bag, shook the bag well, and then threw its contents out before her. With this one stroke we were wiping out all the configural properties we had so dutifully adhered to in her training. "Sink or swim, Peony!" was our message in effect, never supposing we would see her reach the shore. (See Figure 9.4.)

But there she was! Her spontaneous response to this challenge took several forms in repeated trials, all of them reassuring as to the nontrivial character of chimpanzee intelligence:

1. She placed the two spoons together, superimposing one on the other. She did nothing with SAME, as though it were redundant, but put the word DIFFERENT on top of the piece of clay.

2. She placed the piece of clay next to the word DIFFERENT, superimposed the two spoons again, and this time placed the word SAME on top of them.

3. She superimposed the clay, placing one piece on top of the other, and then set the word SAME on top of them (and did nothing with DIFFERENT and the spoon).

4. She wrote out in a linear fashion: "clay SAME clay DIFFERENT spoon."

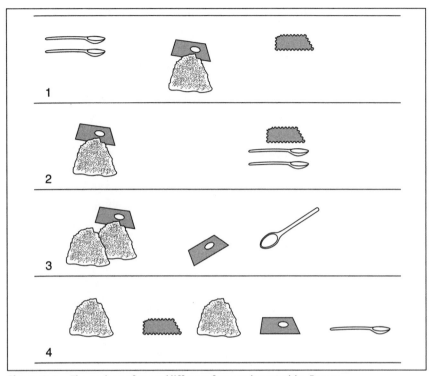

Figure 9.4   The variety of same/different formats invented by Peony.

In subsequent lessons most of these formats disappeared, including our favorite, the linear format. She retained only one format from the original set, and used it consistently. She superimposed the two like objects and placed the word SAME on top of them; then she placed the word DIFFERENT either on, or alongside of, the odd object.

Peony never superimposed the two unlike objects, then placing the word DIFFERENT on them. (Had she done this, of course, she would have had no way of dealing with the remaining object and the word SAME.) Peony's spontaneous constructions strongly suggest that for her, sameness was the primary relation, difference a secondary one.

Not only did Peony and two other animals learn the words for same/different but the words had exactly the desired effect. All three animals—Sarah, Elizabeth, and Peony—could now do what they could not do before they were taught SAME/DIFFERENT; they could match relations, not only the old cases AA, BB, and so on, of course, but novel examples such as

XX, YY, and so on. But SAME/DIFFERENT had broader effects than we had realized at first.

When an individual matches relations—AA to BB, or EF to CD—she is already implicitly doing a simple kind of analogy. She is saying that the relation between A and A is the same as that between B and B; that A is to A as B is to B. Let us make this explicit by writing the relation as an analogy: A:A same B:B; E:F same C:D.

Is this analysis sound? Is the matching of relations really the equivalent of human analogies? Will such a formal argument hold up when tested? It did indeed. That chimpanzees can do analogies was first shown by the animal learning psychologist Doug Gillan and his associates Woodruff and Premack. They gave Sarah incomplete analogies of the kind shown below:

> *big circle: small circle*
> SAME
> *big square: ?*

along with two or three alternatives, and required to choose the one that would complete the analogy. Sarah was successful right from the first test, doing as well on the opening trials as on the later ones, performing at her usual 85 percent correct level. Teaching Sarah SAME/DIFFERENT enabled her to complete analogies from the outset!

In another approach we gave Sarah completed analogies, only some of which were correct, and required her to judge between the correct and incorrect versions by answering SAME or DIFFERENT. The two arguments in the analogy were joined by an interrogative particle—A:A ? B:C—and Sarah was required to remove the interrogative particle and replace it with the plastic words SAME or DIFFERENT. She was as successful in this judgment as she had been when completing the incomplete analogy.

In yet another approach, the comparative psychologist David Oden required Sarah to construct analogies "from scratch." He gave Sarah the analogy board along with either four or five elements, a different set for each trial, and accepted whatever arrangement she made. Sarah, unlike uneducated chimpanzees who merely play with the elements, immediately placed the elements on the analogy board and constructed analogies. She was correct about 60 percent of the time—a mediocre performance but still significantly greater than chance, which is only about 30 percent correct in the four-element case and still lower for the five-element case.

In examining the 240 videotapes of Sarah's performances, Oden made a singular discovery. He found that Sarah engages in self-correction or "editing," a kind of behavior rare in nonhumans. Sarah corrected when the three elements she had placed on the analogy board contained an error, one blocking the possibility of completing the analogy. In other words, the analogy could not be made complete without first correcting the error.

For example, on one occasion she placed A:B on one side of the analogy, then placed B′ across from A. This blocks the possibility of an analogy; no fourth element could be added that would produce an analogy. On this occasion Sarah moved B′, placing it across from B, and then went on to complete the analogy.

Although Sarah left most of her incorrect constructions alone, she edited fifteen of them, fourteen of them correctly. It was a surprise to see metacognition in Sarah, for correcting one's own previous action is rare in both young children and animals. On the other hand metacognition is commonplace in human affairs, and much of human achievement depends heavily upon it. Authors confess to having revised thirteen drafts before releasing a work, and painters and composers are almost as prone to corrections and changes. We are often told that the symphony we are about to hear is the fourth and final version, other versions having been squirreled away in drawers or suitcases. But self-editing is not confined to art and science, even though these fields are notorious for its use. Self-editing appears in daily life: The family chef may revise her recipe repeatedly, before giving it her seal of approval.

Given the extent to which self-correction infiltrates human affairs, its absence in animals may seem a great mystery. But is it really so mysterious? Correcting one's previous work depends on *having* previous work, that is, on having technologies that produce lasting works, and animals have no technologies of this kind. Even spoken stories were not edited because stories did not change significantly until people had written language. While we can be confident that hunter-gatherers "edited" their tools, they did not edit their stories.

Functional Analogies

All the analogies we have looked at thus far have been perceptual, and depend on corresponding physical properties: The large ball is to a small ball as a large pencil is to a small pencil, and so on. But analogies also concern functional relations, as seen in Figure 9.5; for example:

> can opener is to can: as key is to door
>
> paint brush is to painted can: as pencil is to written paper

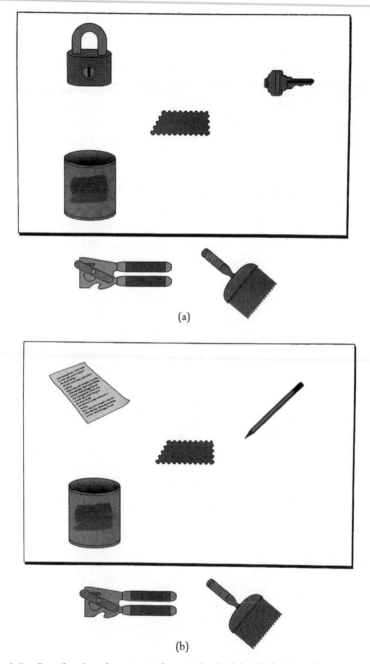

Figure 9.5 Functional analogy tests given to Sarah: (*a*) A lock is to a key as a can is to a can opener; (*b*) marked paper is to a pencil as a painted can is to a brush.

In order to solve functional analogies, the individual must recognize the equivalence of different forms of an action. But how does he do this? Turning a key and operating a can opener do not have the same appearance. Furthermore the objects involved in the two actions—a padlock and a key; a can opener and a can—are not physically alike. Thus the equivalence of the two acts cannot lie in the acts themselves.

The equivalence lies in the goal one attributes to the acts. An individual opens a lock so that he can enter a previously closed space. An individual opens a can so that he can gain access to its contents. The goal in opening is to move an object from one location to another, from inside to outside; the object moved may be inanimate (the contents of a can) or animate (the individual himself).

While functional analogies traditionally are considered more demanding than perceptual analogies, Sarah made no more errors on functional analogies than on the perceptual. The analogies we cited above are two of those she solved correctly.

Sarah was highly familiar with keys and locks (not to mention bottles, doors, cabinets) and saw can openers in operation virtually every day while observing the preparation of her food. An emergency phone call we received at about two in the morning testified to her expertise in opening: Sarah had escaped from her cage, having opened the lock with a key she had seized from the night watchman (he had ventured too close to her cage)!

That Sarah is capable of attributing goal was shown by her success on the theory-of-mind tests discussed in Chapter 7. The attribution of goal underlies the concept of an intentional object and is a basic part of the psychological module, a module that the chimpanzee probably shares with the human to some degree.

We understand action, the action of intentional creatures—for example, eating, drinking, fighting, copulating—by the goals we attribute to actors, not by the physical properties of the action. Action is a unique perceptual category. Other perceptual categories—those of objects, sensory properties, relations—have no hidden or inferential level. They are understood strictly on the basis of their observed physical properties. Even the slightest difference among objects captures our attention, leading us to give the objects distinctive names. For example, despite their similarity we meticulously separate mandarins, tangerines, and oranges.

Now consider how willingly we ignore physical differences when naming actions. Consider for example the diversity of the motions we are content to call "eating": birds pecking seeds, carnivores tearing at chunks of meat, infants suckling, people placing food into their mouths with hands,

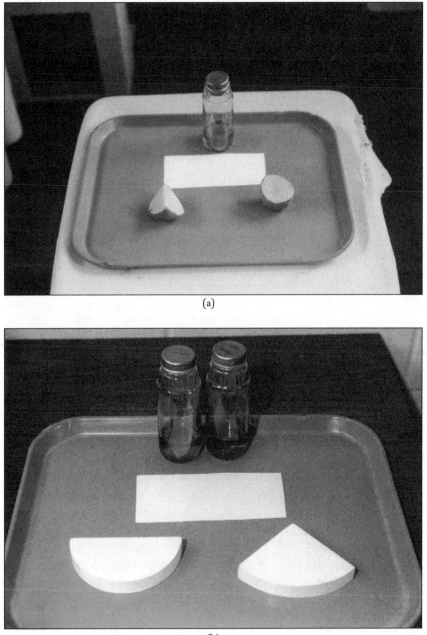

(a)

(b)

Figure 9.6   A match-to-sample test for conceptual proportions. In (a) the sample is matched to the correct alternative, but in (b) and (c) the items making up the sample must be combined in order to match the correct alternative.

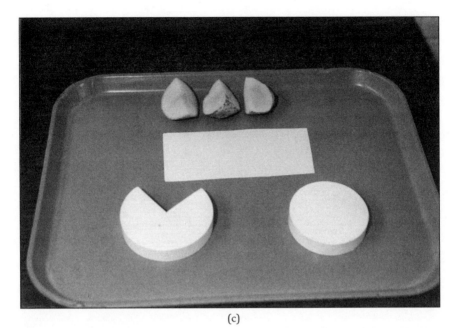

(c)

Figure 9.6   (*Continued*)

forks, or chopsticks. What counts in this case is the goal, and since all the creatures are realizing the same goal, that of introducing food into their mouths, we give all of the actions the same name.

Conceptual Proportions

Even the untrained chimpanzee can readily match proportions; can match half an apple with half an apple; a quarter of an apple with a quarter of an apple; half glass of water with a half glass of water, and so on. But the animal taught SAME/DIFFERENT produces yet another surprise: It can match half an apple to a half glass of water! (See Figure 9.6.)

The untrained animal is restricted to the matching of physically similar proportions. The "educated" animal can match the conceptually similar proportions of all conceivable objects—of apples to glasses of water, of glasses of water to wooden disks, and so on.

It can also "add" proportions. As seen in Figure 9.6c, when given samples consisting of two or more proportions—for example, one quarter of an apple and one half of an apple—the animal combines the separate propor-

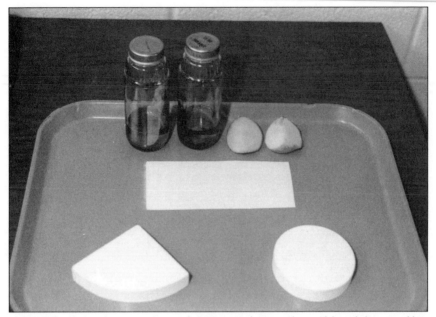

Figure 9.7   A match-to-sample test for conceptual proportions. Although items making up the sample differ, they must be combined in order to match the correct alternative.

tions and selects an alternative equal to their sum; in the above case, three-quarters of an apple. And in the most impressive version of this problem, the animal combines proportions of *different* objects—for example, one-quarter of an apple and one-quarter of a glass of water—and then selects their sum, in this case, one-half. It can even select one-half of a large wooden disk, an object that has nothing to do with either apples or glasses of water. The large wooden disk was designed in the science instrument shop according to formula, so that all of its proportions were of exactly the same size—one-quarter of a disk was of the same size as a half-disk, and so on. This ruled out the possibility that the animal was selecting the alternative that matched the *size* of the sample. (See Figure 9.7.)

If chimpanzees were human, we would be sure they were using numbers to solve these problems. We would be certain that they represented one-quarter of a glass of water, of an apple, of a disk, and so forth by the numbers 1, 4, and so on, and that therefore they would have no difficulty in solving the problems. However, chimpanzees do not have numbers, and even if they did, the use of numbers would turn the proportions into fractions—¼, ½, and so on—and fractions are a problem even for children.

In fact, the system that enables the animal to solve the proportions problem is one we have already encountered: the analogy, a capacity which SAME/DIFFERENT confers on the animal. The analogy provides a perfect format for comparing proportions of physically unlike objects. For example, to match one-quarter of an apple with one-quarter of a glass of water, both can be pictured as a proportion of the whole object, and the whole represented as an analogy:

> *one quarter apple: whole apple*
> SAME
> *one quarter glass water: whole glass water*

Repeated Trials

In discussing analogies we invented a new chronology to simplify our account. The true chronology was more complex, less dependent on thought than on luck or serendipity, the latter often playing a sizable role in science.

In the course of comparing animals that had and had not been taught language, we found, more or less accidentally, that some chimpanzees can match relations. In fact the language-trained animals could manage a number of problems, an entire family of tests, including causality, analogies, and the like, that the other animals could not. Naturally, we thought the effect depended on language.

But language is many things—words, sentences, the ability to ask questions, describe conditions, and so on—and to find out which of these components is critical required a series of tests. The upshot was a surprise: Only SAME/DIFFERENT counted. Had we taught the entire language but left out SAME/DIFFERENT, there would have been no effect.

In the course of conducting these tests it was essential to run a control group: animals that were not taught language at all but simply were trained in the matching problem. The animals gave us a real surprise! Because these animals were older, they tolerated what the younger animals had refused: repeated trials. In the course of being given up to 300 trials of the same problem, these older animals gradually learned to match like relations, AA to BB, and after another 100 trials, to match unlike relations, EF to CD. Moreover they learned these problems without feedback; that is, they were not "told" when their choice was correct or incorrect. All their choices were approved.

The fact that they learned the problem as they did, gradually and without feedback, is compatible with the idea that these animals learned to develop their own "names," different mental reactions to the alike and unlike relations. This kind of learning often is called "perceptual" learning. What may also be compatible with the idea of perceptually learned names is that while these animals were successful in matching relations, they remained unable to solve analogies.

Evidently their "homemade" words did not quite have the power of those "store-bought" words, the plastic words SAME/DIFFERENT. For when the animal is taught SAME/DIFFERENT it can not only match relations but solve the entire family of tests—analogies, causality, and the like—and do so in one fell swoop. The names that the chimpanzees learned in the context of repeated trials lack generality, and evidently apply only to the specific problem in which they were learned.

Can Monkeys Use Labels?

What is unique about the chimpanzee's success with analogies is its ability to use labels: either implicit labels it has itself produced, or the plastic words SAME/DIFFERENT, explicit labels it has been taught. In first applying a label to the relations between pairs of objects, then comparing the relations between the pairs—applying the same operation at two different levels, a simple act of recursion—the chimpanzee invades human territory. It performs an analogy.

Is there evidence that any other species, rats or monkeys perhaps, makes use of labels?

Monkeys have been trained to push a left button when two objects are alike (AA), and to push a right button when two objects are not alike (CD); that is, they have been trained to respond to the relation between objects. This is a problem that does not require labels. The monkey needs only to superimpose the objects (or images of the objects) in both pairs, and push the left button when the two images match (or superimpose) and the right button when they do not.

There is a more complex problem a monkey might solve as well, one that involves not a single relation but pairs of relations: AA:BB versus AA:CD. The requirements would be those for the simpler problem: When the paired relations are the same, push the left button; when they are not the same, push the right button.

While this problem seems to be an exact match of the analogies given the chimpanzee, in fact it is not the same but a far simpler problem. The relations the chimpanzees solved consisted of objects—for example, two apples, two spoons, a scissor and a doll—whereas those given the monkey consisted of patterns composed of dots and lines—mere sensory properties.

Dots vary in their size, number, spacing, and so on. Lines vary with respect to such things as thickness, number, and curvature. As sensory properties, their identity will be registered automatically by innate circuits in the brain. There is no need to label relations that are composed of patterns. In judging the relations between objects, however, there are no innate circuits that automatically register the sameness/difference of pairs of objects. So, instead, one must label the relation.

Although monkeys may learn to respond correctly when the two relations AA:BB are alike, will they be able to learn to respond correctly when the relations are not alike CD:EF? Both AA:BB and CD:EF are cases of "same," but the sameness of unlike relations is far more difficult to recognize than is the sameness of like relations.

But how about the rat: Can it respond to "analogies" that consist of sensory patterns? Probably it can, because, as we just said, the difficulty of performing analogies does not arise until there is a need to use labels.

Limitations on Chimpanzee Analogies

There is no evidence that chimpanzees spontaneously form analogies. Indeed, there is no evidence that they carry out a precursor of the analogy: Divide the world either mentally or physically into elements. Only when the division has been made for a chimpanzee by the human and the "pieces"—the big and little circles, the acts of opening doors and cans, etc.— given to it, does the chimpanzee arrange them in an analogical structure.

While the transition from matching objects to matching relations is notable enough, it leads nowhere in the hands of the chimpanzee. The demonstration is confined strictly to the laboratory. The test outcome reveals, however, a fact that could easily have been missed: Conceptual equivalence does not belong to humans alone—we are not the first to escape from the clutches of physical similarity.

In the human, however, the transition from matching objects to matching relations is not a mere demonstration but has rich practical consequences. It prepares the child for a new way of processing information, and for solving problems of a powerful kind. Once the child can match one relation to another he can relate problems he has already solved to those he has yet to solve. Analogical reasoning of this kind, though a bit frail, can be found in children as young as two; cases of greater solidity appear in four-

and five-year-olds, with truly impressive pieces of analogical reasoning appearing in eight- to twelve-year-olds.

The history of science is replete with theories and laws that have arisen out of analogical thinking. These include no less than evolutionary theory itself, the analogy which Darwin saw between Malthus's account of human population in the face of limited resources and the struggle for survival engaged in by both plants and animals. One could also cite the likeness between electricity and magnetism which gave rise to Maxwell's theory of electromagnetism, and that between mind and computer which facilitated Alan Turing's work.

Note

1. While some birds, such as corvids, can be taught to match like objects, this cannot be said of pigeons. Wasserman, however, has found pigeons able to match stimulus patterns containing repeated elements. Indeed, once trained to match such patterns, pigeons then can transfer to new patterns of repeated elements.

Is this comparable to responding to the equivalence of objects, or is there a fundamental difference between recognizing the identity of patterns and that of objects? A simple test could answer this question. Having taught the pigeon to recognize the identity of patterns, one would have to ask: Does recognizing the identity of patterns have an educative effect? Has it prepared the pigeon to recognize the identity of objects? This important question has not yet been addressed.

Chapter 10
Equivalence and Its
Instruments of Discovery

Analogies and their offshoots—metaphors and similes—intrigue us with the unsuspected connections they reveal. Shakespeare was the unrivaled master of their use; his comparison of the shining beam of a candle and the performance of a good deed is only one of the innumerable examples of equivalences that awaken our delight, increasing our appetite for other cases in which disparate ideas are tied together.

Metaphors and similes, brought to a pinnacle by Shakespeare, are confined to human and language, but they are foreshadowed by certain primitive equivalence devices which are *not* confined to humans. Humans share such devices as intermodal equivalence, categorical perception, somasthesia, and even stimulus generalization with many other species. These devices too, in their simpler way, connect one event with another, and in so doing establish an equivalence of sorts.

Intermodal equivalence allows an individual to discover the equivalence between how an object feels and how it looks, an equivalence that even infant monkeys can recognize. In a lighted area, they will search for objects—such as spheres, and cubes—that were previously placed in their mouths in the dark.

Somasthesia links sensations of different kinds—for example, colors and sounds, so that some people see a color when they hear a particular musical tone. Musicians and painters are likely to experience associations of this kind. The more common form of somasthesia which everyone experiences equates sensations on the basis of their intensity: loud sounds with bright lights, strong tastes, and so forth.

Intermodal equivalence and somasthesia reflect the structure of the nervous system, but other primitive equivalence devices reflect the structure of the world. Objects and events in the world repeat themselves, but their repetition is seldom perfect. Stimulus generalization and categorical perception overlook the imperfection and compensate for it. In stimulus generalization, for example, a pigeon trained to peck a red key will peck (though less vigorously) a pink key, if the red key is not available. The bird's pecking will then decline in inverse proportion to the similarity between the two colors, according to a law that the perception theorist Roger Sheppard has shown to hold for all species.

Categorical perception goes a step beyond stimulus generalization. In this case an individual will completely ignore the minor variations, will treat all the variants as "the same." For instance humans treat all variants of a phoneme—the basic building block of language—as the same, just as crickets treat all variants of their mating calls.

The Pursuit of Equivalence

Humans not only treat diverse events as alike; from an early age they actively pursue experiences of equivalence. Ten-month-old infants touch physically alike objects consecutively; for example, touch one red block after another, then one green block after another. The infant goes beyond this temporal sorting of like objects one short month later, when he begins to sort like objects in space, placing the red blocks in one location, the greens in another. While chimpanzees engage in temporal sorting—they touch like objects consecutively—they do not advance to spatial sorting, placing like objects in separate locations.[1]

Although animals do not *spontaneously* place like objects together, they can be trained by a technique known as *discrimination learning* to perform what "looks like" sorting; for example, to place red objects in one container, green objects in another. But we can easily show that what the animal has been trained to do is not equivalent to the sorting which children do naturally. If we remove the red and green objects, replacing them with pink and aqua objects, the animal will now conform to the "dictates" of stimulus generalization and place pink objects in the red-object container, the aqua objects in the green-object container. This is something the child will not do. A child who has been sorting red and green objects will, if given pink and aqua objects, reject these objects and all others that are merely similar to red and green. Sorting is a categorical (not an analogical) operation, and unlike the animal's discrimination learning, sorting does not conform to stimulus generalization.

The Individuation of Objects

Making the decision that the object we are looking at now is the same as the one we saw earlier represents a fundamental form of equivalence judgment. Although generally this is an easy decision for an adult, is it equally simple for the child?

Children are, if anything, highly conservative. They assume—unless forced to abandon the view—that the object they are looking at now is the same as the one they saw earlier. What would force a child to surrender this conservative position? The child will renounce the position only if, in order to maintain it, she must violate the spatiotemporal intuitions arising from her physical module.

If for example a child walks upstairs to his bedroom and sees, on his bed, a toy car exactly like the one he just left downstairs, he may puzzle about where the "new" car came from; but he will not "accept" this as the same car he just left downstairs because he is constrained by his physical module. The same object cannot be in two places at once. On the other hand if one day his toy car turns up dabbed with a spot of green paint, a dented hood, rust on its roof, the child will accommodate these changes to his conservative view. Featural changes do not have the gravity of spatiotemporal criteria; and the child will accept the car, despite its unexplained changes, as being his old car.

Indeed the developmental psychologists F. Xu and Carey make a further claim: that ten-month-old infants do not use featural information at all when deciding when an object is new. They claim that ten-month-olds differ in this regard from twelve-month-old infants; the older infants use both features and spatiotemporal information in deciding when an object is new, whereas the ten-month-old uses *only* spatiotemporal information. The researchers base their claim on the following study.

Young infants, after having been shown two toy dogs in a first scene, are, in a following scene, shown one dog. The ten-month-old looks longer at the final scene, because it violates his spatiotemporal intuitions. But if the two dogs in the first scene "turn into" two toy frogs in the final scene, the ten-month-old does not look at it longer, and is not surprised. The twelve-month-old, however, is surprised. This study suffers from a serious drawback, unfortunately: It places *number* into competition with *features*.

Number is known to be a perceptually dominant criterion, and in a ten-month-old it may be strong enough to overshadow features. If so, when the features of objects change while their number does not, as witnessed in the above study, number may override features and the infant will show no dishabituation for features. Really, though, this drawback of having placed numbers and features into competition is a minor weakness of the test. The serious issue concerns the interpretation given these results by the experimenters.

What is it that develops in the human, Xu and Carey ask, which permits the twelve-month-old to take the features of objects into account? Names, they answer. Infants now learn the names of objects. And when they do they are able to use features in individuating objects. But how would an infant (who does not use features when individuating objects) learn the names of objects? There is only one possibility: through the use of spatiotemporal factors. In other words a ten-month-old, having learned that the object in the "left-hand corner of the room" is called *chair*, will be surprised when the infant's mother, having moved the object to the center of the room, still calls it *chair*.

The Xu-Carey hypothesis appears to have things turned around: A child *cannot* learn the names of objects until it first uses features in individuating them. Names of objects, we suggest, are associated not with perceptions but with representations. If this is true, then the finding that some young infants have names for objects can have only one meaning: They have formed representations for these objects, and therefore can name them.

Pity the animals in the wild, if the Xu-Carey hypothesis is correct! Not having names for objects, they are unable, of course, to use features in individuating them. Hence they can never know where specific objects are. Such lives would be strange indeed! Animals could recall that something was behind the bushes, but not what that "something" looked like. Fortunately, we need not seriously pity animals in the wild, for both of the predictions have been disconfirmed; one by an "ancient" animal study, the other recently.

Monkeys that watched the animal psychologist Edward Tinklepaugh place a bit of a banana under a container turned irate when, upon lifting the container, they found lettuce instead—a clear indication that monkeys *do* take features into account when individuating objects! This fact was further confirmed in a recent field study which showed (what no one could reasonably have doubted) that monkeys definitely can locate different objects and therefore must use features in individuating them.

Concepts as Mental Representations

Concepts are a major source of equivalence. They lead us to form categories, which is to say, to give a common name to diverse objects and treat these different objects as being the "same." Concepts are mental representations. They depict the conditions that an object must fulfill in order to belong to a category. Concepts, therefore, are in the brain/mind.

Categories, by contrast, consist of the objects themselves: the cabbages, peas, carrots, and so on that are on display in the same (vegetable) section of the supermarket! Concepts are inside, found in the head; categories are outside, found in the world.

Humans, animals in lesser degree, have hundreds, perhaps thousands, of concepts. But where do concepts come from, and how do we acquire them? How might a child, for example, acquire the concept of "animal"? Do infants enter the world with an image of "animal"? Indeed, perhaps infants even enter the world with images of *all* the objects they expect to see—and check them off as they encounter them. (This possibility might explain why children, as they move about their world can be heard to mumble, "Well, only one hundred and forty-three to go . . ."!)

Alternatively, perhaps the child enters the world with a mind that is quite blank and, out of chance encounters with objects that are similar, starts to form concepts. The child's experience with animals may begin, for instance, with the friendly dog that his father holds for him to pet; be followed by an encounter with the neighbor's pet rabbit; and a week later, a trespassing cat. Observing the similarity among the three furry objects the child starts to form the category "animal." A handy little process, in which all goes well until the child encounters a fish, some frogs, a lizard, and so forth (his first hairless animals).

Although the above examples are caricatures of entirely opposing views of concepts, the innate versus the learned, they both are guilty of the same error: They treat concepts as the identification of objects. Concepts do not depend on objects or on their identification. Concepts depend on processes, processes that explain the actions of objects. The following treatment of *animal* provides a clear example.

Animals are self-propelled and goal-directed. They are intentional. They move head-first. Children recognize these basic acts in which all creatures engage. They recognize eating; probably fighting, even perhaps copulation. They recognize these processes in their own species and perhaps in all species. This capacity is true of creatures other than the human. When a laboratory monkey was fed by its trainer, the raven housed across from it made a din, clacking its enormous beak across the bars of its cage. And on alternate days, when the raven was given the first feeding, the monkey screamed, thrusting an angry arm out of the cage in the direction of the raven. A nice example of the recognition of *eating*.

Children understand intentionality; they understand head-first movement, eating, and even "jealous rage," because these are largely modular "ideas" that come from the psychological and biological modules. The origin of jealousy and of emotion in general, however, is unclear. Is emotion modular? If it is, would it not be found in the psychological module? Most but not all emotions arise from social interactions. Children can recognize facial expressions that identify emotions, factors suggesting that emotion may have evolved so as to facilitate social communication.

But emotion is not confined to social species. The over 50 percent of species in the world that are nonsocial also have emotion. Emotion plays two roles, neither of which is involved in social communication. In addition to increasing the vigor of action, emotion enhances memory. Events that are associated with emotion are far better remembered than events not so associated.

Some have argued that every species has an inner essence, one resistant to surface change, and that children recognize this essence. Evidence for this view is said to be provided by the fact that if a skunk is painted blue, children say it is still a skunk. But if young children "understand" inheritance, as tests indicate they do, they will endorse far more than the idea that a skunk remains a skunk even when painted blue! Children who understand inheritance will recognize that the offspring of a skunk (that has been painted blue) will have the usual white stripe of any other skunk. Children seem able to contrast nature with nurture as illustrated by their ability to contrast inheritance with contagion (see Chapter 1). They understand that inheritance concerns the transmission of permanent characteristics, contagion the transmission of conditions that are temporary.

Animals are indeed diverse, though perhaps no more so than any other natural category; however, the focus on the physical diversity of animals (and the supposed need for concepts like "inner essence") comes not from the world but from the laboratory practice of studying concepts using toy animals and pictures. Stuffed animals have very little in common. They do not eat, reproduce, or exhibit emotion, nor are they goal-directed. Stuffed animals—because they come in all possible shapes, sizes, and colors—emphasize diversity. By contrast, animals that move or act call attention to processes that explain the commonality of animals through their actions.

What is the advantage of forming categories, and what do we gain by having them? One often cited advantage is offered through this commonplace answer: The formation of categories enables us to prepare for the future, helping us to anticipate that "new" members will have the same properties as those of familiar members. In other words we can expect unfamiliar "fruit" such as guava or cherimoya to have an edible pulp, sweet taste, and probably annoying seeds. Predictions of this kind, on the average, *do* pan out, otherwise we certainly would have rid ourselves of the need for categories. Occasionally, however, they go awry. One day we encountered the frightened face of a visitor who pointed with great alarm to what she called the largest insect she had ever seen. An insect with a truly frightening stinger! This turned out to be a hummingbird, a not-very-birdlike bird, unknown in her part of eastern Europe. Of course she would not have made this error if she had not been the "victim" of categories.

For classical concepts such as that of the triangle it is possible to provide a rule or definition that encompasses all varieties. A "three-sided figure" holds equally for all triangles: isosceles, skaline, obtuse, equilateral, and so on. And when definitions of such natural concepts as "animal" favor function over features, they too can approximate the closure of a classical concept, providing definitions that encompass nearly all varieties. It is only when the definition ignores process in favor of features that the hope for a classiclike rule is lost.

Of course not all concepts are like that of "animal," a concept that concerns objects that move and that can be unified through the common processes that explain the movement. Many concepts concern objects that do *not* move, such as vegetables and trees. What links the diverse members of these categories? Can we claim that they have an inner essence, an essence which can be found once we have peeled away the surface diversity? And what could that inner essence be, other than the genetic structure of the group?

Such a structure, since it is known to only a handful of scientists, could not possibly be the basis on which people form the category! Ludwig Wittgenstein, the chief philosophical troublemaker of the last century, turned the above argument around by dismissing inner essence and placing all his emphasis on "surface" detail.

Wittgenstein introduced the idea of family resemblance. This can be illustrated by the Smith brothers, a group of largely bearded men who, though easily individuated, bear a striking resemblance to one another, a resemblance based on a crisscrossing of similarities, with different members of the group sharing different similarities. In other words, what members of a category have in common is not an inner essence, or a set of necessary and sufficient conditions that all members share, but a simple crisscrossing of similarities.

Wittgenstein's favorite illustration of family resemblance was the concept of *game*. He urged his readers not to look up "game" in the dictionary but to look instead at actual games and discover for themselves what games have in common. This is a strange example for Wittgenstein to have chosen, however, for if we take his advice and actually look at various games we find ourselves hard-pressed to find the crisscrossing similarities that are supposed to make games analogous to the Smith brothers. Where are the crisscrossing similarities to be found between polo, checkers, horseshoes, mahjong?

Games are not a family resemblance concept, we suggest, but a classic one, defined by three ideas: win, lose, and non-life-threatening. When you can experience the possibility of winning or losing without great risk, the activity in which you are engaging is a game. Further, you can enhance the thrill of playing games by increasing the risk, which is done regularly by linking winning or losing to money. What playing polo and playing Chinese checkers have in common is not crisscrossing similarities but the possibility of non-life-threatening victory or loss. Play and games are highly similar concepts but differ, in that games depend on rules. One can *play* without playing *games*.

Classic studies by the cognitive psychologists Michael Posner and Steven Keele establish that humans remember categories by using a combination of examples they actually experience and "examples" they construct. A constructed example, called a *prototype*, represents the category better than any actual member of it. In a family-resemblance concept such as the Smith brothers there is a best member, the prototype, a Smith brother who represents the family better than any other brother. The sum of the differences between the prototype brother and other brothers is less than for any other member of the family. When people are asked to name a vegetable or an animal, they are most likely to mention the prototype—a potato or a dog. They recognize pictures of the prototype more quickly than those of other members of the category. These facts about how family-resemblance-type categories are processed seem to distinguish them nicely from such classic concepts as number or letter. But when cognitive psychologists S. Armstrong, Henry Gleitman, and L. Gleitman asked people to declare the first number that came into their heads and timed how long it took them to recognize pictures of the number, they found that people recognized this number far more quickly than other numbers. The same results would be found, no doubt, for letters of the alphabet. Evidently prototypes are not unique to family resemblance, for when categories are defined by formal rules, as they are with numbers and letters, people construct prototypes which summarize their experience by means of those categories. In other words humans construct prototypes not as a substitute for formal rules, but as an intrinsic part of how they process information.

The developmental psychologist Leslie Cohen reports that even infants use prototypes when they categorize. While the categories tested in the three-month-old infant were simple, those of the ten-month-old were more complex. Nevertheless all infants responded to the prototype of a category as though it were a highly familiar object when, in fact, the infants had never seen the prototype before!

As of now we have no evidence that animals use prototypes. If they do not, this would suggest that animals have not evolved the resources needed to construct a prototype, but remember categories solely in terms of the examples they experience. It will not be a surprise, though, if future research modifies this view.

Wittgenstein's second major contribution to the discussion of *concept* and *category* is to be found in his dissection of the idea of similarity. Although categories clearly depend on the similarity of their members, the attempt to explain category by using the idea of similarity falls short. Any pair of objects can be made to seem more similar than any other pair simply by choosing the right features.

Polar bears and ice cream bars, for example, can be made quite similar by focusing on temperature. If, however, we seriously propose to place polar bears and ice cream bars in the same category, we will be ridiculed and advised that temperature is a foolish criterion to use. The criterion is not an inherently foolish one, however, in that temperature is a wise criterion to use when placing North and South poles in the same category.

Similarity alone is uninformative—that is Wittgenstein's point. Similarity becomes informative only when given relevance by a theory. We need to have a conceptual understanding of polar bear, ice cream bar, and the two poles if we are to distinguish wise from foolish similarities, that is, similarities that "count" from those that should be ignored. Wittgenstein's argument that all pairs of objects are equally similar, however, is true only under special conditions.

Objects are potentially equally similar *only if we are completely unbiased* in how we perceive the world, only if we are just as likely to attend to some features as to others. But living creatures do not perceive the world in an unbiased way. They attend to some features when looking at certain objects, different features when looking at other objects. They do not sample features randomly! All species are well known to perceive the world in highly biased ways![2]

Categories in Animals

How do animal categories and the concepts on which they depend compare with those of humans? Because animals draw many distinctions that have the "character" of categories, we speak of animal categories. But are we correct in doing so? Are we granting the animal more than is warranted?

This issue was raised earlier, in Chapter 5, with respect to vervet calls—no doubt the world's most celebrated animal category. We credit the vervets with having the categories of *python, eagle,* and *leopard* because vervets make different calls for the three species that prey on them. But are vervet calls accompanied by mental representations? If the vervet were played a tape of its call for leopard, could it inform us that the leopard is four-legged, runs on the ground, has spots and climbs trees? The lack of appropriate tests makes it impossible to say. We do not however need tests to observe that the vervet has no conceptual understanding of predators: that it does not know that eagles, pythons, and leopards are biological entities and therefore are born, grow old, and die. But if there is neither mental representation nor conceptual knowledge associated with the vervet categories, what is the relation between such a category and the human category? Using the same term for both cases is, to say the least, misleading.

Other categories granted to animals are those of kin, gender, and sexual maturity: Virtually all species can recognize kin, distinguish male from female members of their species, and distinguish the sexually mature from the immature animals.

Really, though, these "categories" of gender, sexual maturity, and so on are little more than perceptual devices enabling a species to react differently to certain stimuli. The reactions are limited. In some cases, for instance kin recognition simply inhibits the aggression that animals otherwise would direct at one another. There is of course no understanding of genealogy, no conceptual entailment of any kind, and this is as true for the chimpanzee as for the bee.

Adult members of many species—chimpanzees, dogs, cats, monkeys—will accept mauling from their young that they would never tolerate from adults. Worker bees defend their genetically identical sisters with greater vigor than they do their brothers, often to the point of self-sacrifice.

Are there animal categories more comparable to human categories; categories, for instance, where the instigating stimuli involve objects as opposed to merely a feature or an assembly of features; categories where there is at least some measure of conceptual entailment? While the "natural" categories claimed as being possessed by the pigeon—those of tree, fish, person—might be seen as good candidates, claims for them were based on flawed tests.

The claims for pigeon categories began with a photographer who was instructed to take a large number of photos of largely comparable natural outdoor scenes. In one experiment half of those photos included a person, while the other half did not. The reinforcement theorist Richard Herrnstein and his associates used the photos to train their pigeons, showing their birds twenty of the photos, ten that contained a person and ten that did not. The pigeons were trained to *peck* at the photos that contained a person and to inhibit pecking (*not peck*) at the photos that did not contain a person. Another group of birds was trained to do the opposite. After the birds had learned the problems, they were shown new photos involving slightly different scenes, some of them including new persons. The birds performed correctly, about as well on the new photos as they had on the originals. On the basis of this test Herrnstein and his associates claimed the pigeon had the category "person."

This experiment has two kinds of errors, the first of them being easy to correct. Although the experimenter claims the pigeon is discriminating *person* from *nonperson*, he has not proved the claim. If he had placed a monkey in one of the nonperson photos (or even a horse, dog, etc.) he might have been in for a surprise, because the pigeon may discriminate animals from nonanimals (as opposed to person from nonperson) and peck those photos, too. In other words, until the bird is given a choice among humans *and* other animals, and then is shown to peck only at humans, we cannot be sure. Another "distractor," a scarecrow, should also have been tested, since birds are said to confuse them with people.

Unlike the first error the second error is serious, and difficult to correct. The experiment does not provide us with an answer to the key question: When shown the photo of a person, what does the pigeon perceive, a distinctive kind of object more or less like that a human perceives? Or does it perceive an assembly of features, a list rather than an organized entity? The positive transfer, the success of the bird in responding to new photos, does not answer the question. Positive transfer is compatible with both alternatives.

The perception psychologist John Cerella attempted to answer the key question by training pigeons to respond to the cartoon character Charlie Brown. After training the birds on Charlie's normal form, he divided the cartoon form of Charlie Brown into three segments—head, torso, legs—and then recombined the segments into both normal and abnormal combinations. The pigeons responded to the normal and abnormal combinations in the same way: to a figure with legs on top, torso on bottom, and head in the middle, no less than to a normal figure with head on top, torso in the middle, legs on the bottom!

The failure of the pigeons to discriminate the order of the body segments could have two explanations. The pigeon may be a clever bird, able to reorder the figures in its mind; this is what five-year-old children do when given a picture story in a scrambled order. While three-and-a-half-year-old

212 ORIGINAL INTELLIGENCE

children cannot mentally reorder the story and therefore can make no sense of it, the five-year-old understands scrambled stories as well as normal stories. Do pigeons mentally reorder scrambled bodies the way five-year-olds reorder scrambled stories? A more likely alternative is that pigeons respond to features, not figures. Pigeons do not respond to changes in the construction of body segments because such changes have no effect on the features themselves.

Determining what another creature perceives—that is, whether or not it perceives what you perceive—is difficult under the best of circumstances. The question becomes additionally difficult when the other creature lacks humanlike intelligence and cannot be tested as humans can be. The intelligence of a species sets limits on the tests that can be used to explore its mind. For this reason questions of mind are far easier to answer for chimpanzees than for pigeons.

If for instance we give the chimpanzee a photo of a face, we can pretty well tell whether it sees a facelike object (more or less like the one we see) or an assembly of features (unlike anything we see). Two tests give us an informative answer. First, as we saw in Chapter 2, when Sarah was given the elements of a face—eyes, nose, mouth—she reassembled them. Second, while the young animals did not emulate Sarah, they passed a less demanding test: In the context of the match-to-sample test they matched the nose to a flower, the ear to a bell, the eye to a blinking flashlight, and so forth. Neither the reassembly of the face nor the linking of facial features with their functions are outcomes that would be found in a species that saw the face as a mere assembly of features. But these diagnostic tests cannot easily be given to the pigeon, and the tests that can be given to it fail to provide entirely determinant outcomes.[3]

Verena Dasser attempted to show that rhesus monkeys have a category of *mother* that is somewhat "more" than a mere perceptual reaction to a set of features. Using match-to-sample tests, she gave monkeys a photo of a rhesus mother as the sample, and as alternatives, two photos of young monkeys, one of which was the actual offspring of the rhesus mother. In due time the monkeys being tested successfully matched the offspring to the mother.

Are the monkeys Wittgensteinians? Attuned to family resemblance? Using the physical similarity between a mother and her offspring to identify relationship? Oddly enough, when humans (who did not have the monkey's knowledge of the relations among the troop) were given the same problem, they flunked the test. Humans cannot use physical resemblances among the rhesus monkeys as a cue to maternity. And perhaps neither can monkeys.

Motherhood, or who gave birth to whom, is the criterion humans use when assembling test items; but what is the criterion monkeys use, when matching infants to their mothers?

The biological idea of *motherhood* is almost certainly beyond a monkey or any other nonhuman. A more likely criterion for the monkey is amount of association between two individuals; for how long, or how often, two individuals associate is an observable factor available to every member of a troupe.

But even if amount of association actually is the monkey's criterion, other questions still remain. Must the association be friendly or would antagonistic association count? Does the monkey form a special category for individuals that frequently associate with one another, provided that one of the following is true: One individual is larger than the other; the larger individual is female; the female is sexually mature? Age, gender, and sexual maturity are distinctions that monkeys can recognize, each in a specific context. But the question is: Could monkeys be taught to combine these individual distinctions, and begin to formulate the concept of motherhood?

Intermodal Equivalence and the Concept of Self

If an individual has seen an object but never touched it, or conversely has touched an object but never seen it, will he recognize their equivalence? Numerous approaches have been used to answer these questions.

The comparative psychologists Kim Dolgin, Liz Spelke, and David Premack allowed infant apes and monkeys to touch and feel five different objects. They placed a cube, sphere, or the like in the hands and mouths of the animals in an unlighted room so that the animals could not see the objects. The lights were then turned on, and the infants were shown the objects in pairs. All four of the infants looked at, and reached for, the object that corresponded to the one they had initially felt. Rather than habituate, they preferred to look at the object they had previously touched.[4]

There is a misunderstood relation between intermodal perception and the concept of self. The mirror recognition test is widely construed as a litmus test for the concept of "self." Species such as the chimpanzee and the child pass the test; that is, they touch *themselves* when looking in a mirror. Species such as monkeys and gorillas fail the test, touching the mirror but not themselves. Sometimes these species will reach behind the mirror, as though trying to contact another creature. If a spot of rouge is dabbed surreptitiously on the face, species that pass the test will touch the spot on their own face while looking in the mirror. Those that fail the test touch the spot on the face in the mirror. Do these differences, in response to a mirror, provide us with a litmus test for the concept of self?

The child almost certainly has had her face touched by her mother, and both have explored the child's face with their hands. In this way, the child is provided with a *tactual* representation of her face, a representation provided both by the fingers and by the touched face of the child. We can test this assumption by showing the child two photos: one of her own face, the other of another child. If the child does have a tactual representation of her face she will recognize her own photo as a visual equivalent of it, looking at it longer in an habituation/dishabituation test; and when given a match-to-sample test, she will chose her own photo.

Perhaps chimpanzees tend to pass the habituation/dishabituation version of the test because they too have a tactual representation of their face; like the human, the chimpanzee handles objects and may therefore touch its face. Monkeys will almost certainly fail this test. Except for the manipulative cebus, monkeys do not handle objects and are unlikely to have tactual representations of their faces.[5]

An individual who recognizes the equivalence between his mirror image and his tactual representation of his face will automatically conclude that the spot on the mirror is a representation of a spot on his face and will touch his face. An individual who has *no* tactual representation of his face will not recognize the mirror image as a representation of his face, and cannot recognize therefore that the spot in the mirror is a representation of a spot on his face.

Suppose we follow the "photo" test with the mirror recognition test. What will happen? We predict that species that pass the photo test will also pass the mirror test; while those that fail the photo test will probably fail the mirror test. "Probably," because use of the mirror itself could provide the intermodal stimulation that just might serve as a substitute for a tactual representation of the face. An individual who happened to touch his face or to move while looking in the mirror could receive intermodal perception. It would be tactual-visual in one case, proprioceptive-visual in the other—weak possibilities, compared to the effect of the tactual representation of the face.

Passing the mirror test depends solely on the ability to combine one's mirror image with the tactual representation of one's face. The test has no relevance to a concept of self. Having a concept of self involves far more than mere mirror recognition; it involves the appraisal of what is seen in the mirror. Not only self-appraisal, but social appraisal.

A concept of self is a social construction based on our assessment of the reactions of others. "Am I attractive?" A woman's positive assessment of her mirror image is not the final answer. Rather, she also wishes to know such things as whether men look at her admiringly and whether women use her as a model. If her assessment of self is not confirmed by others, if she fails to attract admirers, a woman's self-appraisal will weaken.

Although a chimpanzee passes the mirror test, there is no evidence that it engages in either self- or social appraisal.

The concept of self presupposes causal reasoning, the ability to reason: "Men pay attention to me because I am attractive." As we have seen, this kind of reasoning is not available to the chimpanzee.

Sensory Experience

Many human concepts that are weak in sensory experience are said to be metaphors that borrow their meaning from concepts rich in sensory experience. It is said, for instance, that "time" borrows its meaning from "space," in that the duration of an event cannot actually be perceived—it is inferred from the distance one has traveled, the amount of work one has done, or some such space-factor. For while we can both see and feel *space*, we can neither see *nor* touch *time*.

Time and space are two of many would-be "saprophitic" concepts, concepts which "live off" the sensory experience provided by another concept. According to the principal advocates of this view of metaphors, George Lakoff and his associates, many concepts, including love, mind, death, idea, and dream are saprophitic. They even have proposed that the concept of *idea* is a metaphor based on the concept of food. Outlandish? The claim loses some of its improbability when we are reminded of such phrases as:

> "I can't get my teeth into his ideas."
>
> "I find much of what he says indigestible."
>
> "I got a bellyful of his ideas last night."

There are also, however, phrases such as "pregnant ideas" and "tortuous ideas" that have little to do with food. Perhaps important concepts are represented by more than just one metaphor! Until recently the evidence for the above claims, though provocative, was never convincing. It consisted entirely of linguistic evidence, of what people actually say. But we cannot simply equate what people say with what they think.

Boroditsky greatly improved the quality of the evidence for Lakoff's claim by presenting new evidence, discussed earlier in Chapter 4, that goes well beyond phrases. Further, she demonstrated an important facet of the argument by showing that metaphorical relations are *asymmetrical*. Concepts that are weak in sensory experience borrow from those that have a strong sensory component. Thus while people think about time more effectively after they have been primed on spatial distinctions, the reverse is not true: Priming people on temporal distinctions does not help them with their thinking about space.

Somasthesia

When it comes to describing some of our most memorable experiences, literal language often fails us and we fall back on our figurative resources. Similes and metaphors are figures of speech that rely heavily on somasthesia, the use of sensations in one domain to describe sensations and feelings in another domain. In talking about our experience with others, for example, we say such things as: John is cold or warm, Ellen distant or close, Ed has a stony or a soft character. In discussing music, we call a voice "velvety"; wine is described as "floral," "flinty," and so on.

Is somasthesia an advanced competence, meaning that it developed late in human evolution? We might think so. The advantage it confers is expressed mainly in figurative language. But somasthesia is a good example of a competence that did *not* evolve as an adaptation for its present use. We can be confident in saying so because somasthesia is present in the chimpanzee, as is shown in the following test.

The test involved two steps. In the preliminary phase the trainer placed a set of three elements, either large or small circles, on a table before the chimpanzee. She would place on the table LLL, a sequence of large circles; or sss, a sequence of small circles; or LLs, LsL, and so on: mixed sequences of large and small circles. The animals were given their own supply of large and small circles and taught to place them in correspondence with those of the trainer—a large circle by each of the trainer's large circles, a small circle by each of her small circles. After the animal had learned to "copy" the trainer, we took the important next step.[6]

In this phase the trainer continued to lay out sequences of the large and small circles; however, we removed the animal's supply of circles and gave them new objects instead: three red and three pink squares of the same size. Without hesitation the animals used the squares as they had the circles, placing them in correspondence with the trainer's sequence. And what was that? Both animals placed the *red* squares into correspondence with the *large* circles, the *pink* squares into correspondence with the *small* circles. Their performance was essentially perfect.

Encouraged by this outcome, we tried a third step. We removed the red and pink squares and replaced them with six new squares, three rough (sandpaper) and three smooth (velvet) of the same size and color. Without hesitation the animals once again placed them in correspondence with the trainer's sequence, *rough* squares with *large* circles, *smooth* squares with *small* circles.

Finally we combined the second and the third steps, giving the animals a supply of red and pink squares on some trials, rough and smooth squares on others. It seems we should have stopped while we were ahead. For one of the animals now developed a peculiar practice that it reserved for trials in which the trainer laid out homogeneous sequences—cases of sequences of all large or all small circles, LLL or sss. The animal copied the homogeneity of the trainer's sequence, laying out sequences of her own that were either all red or all pink, all rough or all smooth, but she did not copy specific features. In other words, when the trainer laid out, say, LLL, the animal was as likely to "copy" the trainer's sequence with three pink squares as with three red ones (or three smooth squares, as three rough ones). Only when the trainer laid out mixed sequences—LsL, ssL, and so on—did the animal resume normal copying, placing red and pink, rough and smooth into correspondence with the trainer's large and small. In other words the animal observed the correspondence between size and color, or size and roughness, on a relative, not on an absolute, basis.

Since somasthesia is found in the chimpanzee it clearly did not develop late in human evolution. In this respect somasthesia resembles other competences that evolved in nonhuman species and later became building blocks of language. Somasthesia is not, however, a structural component of language, despite the formidable role it plays in today's use of language. Did somasthesia always play such a role in language, and if not, when did it join forces with language? The presence of figurative language in the earliest written texts does not help us to answer the question. Writing is itself an extremely late development. Thousands of years of speech preceded writing, and figurative language could have developed either in speech or in writing.

Do hunter-gatherers use similes and metaphors when speaking to one another? Hunter-gatherers have a concept of time, and are facile in its use. Knowing an animal's speed of running, they can quickly translate an estimated duration into the distance an animal can travel, as we saw in Chapter 8. Hunter-gatherers must therefore have analogies for time and space. Analogies, however, are precursors of metaphor and simile, they are not strictly a part of figurative language. Indeed, analogies do not even require language. We are reminded of this fact by the chimpanzee's success in using perceptual and functional analogies, both of which were based on objects, or drawings of objects. The fact that hunter-gatherers use analogies does not tell us whether their analogies influence their language, that is, lead them to adopt metaphors and similes in their speech.

Symbols versus Images

Is human intelligence the equivalent of a computer model of intelligence? Probably not. All information in the computer model is represented by symbols—there are no images. Images, however, play a fundamental role in many aspects of human intelligence.

The idea that human intelligence is based on symbols was encouraged by the work of the English mathematician, Alan Turing. He demonstrated that problems of deductive reasoning could be solved by a machine. The machine "reasoned" by carrying out a set of operations on symbols whose meaning the machine did not know. (As far as the machine was concerned the symbols were merely physical objects with different shapes.) The operations performed by the machine were such mundane acts as repeating a string of words, erasing the string, moving the string from one line to another, and so on. In this mechanical way the machine solved problems of a kind that appear in every schoolchild's book on logic. With apologies for modernizing the sentences:

All *persons* are mortal.

Henrietta [Socrates wife] is a person.

Therefore Henrietta is mortal.

When the two premises were entered into the machine the machine performed its operations on them, automatically reaching the desired conclusion.

Turing's work also was influential because it appeared to solve this long-standing philosophical problem: How does intelligence emerge out of a set of "dumb" molecules? After all, the brain is nothing more than a batch of chemicals. How does a chemical mixture acquire "knowledge"? Turing's demonstration seemed to provide the answer. It did not handle the details—explaining how the chemicals form neurons, how the neurons are interconnected, what signals activate the neurons, etc. But the kind of demonstration it did offer—a machine that reasoned by rearranging the positions of meaningless marks according to prescribed rules—suggested that all the other "details" could be reduced to equally trivial processes, with explanations provided at the proper time.

Calling Turing's invention a "Turing machine" was not a misnomer. Like other abstract thinkers of his ability Turing also was a gifted tinkerer, constructing gadgets that gave physical form to his ideas. The gadgets demonstrated that his ideas worked not only on the printed page but in the real world. During World War II, Turing led a team that designed such gadgets— some became the predecessors of today's computer, and one, by breaking the German code, played a long-unpublicized role in hastening the Allied victory. Few were aware of Turing's monumental contributions to the understanding of mind, the computer, and the British war effort when, in 1954, at the age of forty-two, to escape governmental harassment for homosexuality, then a crime in England, Turing took his own life.

The field of artificial intelligence, which has been built on Turing's breakthroughs, has never rued the inability of the computer to incorporate imaginal representation; to the contrary, the significance of imaginal representation, even its reality, has continued to be disputed. The field of artificial intelligence has taken a stance similar to that of certain philosophers who have always thought that talking of "pictures in the mind" is misguided at best. Until recently, their position was easily defended. Reports of the use of images by various individuals bore the suspected status of all anecdotal evidence. In a sense such evidence could be easily dismissed, for, since no importance was attached to images, there was no pressing need to deny that people experience images when thinking. The images that flooded consciousness were deemed mere epiphenomena.

Although people may be dazzled by the images before their eyes, the real work was performed behind the scenes in the form of Turing-like processes, operating on symbols. There was no conscious access to thinking—no more access than to metabolism, the secretion of urine, or any other vital body process.

It was possible for those holding to this position even to dismiss the remarkable introspections of Albert Einstein, who, in describing his discovery of spatial relativity, said: "Words and sentences, whether written or spoken, do not seem to play any part in my thought processes. The psychological entities that serve as building blocks for my thought are certain signs or images, more or less clear, that I can reproduce and recombine at will." Einstein describes these images, which involve everyday machinery and activity—moving elevators and trains—and tells us, that, in picturing himself jumping up in a rising elevator, he was helped to grasp the nature of space!

Recent experimental work has removed imaginal representation from the realm of anecdote, giving it a status comparable to that of any other scientific finding. Models of imaginal representation and processing proposed by Roger Shepard, by the cognitive neuroscientist Stephen Kosslyn and his associates, and others, have made predictions of novel findings not predicted by models of symbolic representation, and these have been confirmed. Perhaps the single most graphic demonstration of imaginal thinking is the evidence for two independent forms of mathematical thinking, one based on words, the other on images.

Dehaene and his associates trained bilingual students, proficient in Russian and English, to solve simple addition problems in two different ways. In *exact* addition, the individual was presented with a two-digit addition problem and trained to select the *correct* answer from two alternatives, one being the exact answer and the other off by just a single digit. In *approximate* addition, the individual was presented with the same two-digit addition problem and trained to select an answer from two alternatives, both incorrect, but one a closer approximation to the correct answer than the other. The instructions given the students emphasized that the correct answer required calculation, whereas an approximate answer could be reached by guessing. All the students were taught each kind of problem in both English and Russian.

Brain images, taken while the students were solving the problems, showed that distinct parts of the brain were activated by the two methods of solving the problem. Exact math activated only one side of the brain, the left inferior frontal circuits also known to be used when generating associations between words. Approximate math activated both sides of the brain, mainly the parietal lobes, which are known to handle analogies and other visuospatial mental transformations. Striking behavioral differences were also associated with the two procedures.

For problems that had been learned with exact math, there was a cost in shifting from one language to the other. If the student had learned the problem in Russian he was "slowed down" when required to solve the problem in English, and vice versa. This suggests that solutions learned with exact math are stored in words, and that shifting to new words has a translation cost.

For problems that had been learned with approximate math, there was no translation cost. The student was not slowed down when required to solve a problem using a language different from the one used in training (equally true for both Russian and English). This suggests that solutions learned with approximate math are not stored in words; instead they are represented with the mental "numerical" line that was discussed, in the context of the child's mathematical module, in Chapter 1.

Further, for problems learned with exact math, new problems took longer to solve than old ones—again suggesting the use of specific words in representing solutions to the problems—but for problems learned with approximate math, new problems took no longer to solve than old ones. This suggests that solving a new problem by "moving" to a new location on the mental line had no cost, unlike the translation cost of solving new problems whose answers are stored in words.

This combination of results, which includes both neural and behavioral data, puts to rest the old stories circulated for years about the "phony" status of imaginal representation. It puts to rest the old view that a consciousness of images experienced when solving a problem is epiphenomenal and bears no relation to the real thinking that is going on unconsciously in the form of Turing-like operations on symbols. This resolution to the issue raises a question that should have been asked far earlier: Why would a kind of epiphenomenal smokescreen, one that bears no relation to real thinking, have evolved in the first place? Images are not cost-free: They take time, occupy neural space, and reduce one's ability to do other things. As a rule, costly processes that have no adaptive value do not evolve.

Artificial intelligence presents the mind as a thinking machine, which is to say a Turing machine, wedged between perception on the one hand and action on the other. Occasionally the field apologizes for not having come up with an explanation for perception and action—for not having connected them to thinking—and once again drops a promissory note to do both when the time is ripe. But the artificial intelligence conception of mind is not one that can be corrected by simply adding perception and action to symbols. The human mind is not a Turing machine. Turing machines cannot solve math problems using imaginal representation, because they do not have imaginal representation. And we can be confident that problems involving numbers are not the only ones solved by images. Perhaps all problems in which one attempts to *guess* rather than to *calculate* an answer incline one to use imaginal representation.

It is a major error to suppose that perception and action are independent processes that can be arbitrarily tacked on to thinking when our progress permits. Perception and action are integral parts of thinking. To begin with, imaginal thinking, which plays an important role in all thinking, is itself affected by perception. The major imaginal theorists, Shepard and Kosslyn, for example, have sought to show the constraints that perception imposes on imaging—that what we "image" is affected by what we perceive—and have tried to explain the interaction between the two processes.

Actions and images are no less intimately connected than are perception and images. Our most important images are the dynamic images which comprise the major vehicle of personal memory. These images depict episodes from our past—events of a birthday party, a war experience, the aftermath of a tornado, a wedding celebration, etc.—in which we "see" ourselves interacting with others, what we did to them, how they reacted to us. Much of the original emotion that accompanied the episode is mysteriously preserved by the image. Why this is so, and why, in general, emotion is far more acutely linked with imaginal than with symbolic processes, simply is part of our overall ignorance of both emotion and image.

Neither image nor emotion is inherently incompatible with the computer. Both can be made a part of the computer once our knowledge of imaginal and emotional thinking has permitted us to write programs enabling the computer to make use of image and emotion that is comparable to the human use. When we can design a "Turing machine" based on images, we will honor the image in the way we presently honor the symbol.

Is the widespread guess, that images are more primitive than symbols, correct? The guess mistakenly confuses symbols with natural language, the language we use when communicating with one another. But we can assume an earlier language, a language inside the head, used strictly for thinking, not for speaking. This machine language will differ from natural language in several key respects: There will be no ambiguity in machine language, no words that have multiple meanings, no polysemy, no meanings that are represented by more than one word. And of course there will be no duality of patterning, because words in machine language are never spoken!

How has machine language, an innate system, evolved under the constraints of individual thinking, as compared with natural language, another innate system, but one that has evolved under social constraints? If we take Lakoff seriously, machine language is a very limited system, consisting exclusively of prime concepts, concepts rich enough in sensory experience to stand on their own two feet. There are no saprophitic or secondary concepts in machine language because these are learned, not innate, concepts (learned, as analogies to prime concepts). On this view animals, especially "higher" animals, may possess a machine language very comparable to the human version. If so, the difference in human and animal concepts would consist exclusively of saprophitic or secondary concepts. Humans—especially educated, modern humans—have a large repertoire of such concepts; in fact most of their concepts are of this kind; whereas animals have no saprophitic concepts because they are incapable of forming analogies.

There is a second reason for not regarding the image as being more primitive than the symbol. In solving problems, humans do not inevitably start with an imaginal approach. Humans have a bias. Some solve reasoning problems symbolically, by taking an algebraic approach, others use Venn diagrams, taking an imaginal approach. Others, though a minority, are adept at both. The very fact that some use Venn diagrams to solve reasoning problems is further evidence that the human mind is not a Turing machine.

Al Newell, who through his work with his celebrated colleague Herb Simon was a leading pioneer of artificial intelligence, once exalted the symbol by pronouncing it the most important step in the evolution of intelligence. Newell, like others writing on this topic, thought of intelligence and symbols in the same breath. When we asked the noted neuroscientist Ira Black to speculate about changes in the brain that may have accompanied the great advance in intelligence produced by the evolution of the symbol, Ira's answer came as a considerable surprise.

Ira began by suggesting that symbols can probably be found in bacteria! Bacteria have been the site of surprises before, not the least of which is sexuality; but sexuality is, after all a primitive. We found the idea of symbols in the bacteria a far greater surprise. But Black suggested that symbols are too valuable a device not to have been designed early by evolution. Symbols, whereby one item stands for another, can make an enormous contribution to the efficiency of any complex process, and metabolism, Black observes, is a highly complex process to which symbols could make a significant contribution. He noted that environmentally influenced molecules that "mediate" the regulation of remote biochemical pathways are, in a sense, representing environmental conditions; they "stand for" them.

But are the molecules really symbols? Do they genuinely represent the environment? For a molecule to act as a symbol it must have the same effect upon another effector molecule as the environment had upon it. Black agreed that we have no firm demonstrations of this kind, but he considered it a genuine possibility. He repeated his argument: A device as valuable as a symbol would have been put to use early by evolution, and is unlikely to have been left to such a latecomer as intelligence.

Although we tend to think of intelligence as a complex process and of digestion as simple, this view is not an informed judgment but a bias. Symbols may well have facilitated metabolic processing just as they facilitate the processes of intelligence.

A conjecture of this kind raises another. Not only symbols, but other operations we associate with intelligence—those of memory and learning, for example—may have evolved at the molecular level in domains other than intelligence. A simple, first-order level of intelligence could consist exclusively of these kinds of operations—operations that did not evolve in the context of intelligence—this would contrast with a second level containing operations that did evolve in the context of intelligence. Operations such as imitation, analogies, reasoning of various kinds, and pedagogy may have no duplicates at the molecular level. These evolved explicitly in the context of intelligence. With this conjecture, concerning two levels of intelligence, we close the experimental chapters of this book.

Notes

1. Not all of the chimpanzee's temporal sorting concerns objects are as pedestrian as red blocks. Occasionally its consecutive handling of objects reveals a more interesting equivalence, such as, for example, when Sarah, at about eleven months of age, boldly lurched forward to touch the hem of a woman's coat. The woman, a complete stranger to Sarah, was wearing a coat of an unusual blanketlike fabric. After feeling the coat, Sarah scooted back to her crib and palpated her own blanket. Her blanket and the woman's coat were of the same fabric. Sarah handled her blanket, placed her face against it, and looked intently at the visitor's coat in a kind of implicit judgment of sameness.

   This act by Sarah revealed an aspect of equivalence that we had overlooked—its motivational force, the "magnetic pull" exerted by the experience of equivalence. The force must be appreciable. In Sarah's case, it brought her into the presence of a stranger—an aversive object for a young chimpanzee. It seems likely that one could actually measure the motive force of equivalence (rather than speculate about it) by inserting its experience into the reinforcement paradigm in this way: Require Sarah to press a lever in order to have the opportunity to experience equivalence. The increase in her lever pressing for equivalence might well compare favorably with that for food or water.

2. It is tempting to build on the fact that species perceive the world in a biased way and argue that categories exist only in the mind and have no external reality. Categories are simply a biased way of perceiving the world. We settle on one set of features when we see fruit, select an entirely different set of features when we see animals, yet another set for flowers, and so forth. In other words according to this argument, the categories *fruit, animals,* and *flowers* do not really differ in the way they are normally considered to do. They differ only in terms of the features that we attend to when perceiving these categories.

   But if the categories do not themselves exist, why do we activate different features when attending to different categories and why do we have such biases? An obvious answer comes from evolutionary theory: It is existing category differences that explain the biases. These differences maximize our perception, enhancing our ability to discriminate one category from another.

3. The animal psychologist S. L. Greene sought to overcome the ambiguity of the original test by introducing a new question: Does the pigeon really use the cate-

gory *person* when solving the problem, or does it simply memorize the individual photos, learning to respond to some stimuli and to inhibit its response to other stimuli? The ability to memorize all the stimuli might seem a formidable task, but pigeons are known to excel at memorizing.

To answer her question, Greene abandoned the normal categorized version of the problem (in which one set of photos contains persons and the other does not) and used an uncategorized version. Now both sets of photos were a mixture, consisting of scenes that did and did not contain persons. The two sets did differ, though, in that the people who appeared in the one set were different from those who appeared in the other.

The pigeons quickly solved the uncategorized problem, indicating that they are quite capable of solving the problem by memorization. Does this mean pigeons never use category, and solved the categorized version of the problem by memorization, too? The animal psychologist Wasserman contests this conclusion. Wasserman compared the rate at which pigeons learn the categorized, uncategorized, and partially categorized version of a problem, and found that they learn the categorized version fastest. This is not an informative outcome, however, for it does not establish that the birds use category in solving the problem; indeed, his findings are completely compatible with memorization. Speed of learning should be inversely proportional to the overlap between the features of the two sets: fastest for the category case, because overlap in features between the two sets is minimal; slowest for the completely uncategorized case, because overlap in features is maximal; and intermediate for the intermediate cases.

Perhaps it would be helpful to compare children and pigeons with respect to their learning of these problems. Since we know that children do use categories, not assemblies of features when solving such problems, a significant overlap between the performance of the two species would suggest that pigeons also use categories, not assemblies of features.

If we were to compare pigeons and children with respect to their learning of the categorized and uncategorized versions of the problem, we might be in for a surprise. If children were to learn the categorized version faster than pigeons, no one would be suprised; the surprise would come from the other direction: Children might have greater difficulty than do pigeons in learning the uncategorized version of the problem. In the child's eyes, all persons belong to the same category. He will therefore tend to respond to all persons, meaning that he will have difficulty learning to inhibit responding to some persons while continuing to respond to others. The pigeon will not have the child's problem. By discriminating between the *features* in the two sets of photographs, it can learn the the categorized and the uncategorized problem in the same way. It may however learn the uncategorized problem somewhat more slowly, owing to the overlap of features between the two sets of photographs.

4. When the infants were shown pictures of some of the five objects, followed by pairs of the objects themselves, they looked *away* from the object whose picture they had seen, thereby demonstrating a classic habituation effect. The pictures and objects both were perceived visually and thus were apprehended by the same modality. It is only when objects are apprehended by *different* modalities that individuals, humans and animals alike, prefer the object they already have seen or

touched. In other words when representations come from different modalities, individuals prefer equivalence; they avoid equivalence, however, when the representations come from the same modality.

    This study is a replication of an earlier test by Meltzoff and Borton. Kim Dolgin carried out all the actual research on human infants, which involved testing infant monkeys (patois and drill) and apes (chimpanzee and orangutan). We are indebted to the Philadelphia zoo for the use of these animals.

5. One might try to enable a monkey to pass the mirror recognition test by doing for it what it does not do for itself: gently palpate the animal's face, giving the monkey a tactual representation of its face.

6. The chimpanzees could not be said to have copied the experimenter, for when they were given more circles than were needed to make an exact copy, they continued to add circles after they had completed the sequence. Unlike children, chimpanzees do not show spontaneous one-to-one correspondence. Fortunately, strict copying is not a requirement for the test of somasthesia.

Conclusion

In the preceding chapters we have developed a theory of the human mind. As promised in the Introduction, we now describe an education that suits this mind. Not a complete education, but provisional examples that lead to a complete education. The examples consist of lessons for young children.

A theory of education could only be derived from understanding the mind that is to be educated. As we have seen, the modules are the original "teachers," guiding the initial learning of the infant, laying the ground work for language, arithmetic, theory of mind, music, and so forth.

What has evolution prepared the child to learn? Of the topics for which the child is prepared, are there any that are overlooked? Not taught at all? Are there topics for which evolution has not prepared the child but which must be learned nevertheless, and could be more readily learned if they were linked to topics for which the child has been prepared? Finally, is evolution as flawless as the impression given? Or has it failed on occasion, and endowed the child with false intuitions that need to be corrected?

We communicate with one another, using language. But how accurately? Are misunderstandings common, or are they rare? We "navigate" in space every day, returning to old locations and seeking out new ones. But how accurately do we find our way? In looking for new locations, are we seriously lost some of the time, or a bit lost most of the time?

How accurate are the mental states that children attribute to one another? For that matter, how accurate are the mental states that adults attribute to one another in their daily lives? Ethological information, the kind of data that tell us what humans actually do in their daily lives, is not easy to find.

Children do not receive instruction in the use of their fundamental competences—they are not taught to gauge the accuracy of the mental states they attribute to others. They are not taught to minimize misunderstandings when talking to one another, nor are they taught the most efficient way in which to find a new location. Is this because the accuracy of our fundamental competences cannot be improved, or because procedures have yet to be designed that will aid us in accomplishing the task? The following is a procedure for improving social competence, one based on an approach that is familiar to the reader.

Lesson One: Social Competence

A small group of toddlers, two and a half to three years of age, gather in a classroom where a teacher asks them questions while showing them a series of videotapes. In the first videotape the toddlers see a small group of children (a few years older than they are), playing with toys while lounging on a rug in a classroom. Betty, a curly-haired child who has been playing with a doll, makes her way over to Tommy, a sturdy child who is coloring, and begins to talk to him in a friendly way.

The teacher hits the PAUSE button, and asks, "Why did Betty stop playing with her doll and go over to talk to Tommy?" While most of the children may not reply, one or perhaps two of them may say "She wants his coloring box."

The teacher now pushes PLAY, and the children see that the answer is correct: Betty *does* ask Tommy to let her play with his coloring box. But rather than grant her request, Tommy neither speaks to nor looks at Betty but simply shakes his head from side to side and continues to color.

"What will Betty do?" the teacher asks. "What do you think, Roger?" Roger has no idea. Another child interrupts, to suggest that Betty might ask for help from her teacher.

When the videotape continues we see Betty's teacher showing Betty how to operate an unusual toy: a small car that shoots harmless sparks from its wheels as it moves forward. Betty takes the toy car over to Tommy and runs it by him. He stops coloring. Betty returns to her play area and continues to operate the car.

Once again the teacher stops the videotape and asks, "What will Tommy do now?" Three toddlers answer. One says: "He will grab the car." The other two suggest: "He will give Betty the colors, and Betty will give him the car." Their prediction is confirmed when the teacher activates the videotape.

The children see Betty and Tommy engage in a peaceful exchange, with Tommy bringing the box of colors to Betty and Betty handing him the toy car. Toddlers of around two and a half years of age do not barter; that is, they do not exchange objects with one another. Children of five or six years of age do so, although not always in as smooth a fashion as shown in the videotape.

Simple films such as these can achieve several purposes. In addition to exposing the child to the diagnosis of motives in social situations, they also can acquaint the child with examples of peaceful resolutions to social conflicts. A film can implicitly ask further questions; for instance, "When a child is diagnosing the motives of the characters in the film, what is the source of his or her hypothesis?" Is the child who "interprets" Betty's friendliness as "angling" for Tommy's colors herself a child who uses angling as a strategy?

Since the "lesson" described above has not been tried out on a large scale, it would be foolhardly to claim that it can actually improve the accuracy of the mental states that young children attribute to others. Nevertheless, several considerations recommend such a lesson, for in general the best way to sharpen a skill is to *use* it, especially if its use leads to some measure of success. In the use of lessons such as this one must suit the social situations depicted in the videotape to the competences of the children, starting with simple situations that increase in complexity as the children advance.

The videotape offers an ideal teaching device. It permits the child to form a hypothesis concerning what the characters in the film will do, and to then check the accuracy of his hypothesis against what the characters actually do. Of course, a teacher must be well acquainted with her films—interrupting them at precisely the right points and allowing tension to build up concerning the resolution of a problem in which each child has a stake. How *indeed* will Betty get the colors from Tommy?

The question of "how" to teach social competence is not one that has been widely addressed. Literature has often been recommended as a means of instruction in the subtleties of human motivation, and very likely it is. A most pleasant one it is, besides. But toddlers cannot profit from *The Magic Mountain* or *War and Peace*. Children need "stories" they can understand in their very earliest years, and short, filmed stories are a helpful introduction for children who cannot yet read.

Lesson Two: Morality

How does an individual satisfy both his own needs and those of the social group of which he is a member? This is the key question for morality. This is not an issue that many species face, because somewhat more than 50 percent of species are not social. But humans, an intensely social species, face the problem of morality with a vengeance. Humans do not have a module that "teaches" them morality, nor could they have such a module, for morality is not a unitary topic like that of language or number. Fortunately, however, humans do have at least three social dispositions that are highly conducive to morality.

1. Children are empathic. By eighteen months of age children recognize the distress of others and, in nearly all cases, attempt to relieve it.
2. Children are pedagogic. From an early age, children are disposed to teach one another.
3. Children assign value to interactions. From about ten months of age children assign value to acts they observe one individual performing on another, and they gauge as positive and negative not only the caresses and hits directed at them personally but the caresses and hits other individuals direct at one another.

All of these dispositions—empathy, pedagogy, and the assignment of value to the acts of others—share a quality that makes them potential contributors to morality. Why? Because the beneficiary in all these cases is *not* the child himself—the benficiary is the other individual!

Many suppose that evolutionary theory has an important contribution to make to the clarification of morality, and that the concept of altruism is critical. Altruism, like empathy and pedagogy, is a willingness to serve others despite the cost to one's self. Although evolutionary theory of an earlier period found it difficult to explain how such a disposition could evolve, they did arrive at two answers: kin altruism and reciprocal altruism.

Kin altruism is illustrated in the thinking of the evolutionary theorist W. T. Hamilton, who formulated the concept. In the haplodiploid social insects, such as bees, the average fraction of genes shared by sisters is three-fourths, an amount greater than the one-half they share with their mother, the queen bee, or the one-quarter they share with their brothers. Were a female bee to lose its own life in the course of defending its sisters, the act still would contribute positively to the evolution of the bee's own genes, provided it saved at least two of its sisters (or four of its half-sisters), for it would leave behind more of its genes than if it had saved its own life.

Reciprocal altruism, a concept introduced by the evolutionary theorist R. L. Trivers, purports to explain the assistance that genetically *unrelated* individuals give to one another. "If you scratch my back, I'll scratch yours," is a pithy account of the basic idea of reciprocal altruism. This form of altruism depends on certain basic preconditions, however. First, individuals must be able to identify one another—a condition that most species, vertebrates in particular, can meet; second, individuals must be able to remember both the assistance they have given to others and the assistance others have given to them. In addition they must be able to remember not only when their assistance was reciprocated but the number of times they assisted others without having been assisted in return. And individuals must be prepared to punish—to expel from the group—an individual that fails to reciprocate. Reciprocal altruism will not work unless "cheaters" are punished.

Among humans, the idea of reciprocal altruism would require an additional factor. The individual would have to be able to translate the value of one act into that of another, for Harry may water Tom's hedge on weekends while, during the week, Harry's son jumps into Tom's SUV and is driven to school along with Tom's children. How many rides equal one watering?

The evidence for kin altruism in insects is compelling. But humans have mechanisms that can override genes. In civil wars and revolutions, when opposing belief systems are activated, both patricide and fratricide are observed: Fathers kill sons, sons kill fathers, and brothers kill brothers.

While the evidence of kin altruism is compelling, that for reciprocal altruism is not. Vampire bats once were thought to share blood in a manner compatible with reciprocal altruism, but recent data suggest that sharing takes place not between unrelated individuals but between kin—mothers and infants, for example.

Does reciprocal altruism explain cooperation? Cooperation has several levels. At its lowest level, cooperation involves the synchronized behavior of two or more individuals as they pursue a common goal, a kind of cooperation seen among chimpanzees. Chimpanzees hunt opportunistically. While passing through an area they may spot a favorite prey, a young colobus monkey, whereupon some members of the group will climb the tree and others station themselves at the possible escape points. It can be said that the chimpanzees pursuing the monkey and those blocking the exits are cooperating, are synchronizing their behavior in pursuit of a common goal.

Cooperation has a higher level, however, one found only in humans. Before working together, humans form a contract, an agreement to share. This kind of cooperation does not conform to reciprocal altruism. It does not require individuals to remember what they gave, what they were given, when they gave, and so forth, and places no burden on memory. Only one thing needs to be remembered: where the individual placed his contract for safekeeping.

Animals not only cannot form an agreement to share because they lack language, but they also have little disposition to share. Rather than share, the successful chimpanzee typically attempts to run off with the victim's body, relinquishing pieces of meat only to those bold enough to grab or to beg vigorously for it—in the manner that the cognitive anthropologist Glynn Isaac aptly has called *tolerated scrounging*. Cooperation without an agreement to share lasts a matter of minutes, the duration of an opportunistic hunt. Cooperation with an agreement to share may last for years—even a lifetime.

The lesson in morality for children, then, exploits the three prosocial dispositions of empathy, pedagogy, and the attribution of value, building a moral platform that is centered on helping the other one. Empathy appears in infants as young as eighteen months of age, and a clear picture of empathy has been given us through a study done by the German developmental psychologist Doris Bischof.

In this study, children encounter an adult female "playmate" whose teddybear breaks in the course of play. The adult weeps and grieves, saying "My teddy is broken!" The children go to her side, speak to her consolingly, pat her, and in some cases attempt to fix the teddybear. Some ask their mothers to help fix the toy. (At this age, children are more comfortable when accompanied by their mothers in the classroom.)

Despite all of the above, two of the fifty children tested, one a boy and the other a girl, while recognizing the distress, still "gloated," parading around the victim, stomping their feet and shouting! The ability to recognize the distress of another individual apparently does not lead automatically to empathy. As Bischof notes, it can just as easily lead to sadism, to exploiting the vulnerability of the distressed individual. Happily, Bischof's data suggest that very few children take the sadistic path.

What produces empathy? Is it the condition—in this case, the broken teddybear? What if the teddy broke but the victim did not cry? Would the children then console the adult? Is it grief and tears? (If the teddy did not break but the victim cried anyway, would the children still console her?) Or does empathy require both factors, both the accident and the tears? We do have tests that could decide, but they have yet to tease these alternatives apart.

Because the six-month-old merely cries when hearing another infant cry, whereas the eighteen-month-old, rather than cry, attempts to comfort a crying infant, Bischof argues that the presence of empathy demonstrates that eighteen-month-old children do have a sense of self. The difference can be explained more simply, however. The six-month-old does not cry in response to a crying infant, but to the sound of crying itself. The infant will respond in the same way whether the cries come from a victim or from a loudspeaker. (In this respect, she is like the vervet monkey that also responds the same way whether cries come from another vervet or from a loudspeaker.) The eighteen-month old child, by contrast, is responding to the distress of a child, not to the sight or sound of distress. When she is shown a film of a distressed child she will not try to comfort it.

Fortunately, there is no need to teach the child empathy. Thanks to home "lessons" from mother and/or caretakers, the child already is well schooled in empathy. Long before an infant is eighteen months of age he will have bumped himself and scraped his knee, have fallen down and hurt himself, and been consoled by his mother and family.

While we need not teach the child empathy, we can strengthen his disposition to practise it by giving him the opportunity to do so. And we could do that by repeating Bischof's study, but using it now as an exercise in empathy. We could change the victim, her distress, the conditions that produce her distress; provide the child with broad experience of the kinds of occasions in which he may be called upon to act empathically; show the child examples of successful empathy in videotapes in which children console victims and succeed in relieving their distress. Once again, though, we face an ethological question for which there is no answer: How often does a child, in the normal course of events, engage in empathy: receive it, observe it, practice it?

Is there anything one can do to reduce the small percentage of children who gloat? Children who respond sadistically almost certainly have not invented sadism. Nor have normal children invented empathy. Although children may vary in benevolence, Bischof's data are less a measure of sadism in children than a measure of their parents and an aberrant home. Are there remedial steps that might be taken? Perhaps merely showing the parent films that compare the reaction of his child to the reactions of the other children, vis-à-vis the victim. Or by showing the empathic reaction of other children to the rare child who has failed to show empathy.

In pedagogy, as in empathy, the target of assistance is an "incapacitated" individual. In the case of empathy the target is a victim of a mishap, whereas in pedagogy the target is an individual who is unable to carry out a task: She cannot color "inside the lines," her block tower topples over, she consistently places her doll's shoes on the wrong feet, and so on. And despite the differences between pedagogy and empathy, there is an emotional impetus in both cases. Confronting another individual's distress can be deeply unsettling—there is a measure of emotional upset when one sees acts that fall short of one's own aesthetic standards.

The best approach to take toward strengthening the child's pedagogic disposition is, once again, to "exercise the disposition," to give the child opportunities to teach others who are confronted by tasks they cannot perform. The child is shown videotapes of children teaching others to color within the lines, build towers that are not faulty, properly dress the doll—examples of successful pedagogy. A good first step in the encouragement of pedagogy is to increase the child's own competence, for a child cannot teach others (to color properly, build towers, dress dolls) unless he is himself competent in these tasks.

The third prosocial disposition—assigning value +/- to acts performed by others—is probably the most automatic of the three dispositions and therefore the least needful of being exercised. The three dispositions—empathy, pedagogy, and assigning value +/- to acts performed by others—are innate dispositions, an integral part of the child. Empathy and pedagogy are amenable to broadening and strengthening, whereas the assigning of value +/- is so nearly automatic as to require no strengthening. The three are not, however, the sum total of the child's innate social dispositions. If they were, building a moral platform for helping others would be simple indeed. The child has other dispositions that are far less amenable to morality.

For example, when a four-year-old child is asked to oversee the division of a cake he will agree to accept a smaller piece, provided that his accepting a smaller portion has this consequence: Another child will receive a still smaller portion! In other words even at this tender age the child is interested, not in having a large portion per se, but in having a portion larger than another receives. This is reminiscent of the case of an esteemed scientist who, in setting his terms for a job at a university eager to hire him, demanded, not a fixed salary, but a sum greater than that paid anyone else, including that of the president of the university and the football coach. At any rate, our point here is that when adjusting one's aspirations for teaching morality, one must take into account *all* of the child's dispositions. The discovery of negative dispositions serves only to increase the desirability of strengthening those that are positive.

Notice that the prosocial dispositions—empathy, pedagogy, etc.—do not depend on either kin altruism or reciprocal altruism. Children do not restrict their assistance to kin, nor do they teach or console only those who have assisted them. The many children who consoled the distressed victim in the Bischof study had never previously been consoled by her. When a child has been taught or consoled by its parent, rather than being disposed to now console or teach its parent, as reciprocal altruism requires, the child is disposed to teach or console another individual, one who is in need of help.

The errors we have found in what evolutionary theory has to say about social behavior are not a surprise. For the theories espoused by evolutionary theory did not result from studies of social behavior but from an attempt to rescue evolutionary theory from the problem of altruism. Ironically, the problem of altruism has since disappeared because evolutionary theory now accepts what it rejected earlier: evolution at the level of the group as well as at the level of the individual. Dispositions in which an individual serves others at a cost to himself are no longer a problem. They can readily evolve. They will benefit the group.

Lesson Three: Physics

Because modern physics has left the intuitive content of the infant's physical module far behind, the physics module presents a unique challenge to education. While there have been equally consequential developments in modern biology—evolutionary theory, genes, DNA—the situations in physics and biology are not alike. Modern ideas in biological theory, while highly novel, are not counterintuitive. As opposed to colliding with modular intuitions, as did modern physics, evolutionary theory collided with a cultural artifact, religion; with the biblical, or Adam and Eve, account of creation. Modern biology, consequently, unlike modern physics, is not called upon to correct unsound modular ideas.

The intuition that large objects fall faster than small objects is given us by our physical module, and conforms of course with what we actually see. The basic laws of physics, however, cannot be discovered in the observed world. To discover the basic laws one needs a hypothetical world, an uncontaminated world—Galileo's world. For only in such a world can one see that all objects fall at the same speed. Only in such a world can one see that objects, once placed in motion, never come to rest.

How shall we "tell" a toddler about *friction*, the contaminant that is the source of our mistaken intuitions that large objects fall faster than small ones? Using simple animations, we show the child what friction consists of and how it works. Moreover, with the help of her physical module the child will understand what she is shown—and its consequences.

Using simple animations we show the child a screen consisting of "air" that is filled with particles of various sizes, dancing about in Brownian movement. A feather and a rock start to descend from the top of the screen. The child sees the objects falling, colliding with the particles as they do so. The rock successfully bumps particles aside and reaches the ground first.

A magic vacuum cleaner appears at the scene's end and sucks up some of the particles. The "air" begins to clear. Once again the feather and the rock descend, and the child can see that the feather has an easier time of it. The rock and feather now come close to landing at about the same time. The magic vacuum cleaner next completes its task, leaving the air sparkling clean. Rock and feather, now descending through perfectly clear air, no longer collide with particles but fall at the same speed and land in unison.

Can we claim that the child grasps the "idea" of friction? That she understands how friction causes differences in the rate of fall? Or is the child merely delighted by what she sees?

The child's grasp of the idea can be tested in the same way that she was taught—nonverbally—through the use of the most effective of all nonverbal tests: match-to-sample.

As samples, the child is shown two pictures of the "air": in one case filled with particles, in the other case sparkling clean. As alternatives, the child is shown videotapes of falling objects: in one the objects fall at the same speed, in the other they fall at different speeds. Will the child associate objects that fall at the same speed with "clean air," objects that fall at different speeds with "dirty air"?

Animations have the pedagogic force of language. They can *portray* the counterfactual more vividly than language can *describe* it. Rather than use language to explain counterfactual cases to the child, rather than explain in words that there is no friction in a vacuum—we demonstrate the idea.

Animations make it possible to teach science to remarkably young children; and while early instruction is not necessarily desirable in and of itself, it becomes desirable under certain conditions. The use of animations may have the happy result of reducing the number of children who are "put off" by science. How many of the children who find the standard treatment of Galileo forbidding would have the same reaction to the magic vacuum cleaner?

The false intuition that larger objects fall faster than small ones is not the only case in which the child would benefit from the use of education to modify his endowment from evolution. Imitation is another such case. This time we cannot fault evolution; the modern world is the villain.

The child's incredibly well-developed tendency to copy a model was an unqualified boon during the Pleistocene period. Daughters adopted domestic skills by copying their mothers: how to care for an infant, how to scrape a hide, and so on; and sons picked up hunting skills by copying their fathers: how to make arrows, how to track an animal, and so forth. There were few acts carried out by an adult that a child would not have benefited from copying.

Today, the benefit to the child of copying adults is not clearcut. The child who watches TV or movies (and what child does not) is in danger of finding himself squeezing the trigger of a gun—with little understanding of what or why he is doing so. A child may hate another student and/or teacher, possibly with good cause, but (1) if he had not watched TV or (2) evolution had not made him an imitator, he would not be shooting his victim. More likely, he would be hitting the student and shouting at the teacher. But there is far less drama in hitting or shouting than in shooting, and hence they are less likely to appear on TV.

Children have always been shown playful representations that feature violence: cartoons in recent years, Punch and Judy shows in the past. But the characters in these cases—cartoon animals and puppets—do not look like students or teachers. And the violence in which these fanciful figures engage, the exaggerated swats and blows they land on one another, may stimulate not imitation but catharsis—a release from the penchant to carry out violence.

Most children do not realize that they are born imitators and will therefore tend to copy the actions of real-world models. Schools must enlighten the young child; teach him to use this powerful disposition discriminatively, to imitate only appropriate acts and to suppress his tendency to imitate inappropriate ones. This may well require a decision about and training in what is and is not appropriate, but one thing is certain: Essential class time must be given over to this training.

Perhaps we can devise tests that will examine the efficacy of the training. If, in a play situation, a child still picks up a gun and "fires" it at his victim, the training must obviously continue or, better yet, be improved. Presently, we are not experts in how this could be done. How are we to train the suppression of improper imitation, and how to test the efficacy of such training? Tough issues to tackle, certainly, but unavoidable, and very much worth the try.

Lesson Four: The Arts

Evolution has contributed to the arts almost as generously as it has to the sciences. It has given the child not only the music module but a deep aesthetic sense for virtually every phase of human life: the beauty of the face, the grace of movement, the lilt of the voice. In the Athens of Greece's golden age, where some of the earliest true schools were found, aesthetic and academic courses had the same status. Music, music theory, and a special kind of gymnastics emphasizing both body development and graceful movement were standard parts of the curriculum.

Dance

Even though three-year-old toddlers are not adept at movement, they can be taught to dance. Toddlers can walk of course, having started walking two years earlier, but they are not experts at it and their attempts at more complex movements have a comic quality. Film of three-year-olds who are attempting to jump, a movement that is required in both hopping and skipping (which three-year-olds cannot do), show them in a Groucho Marx–like crouch, their shoes seemingly glued to the floor.

Nevertheless, when trained with a combination of models and passive guidance, toddlers soon carry out acceptable hops and skips; and when they do, they are placed in groups of two to four and taught simple dances that combine the movements they have learned. A hop may now lead to a skip, a skip to a walk; two children walk and hop together; move apart; rejoin one another. In other words, the children dance.

After learning simple dances such as these, children will be shown videotapes of their own performances as well as those of others, and asked to judge which are "good and bad." Examples of a "bad dance" can be found in their own earlier performances, as well as in the deliberately inadequate performances of older models. The ability to dance will precede the ability to judge dance. But in time, the child will be able to do both.

No doubt the child's success will not be confined to the acts in which she is explicitly trained, but as all effective learning has demonstrated, the child will transfer her success to a larger set of acts. Toddlers trained to skip, hop, walk (and their combinations) will soon be able to distinguish between the awkward and graceful movements associated with such mundane activities as climbing stairs, brushing teeth, eating meals, ironing clothes, etc. The child's first training in the control of his body may instill a budding sense of self-control that will grow and in time affect all his acts.

Stories

Because children take naturally to "pretend," they are all potential storytellers and can easily be induced to tell stories, especially when provided with imaginative scenes.

Georgie, a small doll, along with a cast of characters—a bird, a ladder, a pair of wings, a kite—are marooned on the moon. The child is asked, "How can Georgie get back to his friends on the earth?" Most three-year-olds will propose a verbal solution, while others may simply place Georgie on the bird and fly him down, carrying out the solution without saying a word.

The children who have simply carried out the solution can be encouraged to comment on the trip by being asked questions such as these:

Was Georgie's trip smooth or bumpy?

Did Georgie get airsick?

Did the bird come right home, or did it stop off for lunch?

Were there close calls with meteors?

Given several opportunities to solve Georgie's problem, children will become increasingly adept with the story. Ultimately they will tell their "Georgie" story without the use of visual aids simply when asked about Georgie. At this point the child has both created a story and memorized it.

But does the child know what a story *is*? While the language module guides the child's acquisition of language it does not "teach" the child what a story is. In general the use of language—to describe a scene, mount an argument, tell a story—is not covered by any module. The child learns these practical topics from experience—in the case of stories by being told stories, by reading them, by forming them himself.

Whether the child has absorbed the idea of "story" can be determined by showing the child a picture-story that has its left-right sequence of pictures out of order. Four-year-old children, shown such a random sequence and asked to describe the individual pictures, are able to give a normal description of the pictures, one that retains the intentions of the characters. Of a picture showing a boy and a dog walking side by side, for example, a four-year-old will say: "The boy is taking a walk with his dog," but the three-year-old child will say "Here is a boy, and over here is a dog"—a description completely lacking in intentional content.

The four-year-old can give a normal description of an out-of-order story because he has a schema, a recipe or mental representation of "story," and can use it to mentally reassemble the pictures into their proper order. But the three-year-old cannot: He does not yet have the story schema, does not yet "know" what a story is.

Combining Dance, Story, and Music

After teaching the children dance and stories we add instruction in music, rhythm, and melody, all of which come naturally to the child thanks to his music module. Then the three artforms are combined and the child is introduced to ballet.

Georgie and Bird are given steps that identify and express their respective characters. Georgie walks and runs while Bird skips and hops. The first unsuccessful efforts by Georgie to mount Bird will be accompanied by sliding sounds from the trombone, and sharp percussion will sound when Georgie actually falls off Bird. The flying trip will be melodic, with violins sparkling as the boy and the bird pass the stars and the Milky Way. When Georgie and Bird land safely on Earth they perform a celebratory pas de deux, to full orchestral crescendo, and Bird brings the house down when, in the course of a pirouette, she fully opens her wings.

The children who participate as dancers (as well as those who sew the costumes, scenery, and so on) will then learn the sweetness of the arts through the jubilant applause of the audience, made up mainly of parents!

Lesson Five: Writing and Reading

While evolution has prepared the child remarkably well, it has not "taught" the child everything she needs to know. Moreover evolution has, in a sense, foiled itself by endowing the human with powerful capacities that enable her to construct systems for which she has no evolutionary preparation.

Reading and writing are such a case; they are based on a symbol system the human has himself invented. Because children have no evolutionary preparation for reading and writing, many find both difficult to learn, and some end up illiterate. This is intolerable because it blocks the child's progress, impairing his ability to acquire information. We cannot hope to cure the problem of illiteracy, but we may be able to mitigate the problem by linking the teaching of reading and writing to speech, a competence for which the child does have evolutionary preparation.

We avoid the standard reading texts (which are the same for all children), and instead invite each child to tell his own story: how he obtained his dog; about his favorite movie; his flu shots; whatever topic provokes the child and leads him to speak spontaneously. The child's speech is recorded and converted into writing, and this personal story then is used to teach the child how to read and write.

The first advantage of this approach is motivational. Children will be interested to see a written version of something they have personally said; it will have a quality similar to listening to one's own voice. More important, when the child produces the sounds herself she will be helped to recognize the equivalence between the sounds and their written version. The equivalence will be recognized first at the level of the words.

The child will hear a word in her own voice and accent and at the same time see the written word that corresponds to what she has said. After experiencing a number of auditory-visual pairings of this kind, the child will begin to decompose individual words and recognize the equivalence between written and spoken syllables. With additional training, the decomposition will go further. The child will recognize the equivalence between the letters and their individual sounds.

Teaching the child to read has this unsuspected benefit: When the child learns to read he begins to understand the "composition" of language. When spoken language, speech, is given a written form, the visual counterpart of the sounds makes the units of speech clear. Illiterate children may not recognize that speech consists of sounds, words, and sentences, and may not recognize that spoken words can be divided into smaller pieces.

Linking speech with writing has the additional advantage of providing an opportunity to improve the child's understanding of a story. As in all uses of language, the construction of a story is not guided by a module but must be learned from experience. In teaching the child to read in this way, the child will tell not one story but several, and the teacher will look for improvement in the structure of the stories. At some point he will compare the child's stories with those of experts, teaching the child what he probably never suspected: that stories have structure.

Writing and speech are simply one case. Fractions and proportions are another. While fractions, like writing, are an invented format and a difficult one for children to learn, proportions are a natural format, one that children—indeed, even chimpanzees—can understand. In this case, too, linking the invented to the natural format will help the children to learn the fractions.

The basic idea of a fraction can be taught to the child by dividing an object into a number of parts equal to that of the denominator in the fraction—eight in the case of $\frac{1}{8}$, six in the case of $\frac{1}{6}$, four in the case of $\frac{1}{4}$, and so on. The child then is shown that the numerator of the fraction equals the number of parts that the numerator successfully "captures" from the denominator—three parts in the case of $\frac{3}{8}$, five in the case of $\frac{5}{8}$, and so on.

A frequent difficulty children have, when learning fractions in the usual way, is their tendency to suppose that, for example, $\frac{1}{4}$ is larger than $\frac{1}{2}$ because 4 is a larger number than 2. When, however, a child is taught to associate $\frac{1}{2}$ with half an apple, and $\frac{1}{4}$ with a quarter of an apple, an error of this kind is not likely to arise.

Analogy is another concept that plays a significant role in the mental development of the child. Analogies too can be taught by linking the concept with a format more natural than the one ordinarily used in schools.

Indeed, sometimes analogies are not taught at all. And if they are, they are taught with the use of words, since words are the natural teaching method for the teacher. But analogies can be understood more immediately by the young child if depicted visually.

Half an apple is to a whole apple as half a loaf of bread is to a whole loaf: there you have an analogy that a three-year old will grasp at a glance; fish is to bowl as dog is to doghouse may require the experience of a four-year old; and grandma is to grandpa as mommy is to daddy, the knowledge of a five-year old. Will a child who is taught analogies in this graphic way benefit? Again, there are no test results. The objective is, of course, not "simply" to introduce (by means of objects or pictures) what could be introduced later on (with words). The objective is to make the child so comfortable and confident in the use of analogies that she will become fluent in their use throughout her life.

A Promising Hand?

The deep characteristics of the human mind, and the historical transformations which these characteristics have undergone, have been examined and analyzed in this book, but not as museum curios. They have been examined in order to gauge the prospects of the species. Did evolution deal the human a promising hand?

The human seems to be no more an inescapable victim of his own savagery than certain events, which mar human history, are an ineluctable part of human destiny. For example, one can picture religion without crusades. Eastern religions especially tell a hopeful story with regard to crusades. Eastern religions have never had the competitiveness or the political streak of Western religions. The crusades and competitiveness seemingly inherent to Western religion are not reflections of innate features of human religious experience; rather, they are simply peculiarities of Western religion. The view we take therefore is that ignorance, not savagery, is our problem. Ignorance of who we are.

We humans must decipher our own complexity alone. It would be marvelous if we could contact qualified parties from elsewhere, exchange views of each other's mind, and speed up the process of understanding in all parties. But we are alone. There are no other problem-solving groups to be found.

Yet the human capacity for problem-solving is extraordinary. For the past twenty years or so humans have finally turned their problem-solving capacity on themselves rather than on other bodies (quarks, neutrons, genes, and so forth), and have begun to clarify both the neural processes and the mental capacities of their own minds. Slowly, and not yet surely, we are beginning to understand who we are, not in the sense of a philosophical treatise but in the sense of science; the only sense, so far as we can see, in which we can hope to defeat the ignorance that is our real enemy. We are now making serious progress in peeling away this ignorance, as this book has shown.

Bibliography

Introduction

Cashdan, E. (1980) Egalitarianism among hunters and gatherers. *American Anthropologist*, 82:116–120.

Conroy, G. C. (1997) *Reconstructing Human Origins: A Modern Synthesis*. New York: W. W. Norton.

Enard, W., Khaitovich, P., Klose, J., Zollner, S., Heissig, F., Giavalisco, P., Niselt-Struwe, K., Muchmore, E., Varki, A., Ravid, R., Doxiadis, G. M., Bontrop, R. E., and Paabo, S. (2000) Intra- and interspecific variation in primate gene expression patterns. *Science*, 296:340–344.

Englesberg, E., Irtr, J., Power, J., and Lee, N. (1999) Positive control of enzyme synthesis by gene C in the L-arabnose system. In W. K. Joklin, L. G. Ljungdahl, A. D. O'Brien, A. von Graevenitz, and C. Yanofsky, eds., *Microbiology: A Century Perspective*. Washington, D.C.: ASM Press.

Gelb, I. J. (1963) *A Study of Writing*. Chicago: University of Chicago Press.

Goodall, J. (1986) *The Chimpanzees of Gombe*. Cambridge, MA: Harvard University Press.

Gould, R. A. (1971) Uses and effects of fire among the Western Desert aborigines of Australia. *Mankind*, 8:14–24.

Holloway, R. L. (1995) Toward a synthetic theory of human brain evolution. In J.-P. Changeux and J. Chavaillon, eds., *Origins of the Human Brain*, pp. 42–54. New York: Oxford University Press.

Ingold, T. (1988) Tools, minds and machines: An excursion in the philosophy of technology. *Technological Culture*, 12:151–176.

Jerison, H. J. (1973) *Evolution of Brain and Intelligence*. New York: Academic Press.

Kaplan, H., and Hill, K. (1986) Food-sharing among Ache foragers: Tests of explanatory hypotheses. *Current Anthropology*, 26:233–245.

King, M. C., and Wilson, A. C. (1975) Evolution at two levels in humans and chimpanzees. *Science*, 188:107–116.

Kitto, H. D. F. (1951) *The Greeks*. London: Hammonds-Worth (Penguin Books).

Leakey, R., and Lewin, R. (1992) *Origins Reconsidered: In search of What Makes Us Human*. Boston: Little Brown.

Lee, R. B., and DeVore, I., eds. (1976) *Kalahari Hunter-Gatherers*. Cambridge: Harvard University Press.

Mauss, M. (1925/1967) *The Gift: Forms and Functions of Exchange in Archaic Societies*, I. Cunnison, trans. New York: Norton.

Pilbeam, D. (1992) What makes a human? In S. Jones, R. Martin, and D. Pilbeam, eds., *The Cambridge Encyclopedia of Human Evolution*, pp. 1–5. Cambridge: Cambridge University Press.

Sampson, G. (1985) *Writing Systems*. Stanford: Stanford University Press.

Straus, W. L., and Cave, A. J. E. (1957) Pathology and the posture of Neanderthal man. *Quarterly Review of Biology*, 32:348–363.

Tobias, Philip V. (1995) The Brain of the first hominids. In J.-P. Changeux and J. Chavaillon, eds., *Origins of the Human Brain*, pp. 61–81. New York: Oxford University Press.

Trehub, S. E. (1987) Infants' perception of musical patterns. *Perception and Psychophysics*, 41:635–641.

Trehub, S. E., and Trainor, L. J. (1993) Listening strategies in infancy: The roots of music and language development. In S. McAdams and E. Bigand, eds., *Thinking in Sound: The Cognitive Psychology of Human Audition*, pp. 278–327. Oxford: Clarendon Press.

Walker, A. (1993) The origin of the genus *Homo*. In D. T. Rasmussen, ed., *The Origin and Evolution of Humans and Humanness*, pp. 29–47. Boston: Jones & Bartlett.

Chapter 1

Atran, S. (1985) The nature of folkbotanical life-forms. *American Anthropologist* 87:298–315.

Atran, S. (1990) *Cognitive Foundations of Natural History: Towards an Anthropology of Science*. New York: Cambridge University Press.

Baillargeon, R. (1986) Representing the existence and the location of hidden objects: Object permanence in 6- and 8-month old infants. *Cognition*, 23:21–41.

Baillargeon, R., Spelke, E. S., and Wasserman, S. (1985) Object permanence in five-month-old infants. *Cognition*, 20:191–208.

Barkow, J., Cosmides, L., and Tooby, J., eds. (1992) *The Adapted Mind: Evolutionary Psychology and the Generation of Culture*. New York: Oxford University Press.

Blakemore, C. (1974) Developmental factors in the formation of feature-extracting neurons. In F. O. Schmitt and F. G. Worden, eds., *The Neurosciences: Third Study Program*. Cambridge, MA: MIT Press.

Boysen, S. T., and Berntson, G. G. (1989) Numerical competence in a chimpanzee (*Pan troglodytes*). *Journal of Comparative Psychology*, 103:23–31.

Brown, A. (1990) Domain-specific principles affect learning and transfer in children. *Cognitive Science*, 14:107–133.

Carey, S. (1985) *Conceptual Change in Childhood*. New York: Cambridge University Press.

Carey, S. (1988) Conceptual differences between children and adults. *Mind and Language*, 3:167–181.

Carey, S., and Spelke, E. S. (1994) Domain specific knowledge and conceptual change. In L. A. Hirschfield and S. A. Gelman, eds., *Domain Specificity in Cognition and Culture*, pp. 169–200. New York: Cambridge University Press.

Cheng, K. (1986) A purely geometric module in the rat's spatial representation. *Cognition*, 23:149–178.

Chomsky, N. (1965) *Aspects of a Theory of Syntax*. Cambridge, MA: MIT Press.

Chomsky, N. (1980) *Rules and Representations*. New York: Columbia University Press.

D'Amato, M. R. (1988) A search for tonal pattern perception in cebus monkeys: Why monkeys can't learn to hum a tune. *Music Perception*, 5:453–480.

Dasser, V., Ulbaek, I., and Premack, D. (1989). Perception of intention. *Science*, 243:365–367.

Dehaene, S. (1992) Varieties of numerical abilities. *Cognition*, 44(1–2):1–42.

Fernald, A. (1985) Four-month-old infants prefer to listen to motherese. *Infant Behavior and Development*, 8:181–195.

Fernald, A. (1989) Intonation and communicative intent: Is melody the message? *Child Development*, 60:1497–1510.

Fodor, J. A. (1983) *The Modularity of Mind*. Cambridge, MA: MIT Press.

Gelman, R. (1990) First principles organize attention to and learning about relevant data: Number and the animate-inanimate distinction as examples. *Cognitive Science*, 14:79–106.

Gelman, R., and Gallistel, C. (1978) *The Child's Understanding of Number*. Cambridge: Harvard University Press.

Gelman, S. A., and Wellman, H. M. (1991) Insides and essences: Early understandings of the nonobvious. *Cognition*, 38:213–244.

Gibbon, J., Church, R. M., and Meck, W. H. (1984) Scalar timing in memory. In J. Gibbon and L. Allan, eds., *Timing and Time Perception*, pp. 52–77. New York: New York Academy of Sciences.

Ginsburg, H. (1977). *Children's Arithmetic: The Learning Process*. New York: Van Nostrand.

Gleitman, L., Newport, E., and Gleitman, H. (1984) The current status of the motherese hypothesis. *Journal of Child Language*, 11:43–79.

Heider, F., and Simmel, M. (1944) An experimental study of apparent behavior. *American Journal of Psychology*, 57:243–259.

Hermer, L., and Spelke, E. S. (1996) Modularity and development: The case of spatial reorientation, *Cognition*, 61:195–232.

Hirschfeld, L. A. (1995) Do children have a theory of race? *Cognition*, 54:209–252.

Hirschfeld, L. A. (1996) *Race in the Making*. Cambridge: MIT Press.

Hulse, S. H., and Page, S. C. (1988) Toward a comparative psychology of music perception. *Music Perception*, 5:427–452.

Karmiloff-Smith, A., and Inhelder, B. (1975) If you want to get ahead, get a theory. *Cognition*, 3:195–211.

Keil, F. C. (1989) *Concepts, Kinds, and Cognitive Development*. Cambridge, MA: MIT Press.

Keil, F. C. (1992) The origins of an autonomous biology. In M. R. Gunnar and M. Maratsos, eds., *Minnesota Symposium on Child Psychology*, pp. 103–138. Hillsdale, NJ: Erlbaum.

Keil, F. C. (1994) The birth and nurturance of concepts by domains: The origins of concepts of living things. In L. Hirschfeld and S. Gelman, eds., *Mapping the Mind: Domain Specificity in Cognition and Culture*, pp. 234–254. New York: Cambridge University Press.

Kellman, P. J., and Spelke, E. S. (1983) Perception of partly occluded objects in infancy. *Cognitive Psychology*, 15:483–524.

Kotovsky, L., and Baillargeon, R. (1994) Calibration-based reasoning about collision events in 11-month-old infants. *Cognition*, 51:107–129.

Krumhansl, C. L., and Jusczyk, P. W. (1990) Infants' perception of phrase structure in music. *Psychological Science*, 1:1–4.

Krumhansl, C. L., and Keil, F. C. (1982) Acquisition of the hierarchy of tonal functions in music. *Memory and Cognition*, 10:243–251.

Kummer, H., and Cords, M. (1991) Cues of ownership in long-tailed macaques. *Macaca fasciularis. Animal Behaviour*, 42:529–549.

Leslie, A. M. (1987) Pretense and representation: The origins of "theory of mind." *Psychological Review*, 94:412–426.

Leslie, A. M. (1995) A theory of agency. In D. Sperber, D. Premack, and A. J. Premack, eds., *Causal Cognition*, pp. 121–141. New York: Oxford University Press.

Lettvin, J. Y., Maturana, R. R., McCulloch, W. S., and Pitts, W. H. (1959) What the frog's eye tells the frog's brain. *Proceedings of the Institute of Radio Engineering*, 47:1940–1951.

Mandler, J. M. (1992) How to build a baby: II. Conceptual primitives. *Psychological Review*, 99:587–604.

Matsuzawa, T. (1985) Use of numbers by a chimpanzee. *Nature*, 315, 57–59.

Needham, A., and Baillargeon, R. (1993) Intuitions about support in 4.5-month-old infants. *Cognition*, 47:121–148.

Pinker, S., and Bloom, P. (1990) Natural language and natural selection. *Behavioral and Brain Sciences*, 13:707–784.

Premack, D. (1990) The infant's theory of self-propelled objects. *Cognition*, 36:1–16.

Premack, D., and Premack, A. J. (1994) Moral belief: Form versus content. In L. A. Hirschfeld and S. A. Gelman, eds., *Mapping the Mind: Domain Specificity in Cognition and Culture*, pp. 149–168. New York: Cambridge University Press.

Premack, D., and Premack, A. J. (1995). Origins of human social competence. In M. S. Gazzaniga, ed., *The Cognitive Neurosciences*, pp. 205–218. Cambridge: MIT Press.

Premack, D. and Premack, A. J. (1997) Infants attribute value +/− to the goal-directed actions of self-propelled objects. *Journal of Cognitive Neuroscience*, 9(6):848–856.

Restle, F. (1970) Speed of adding and comparing numbers. *Journal of Experimental Psychology*, 83:274–278.

Rozin, P. (1976) The evolution of intelligence and access to the cognitive unconscious. In J. M. Sprague and A. N. Epstein, eds., *Progress in Psychobiology and Physiological Psychology*. New York: Academic Press.

Smith, M. C. (1978) Cognizing the behavior stream: The recognition of intentional action. *Child Development*, 49:736–743.

Spelke, E. S. 1988 The origins of physical knowledge. In L. Weiskrantz, ed., *Thought without Language*, pp. 168–184. Oxford: Clarendon.

Spelke, E. S., Breinlinger, K., Macomber, J., and Jacobson, K. (1992) Origins of knowledge. *Psychological Review*, 99:605–632.

Sperber, D. (1985) Anthropology and psychology: Towards an epidemiology of representations (the Malinowski Memorial Lecture 1984), *Man*, 20:73–89.

Sperber, D. (1993) The modularity of thought and the epidemiology of representations. In L. Hirschfeld and S. Gelman, eds., *Mapping the Mind: Domain Specificity in Cognition and Culture*. New York: Cambridge University Press.

Tooby, J., and Cosmides, L. (1989) Evolutionary psychology and the generation of culture: I. Theoretical considerations. *Ethology and Sociobiology*, 10:29–49.

Trehub, S. E. (1987) Infants' perception of musical patterns. *Perception and Psychophysics*, 41:635–641.

Trehub, S. E., and Trainor, L. J. (1993) Listening strategies in infancy: The roots of music and language development. In S. McAdams and E. Bigand, eds., *Thinking in Sound: The Cognitive Psychology of Human Audition*, pp. 278–327. Oxford: Clarendon Press.

Von Uexküll, J. (1957) A walk through the world of animals and man. In C. Schiller, ed., *Instinctive Behavior*. New York: International Universities Press.

Wynn, K. (1992) Addition and subtraction by human infants. *Nature*, 358:749–750.

Chapter 2

Galef, B. G. Jr. (1988) Imitation in animals: History, definitions, and interpretation of data from the psychological laboratory. In T. Zentall and B. G. Galef, eds., *Social Learning: Psychological and Biological Perspectives*, pp. 3–28. Hillsdale: Lawrence Erlbaum.

Hayes, K. J., and Hayes, C. (1952) Imitation in a home-raised chimpanzee. *Journal of Comparative and Physiological Psychology*, 45:450–459.

Heyes, C. M., Jaldow, E., Nokes, T., and Dawson, G. R. (1994) Imitation in rats: Conditions of occurrence in a bi-directional control procedure. *Learning and Motivation*, 25:276–287.

Inoue-Nakamura, N., and Matsuzawa, T. (1997) Development of stone tool-use by wild chimpanzees (*Pan troglodytes*). *Journal of Comparative Psychology*, 111(2):159–173.

Kohler, W. (1925) *The Mentality of Apes*. New York: Liveright.

Meltzoff, A. N., and Moore, M. K. (1977) Imitation of facial and manual gestures by human neonates. *Science*, 198:75–78.

Meltzoff, A. N., and Moore, M. K. (1983) Newborn infants imitate adult facial gestures. *Child Development*, 54:702–709.

Meltzoff, A. N., and Moore, M. K. (1992) Early imitation within a functional framework: The importance of person identity, movement, and development. *Infant Behavior and Development*, 15:479–505.

Moore, B. R. (1992) Avian movement imitation and a new form of mimicry: Tracing the evolution of a complex form of learning. *Behavior*, 122:231–263.

Munn, N. (1974) *Walbiri Iconography*. Ithaca, NY: Cornell University Press.

Myowa, M. (1996) Imitation of facial gestures by an infant chimpanzee. *Primates*, 37:207–213.

Myowa-Yamakoshi, M., and Matsuzawa, T. (1999) Factors influencing imitation of manipulatory actions in chimpanzees (*Pan troglodytes*). *Journal of Comparative Psychology*, 113(2):128–136.

Perrett, D. I., Smith, P. A., Mistlin, A. J., Chitty, A. S., Head, D. D., Potter, R., Broenninmann, K., Milner, A. D., and Jeeves, M. A. (1985) Visual analysis of body movements by neurones in the temporal cortex of the macaque monkey: A preliminary report. *Behavioral Brain Research*, 16:153–170.

Piaget, J. (1962) *Play, Dreams and Imitation in Childhood.* New York: Norton.

Premack, D. (1975) Putting a face together. *Science*, 188:228–236.

Premack, D. (1976) *Intelligence in Ape and Man.* Hillsdale, NJ: Erlbaum Associates.

Premack, D. (1988) Minds with and without language. In L. Weiskrantz, ed., *Thought without Language.* Oxford: Clarendon Press.

Premack, D., and Premack, A. J. (1974) Teaching visual language to apes and language-deficient persons. In R. L. Schiefelbusch and L. L. Lloyd, eds., *Language Perspectives: Acquisition, Retardation and Intervention.* Baltimore: University Park Press.

Rizolati, G., Fadiga, L., Gallese, V., and Fogassi, L. (1996) Premotor cortex and the recognition of motor actions. *Cognitive Brain Research*, 3:131–141.

Tomasello, M., Savage-Rumbaugh, S., and Kruger, A. C. (1993). Imitative learning of actions on objects by children, chimpanzees, and enculturated chimpanzees. *Child Development*, 64:1688–1705.

Whiten, A., and Custance, D. (1996) Studies of imitation in chimpanzees and children. In C. M. Heyes and B. G. Galif, Jr., eds., *Social Learning in Animals: The Roots of Culture*, pp. 291–318. San Diego: Academic Press.

Whiten, A., Custance, D. M., Gomez, J.-C., Teixidor, P., and Bard, K. A. (1996) Imitative learning of artificial fruit processing in children (*Homo sapiens*) and chimpanzees (*Pan troglodytes*). *Journal of Comparative Psychology*, 110:3–14.

Chapter 3

Barnett, S. A. (1973) *Homo docens. Journal of Biosocial Science*, 5:393–403.

Berscheid, E., and Walster, E. (1969) *Interpersonal Attraction.* Reading, MA: Addison-Wesley.

Berscheid, E. and Walster, E. (1974) Physical attractiveness. In L. Berkowitz, ed., *Advances in Experimental Social Psychology*, vol. 7. Reading, MA: Academic Press.

Berscheid, E., and Walster, E. (1978) *Interpersonal Attraction.* Reading, MA: Addison-Wesley.

Boesch, C. (1991) Teaching among wild chimpanzees. *Animal Behaviour*, 41:530–532.

Caro, T. M. (1980) Effects of the mother, object play and adult experience on predation in cats. *Behavioral and Neural Biology*, 29:29–51.

Caro, T. M., and Hauser, M. D. (1992) Is there teaching in nonhuman animals? *Quarterly Review of Biology*, 67:151–174.

Child, I. L., and Siroto, L. (1965) BaKwele and American esthetic evaluations compared. *Ethnology*, 4:349–360.

Dixon, K. K. (1972) Physical attractiveness and evaluations of children's transgressions. *Journal of Personality and Social Psychology*, 24:207–213.

Dixon, K. K. (1973) Young children's stereotyping of facial attractiveness. *Developmental Psychology*, 9:183–188.

Dixon, K. K., and Berscheid, E. (1974) Physical attractiveness and peer perception among children. *Sociometry*, 37:1–12.

Dixon, K. K., Berscheid, E., and Walster, E. (1972) What is beautiful is good. *Journal of Personality and Social Psychology*, 24:285–290.

Ford, C. S., Prothro, E. T., and Child, I. L. (1966) Some transcultural comparisons of esthetic judgment. *Journal of Social Psychology*, 68:19–26.

Fouts, R. S., Fouts, D. H., and Van Cantfort, T. E. (1989) The infant Loulis learns signs from cross-fostered chimpanzees. In R. A. Gardner, B. T. Gardner, and T. E. Van Cantfort, eds., *Teaching Sign Language to Chimpanzees*. New York: SUNY Press.

Inoue-Nakamura, N., and Matsuzawa, T. (1997) Development of stone tool-use by wild chimpanzees (*Pan troglodytes*). *Journal of Comparative Psychology*, 111(2):159–173.

Iwao, S., and Child, I. L. (1966) Comparison of esthetic judgments by American experts and by Japanese potters. *Journal of Social Psychology*, 68:27–33.

Lawlor, M. (1955) Cultural influences on preferences for designs. *Journal of Abnormal and Social Psychology*, 61:690–692.

Leyhausen, P. (1979) *Cat Behavior: The Predator and Social Behavior of Domestic and Wild Cats*. London: Garland.

McElroy, W. A. (1952) Aesthetic appreciation in aborigines of Arnhem Land: A comparative experimental study. *Oceania*, 23:81–94.

Manning, J. T., and Hartley, M. A. (1991) Symmetry and ornamentation are correlated in the peacock's train. *Animal Behavior*, 42:1020–1021.

Møller, A. P. (1990) Fluctuating asymmetry in male sexual ornaments may reveal male quality. *Animal Behavior*, 40:1185–1187.

Møller, A. P., Soler, M., and Thornhill, R. (1995) Breast asymmetry, sexual selection and human reproductive success. *Ethological Sociobiology*, 16:207–219.

Perrett, D. I., May, K. A., and Yoshikawa, S. (1994) Facial shape and judgements of female attractiveness. *Nature*, 368:239–242.

Premack, D. (1984) Pedagogy and aesthetics as sources of culture. In M. S. Gazzaniga, ed., *Handbook of Cognitive Neuroscience*. New York: Plenum Press.

Premack, D. (1991) The aesthetic basis of pedagogy. In R. R. Hoffman and D. S. Palermo, eds., *Cognition and the Symbolic Processes*. Hillsdale, NJ: Erlbaum.

Rogoff, B. (1989) *Children as Apprentices in Thinking*. New York: Oxford University Press.

Samuels, G., and Ewy, T. M. (1985) Aesthetic preference of faces during infancy. *British Journal of Developmental Psychology*, 3:221–228.

Schiller, J. C. F. (1882) *Essays, Esthetical and Philosophical, Including the Dissertation on the "Connexions between the Animal and the Spiritual in Man."* London: G. Bell.

Scutt, D., Manning, J. T., Whitehouse, G. H., Leinster, S. J., and Massey, C. P. (1997) The relationship between breast asymmetry, breast size and the occurrence of breast cancer. *British Journal of Radiology*, 70:1017–1021.

Thornhill, R. (1992) Female preference of the pheromone of males with low fluctuating asymmetry in the Japanese scorpionfly (*Panorpa japonica*). *Behavioral Ecology*, 3:277–283.

Thornhill, R., and Gagestad, S. W. (1993). Human facial beauty: Averageness, symmetry, and parasite resistance. *Human Nature*, 4:237–270.

Chapter 4

Boroditsky, L. (1998) Evidence for metaphoric representation: Understanding time. In K. Holyoak, D. Gentner, and B. Kokinov, eds., *Advances in Analogy Research: Integration of Theory and Data from the Cognitive, Computational, and Neural Sciences*. Sofia: New Bulgarian University Press.

Boroditsky, L. (2000) Metaphoric structuring: Understanding time through spatial metaphors. *Cognition*, 75(1):1–28.

Boroditsky, L. (2001) Does language shape thought? Mandarin and English speakers' conception of time. *Cognitive Psychology*, 43(1):1–22.

Gentner, D., and Imai, M. (1997) A cross-linguistic study of early word meaning: Universal ontology and linguistic influence. *Cognition*, 62(2):169–200.

Gleitman, L. R. (1990) The structural source of verb meaning. *Language Acquisition*, 1:3–55.

Goldin-Meadow, S. (1979) Structure in a manual communication system developed without a conventional language model: Language without a helping hand. In H. A. Whitaker, ed., *Studies in Neurolinguistics*, vol. 4. New York: Academic Press.

Hurford, J. R. (1989) Biological evolution of the Saussurean sign as a component of the language acquisition device. *Lingua*, 77:187–222.

Imai, M., and Gentner, D. (1997) A cross-linguistic study of early word meaning: Universal ontology and linguistic influence. *Cognition*, 62:169–200.

Jusczyk, P. W. (1993) Infants' sensitivity to the sound patterns of native language words. *Journal of Memory and Language*, 32:402–420.

Jusczyk, P. W., Hirsh-Pasek, K., Kemler Nelson, D. G., Kennedy, L., Woodward, A., and Piwoz, J. (1992) Perception of acoustic correlates of major phrasal units by young infants. *Cognitive Psychology*, 24:252–293.

Jusczyk, P. W., Luce, P. A., and Charles Luce, J. (1994) Infants' sensitivity to phonotactic patterns in the native language. *Journal of Memory and Language*, 33:630–645.

Levelt, W. J. M. (1989) *Speaking: From Intention to Articulation*. Cambridge, MA: MIT Press.

Levinson, S. (1996) Relativity in spatial conception and description. In J. Gumperz and S. Levinson, eds., *Rethinking Linguistic Relativity*. New York: Cambridge University Press.

Levinson, S. C. (1994) Vision, shape and linguistic description: Tzeltal body-part terminology and object description. In J. B. Haviland and S. C. Levinson, eds., *Special issue of Linguistics*, 32(4):791–855. Berlin: Mouton de Gruyter.

Lubbock, John (1884) Teaching animals to converse. *Nature*, 547–548.

Lucy, J. A. (1992) *Grammatical Categories and Cognition: A Case Study of the Linguistic Relativity Hypothesis*. Cambridge, England: Cambridge University Press.

Pinker, S. (1989) *The Learnability of Argument Structure*. Cambridge, MA: MIT Press.

Sapir, Edward (1921) *Language: An Introduction to the Study of Speech*. New York: Harcourt, Brace & World.

Smiley, S. S., and Brown, A. L. (1979) Conceptual preference for thematic or taxo-
    nomic relations: A nonmonotonic age trend from preschool to old age. *Journal of
    Experimental Child Psychology*, 28:249–257.
Waters, R. S., and Wilson, W. A., Jr. (1976) Speech perception by rhesus monkeys:
    The voicing distinction in synthesized labial and velar stop consonants. *Perception
    and Psychophysics*, 19:285–289.
Whorf, B. (1956) *Language, Thought and Reality: Selected Writings of Benjamin Lee
    Whorf*, J. B. Carroll, ed. Cambridge, MA: MIT Press.

Chapter 5

Baldwin, D. A. (1991) Infants' contribution to the achievement of joint reference.
    Child Development, 62:875–890.
Baldwin, D. A. (1993) Infants' ability to consult the speaker for clues to word refer-
    ence. *Journal of Child Language*, 20:395–418.
Butterworth, G., and Grover, L. (1988) The origins of referential communication in
    human infancy. In L. Weiskrantz, ed., *Thought without Language*, pp. 5–24.
    Oxford: Clarendon Press.
Cheney, D. L., and Seyfarth, R. M. (1988) Assessment of meaning and the detection
    of unreliable signals by vervet monkeys. *Animal Behavior*, 36:477–486.
Cheney, D. L., and Seyfarth, R. M. (1988) *How Monkeys See the World: Inside the
    Mind of Another Species*. Chicago: Chicago University Press.
Christophe, A., Dupoux, E., Bertoncini, J., and Mehler, J. (1994) Do infants perceive
    word boundaries? An empirical study of the bootstrapping of lexical acquisition.
    Journal of the Acoustic Society of America, 95:1570–1580.
Dooling, R. J., and Brown, S. D. (1990) Speech perception by budgerigars (*Melopsit-
    tacus undulatus*): Spoken vowels. *Perceptual Psychology*, 47:568–574.
Dooling, R. J., Okanoya, K., and Brown, S. D. (1989) Speech perception by budgeri-
    gars (*Melopsittacus undulatus*): The voiced-voiceless distinction. *Perceptual Psy-
    chology*, 46:65–71.
Gelman, S. A., and Ebeling, K. S. (1998) Shape and representational status in chil-
    drens' early naming. *Cognition*, 66:35–47.
Goldin-Meadow, S. (1982) The resilience of recursion: A study of a communication
    system developed without a conventional language model. In E. Wanner and L. R.
    Gleitman, eds., *Language Acquisition: The State of the Art*, pp. 51–77. Cambridge:
    Cambridge University Press.
Greenfield, P. M. (1991) Language, tools and brain: The ontogeny and phylogeny of
    hierarchically organized sequential behavior. *Behavioral and Brain Sciences*,
    14:531–595.
Hauser, M. D. (1993) Do vervet monkey infants cry wolf? *Animal Behavior*,
    45:1242–1244.
Hauser, M. D. (1996) *The Evolution of Communication*. Cambridge: MIT Press.
Hauser, M. D., and Marler, P. (1993) Food-associated calls in rhesus macaques
    (*Macaca mulatta*): I. Socioecological factors influencing call production. *Behav-
    ioral Ecology*, 4:194–205.
Herman, L. M., Richards, D. G., and Wolz, J. P. (1984) Comprehension of sentences
    by bottlenosed dolphins. *Cognition*, 16:129–219.

Hoffman, D. D., and Richards, W. A. (1984) Parts of recognition. *Cognition*, 18:65–96.

Kuhl, P. K. (1981) Discrimination of speech by nonhuman animals: Basic auditory sensitivities conducive to the perception of speech-sound categories. *Journal of the Acoustical Society of America*, 70:340–349.

Kuhl, P. K., and Miller, J. D. (1975) Speech perception by the chinchilla: Voiced-voiceless distinction in alveolar plosive consonants. *Science*, 190:69–72.

Landau, B., Smith, L. B., and Jones, S. S. (1988) The importance of shape in early lexical learning. *Cognitive Development*, 3:299–321.

Macnamara, J. (1982) *Names for Things*. Cambridge, MA: MIT Press.

Markman, E. M., and Hutchinson, J. E. (1984) Children's sensitivity to constraints on word meaning: Taxonomic vs thematic relations. *Cognitive Psychology*, 16:1–27.

Miller, G. A. (1956) The magical number seven, plus or minus two: Some limits on our capacity for processing information. *Psychological Review*, 63:81–97.

Miller, G. A. (1981) *Language and Speech*. San Francisco: W. H. Freeman.

Premack, D. (1976) *Intelligence in Ape and Man*. Hillsdale, NJ: Erlbaum.

Premack, D. (1990) Words: What are they, and do animals have them? *Cognition* 37:197–212.

Ramus, F., Hauser, M. D., Miller, C. T., Morris, D., and Mehler, J. (2000) Language discrimination by human newborns and cotton-top tamarin monkeys. *Science*, 288:349–351.

Rescorla, R. A. (1980) *Pavlovian Second-Order Conditioning: Studies in Associative Learning*. Hillsdale, NJ: Erlbaum.

Rescorla, R. A. (1987) A Pavlovian analysis of goal-directed behavior. *American Psychologist*, 42:119–129.

Saffran, J. R., Aslin, R. N., and Newport, E. L. (1996) Statistical learning by 8-month-old infants. *Science*, 274:1926–1928.

Savage-Rumbaugh, S., Seveik, R. A., Brakke, K. E., and Rumbaugh, D. M. (1995) *Symbols: Their Communicative Use, Comprehension, and Combination by Bonobos (Pan paniscus)*. Monographs of the Society for Research in Child Development.

Skinner, B. F. (1935) The generic nature of the concepts of stimulus and response. *Journal of General Psychology*, 12:40–65.

Smith, L. B., Jones, S. S., and Landau, B. (1996) Naming in young children: A dumb attentional mechanism? *Cognition* 60, 143–171.

Soja, N. N., Carey, S., and Spelke, E. (1991) Ontological categories guide young children's inductions of word meaning: Object terms and substance terms. *Cognition*, 38:179–211.

Struhsaker, T. T. (1967) Auditory communication among vervet monkeys. In S. A. Altman, ed., *Social Communication among Primates*. Chicago: University of Chicago Press.

Tulving, E., and Thomson, D. M. (1973) Encoding specificity and retrieval processes in episodic memory. *Psychological Review*, 80:352–373.

Woodruff, G., and Premack, D. (1979) Intentional communication in chimpanzee: The development of deception. *Cognition*, 12:289–301.

Chapter 6

Baker, L. R. (1991) Dretske on the explanatory role of belief. *Philosophical Studies*, 63:99–111.

Boyer, P. (1993) *The Naturalness of Religious Ideas.* Berkeley: University of California Press.

Dretske, F. (1991) How beliefs explain: Reply to Baker. *Philosophical Studies,* 63:113–117.

Georgopoulos, A. P. (1991) Higher order motor control. *Annual Review of Neurosciences,* 14:361–377.

Chapter 7

Astington, J. W., Harris, P. L., and Olson, D. R., eds. (1988) *Developing Theories of Mind.* New York: Cambridge University Press.

Baron-Cohen, S. (1995) *Mindblindness. An Essay on Autism.* Cambridge, MA: MIT Press.

Baron-Cohen, S., Leslie, A. M., and Frith, U. (1985) Does the autistic child have a "theory of mind"? *Cognition,* 21:37–46.

Bennett, J. (1978) Some remarks about concepts. *Behavioral and Brain Sciences,* 1:557–560.

Brothers, L., and Ring, B. (1992) A neuroethological framework for the representation of minds. *Journal of Cognitive Neuroscience,* 4:107–118.

Cheney, D. L., and Seyfarth, R. M. (1990) Attending to behaviour versus attending to knowledge: Examining monkeys' attribution of mental states. *Animal Behaviour,* 40:742–753.

Churchland, P. S., and Churchland, P. M. (1978) Internal states and cognitive theories. *Behavioral and Brain Sciences,* 1:565–566.

Dennett, D. C. (1978) Beliefs about beliefs. *Behavioral and Brain Sciences,* 1:568–570.

Flavell, J. H. (1988) The development of children's knowledge about the mind: From cognitive connections to mental representations. In J. Astington, P. Harris, and D. Olson, eds., *Developing Theories of Mind,* pp. 244–267. New York: Cambridge University Press.

Flavell, J. H., Everett, B. A., Croft, K., and Flavell, E. R. (1981) Young children's knowledge about visual perception: Further evidence for the level 1-level 2 distinction. *Developmental Psychology,* 17:99–103.

Harmon, Gilbert (1978) Studying the chimpanzee's theory of mind. *Behavioral and Brain Sciences,* 1:576–577.

Leslie, A. M. (1987) Pretense and representation: The origins of "theory of mind." *Psychological Review,* 94:412–426.

Leslie, A. M. (1988) The necessity of illusion: Perception and thought in infancy. In L. Weiskrantz, ed., *Thought without Language.* Oxford: Oxford Science Publications.

Leslie, A. M. (1995) A theory of agency. In D. Sperber, D. Premack, and A. Premack, eds., *Causal Cognition: A Multidisciplinary Debate,* pp. 121–142. Oxford: Oxford University Press.

Lewis, D. (1969) *Convention: A Philosophical Study.* Cambridge, MA: Harvard University Press.

Perner, J. (1991) *Understanding the Representational Mind.* Cambridge, MA: Bradford/MIT Press.

Plooij, F. X. (1978) Some basic traits of language in wild chimpanzees? In A. Lock, ed., *Action, Gesture and Symbol.* New York: Academic Press.

Povinelli, D. J., and Eddy, T. J. (1996). What young chimpanzees know about seeing. *Monographs of the Society for Research in Child Development*, 61, serial no. 247.

Premack, D. (1988). "Does the chimpanzee have a theory of mind?" revisited. In W. Byrne and A. Whiten, eds., *Machiavellian Intelligence: Social Expertise and the Evolution of Intellect in Monkeys, Apes and Humans*, pp. 286–322. New York: Oxford University Press.

Premack, D., and Woodruff, G. (1978) Does the chimpanzee have a theory of mind? *Behavioral and Brain Sciences*, 4:515–526.

Pylyshyn, Z. W. (1978) When is attribution of beliefs justified? *Behavioral Brain Science*, 1:592–593.

Sperber, D., and Wilson, D. (1986) *Relevance: Communication and Cognition*. Cambridge, MA: MIT Press.

Wellman, H. M. (1990) *The Child's Theory of Mind*. Cambridge, MA: MIT Press.

Wimmer, H., and Perner, J. (1983) Beliefs about beliefs: Representation and constraining function of wrong beliefs in young children's understanding of deception. *Cognition*, 13:103–128.

Chapter 8

Bullock, M. (1979) Aspects of the young child's theory of causation. Unpublished doctoral dissertation, University of Pennsylvania.

Bullock, M., Gelman, R., and Baillargeon, R. (1982). The development of causal reasoning. In W. J. Friedman, ed., *The Developmental Psychology of Time*. New York: Academic Press.

Cheng, P. W. (1993) Separating causal laws from casual facts: Pressing the limits of statistical relevance. In D. L. Medin, ed., *The Psychology of Learning and Motivation*, vol. 30. New York: Academic Press.

Cheng, P. W., and Novick, L. R. (1991) Causes versus enabling conditions. *Cognition*, 40:83–120.

Cohen, L. B., and Oakes, L. M. (1993) How infants perceive a simple causal event. *Developmental Psychology*, 29:421–433.

DeLoache, J. S. (1989) Young children's understanding of the correspondence between a scale model and a larger space. *Cognitive Development*, 4:121–139.

Dickinson, A., and Shanks, D. (1995) Instrumental action and causal representation. In D. Sperber, D. Premack, and A. J. Premack, eds., *Causal Cognition*, pp. 5–25. New York: Oxford University Press.

Gelman, S. A., and Kremer, K. E. (1991) Understanding natural cause: Children's explanations of how objects and their properties originate. *Child Development*, 62:396–414.

Hume, D. (1740; 1962) An abstract of a treatise of human nature. Reprinted in A. Flew, ed., *David Hume: On Human Nature and the Understanding*. London: Collier-Macmillan.

Kummer, H. (1995) Causal knowledge in animals. In D. Sperber, D. Premack, and A. J. Premack, eds., *Causal Cognition*, pp. 26–36. New York: Oxford University Press.

Leslie, A. M. (1984) Spatiotemporal continuity and the perception of causality in infants. *Perception*, 13:287–305.

Leslie, A. M., and Keeble, S. (1987) Do six-month-old infants perceive causality? *Cognition*, 25:265–88.

Michotte, A. (1963) *The Perception of Causality*. Andover: Methuen.

Oakes, L. M., and Cohen, L. B. (1990) Infant perception of a causal event. *Cognitive Development*, 5:193–207.

Premack, D. (1992) Cause-induced motion: Intention-spontaneous motion. In J.-F. Changeux and J. Chavaillon., eds., *The Origins of the Human Brain*. Oxford: Clarendon.

Premack, D., and Premack, A. J. (1994) Levels of causal understanding in chimpanzees and children. *Cognition*, 50:238–252.

Schlottmann, A., and Shanks, D. R. (1992) Evidence for a distinction between judged and perceived causality. *Quarterly Journal of Experimental Psychology*, 44A:321–342.

Shultz, T. (1982a) Causal reasoning in the social and nonsocial realms. *Canadian Journal of Behavioral Sciences*, 14:307–322.

Shultz, T. R. (1982b). Rules of causal attribution. *Monographs of the Society for Research in Child Development*, 47(1).

Trabasso, T., and van den Broek, P. (1985) Causal thinking and story comprehension. *Journal of Memory and Language*, 24:612–630.

Watson, J. S. (1984) Bases of causal inference in infancy: Time, space, and sensory relations. In L. P. Lipsitt and C. Rovee-Collier, eds., *Advances in Infancy Research*. Norwood, NJ: Ablex.

Watson, J. S. (1966) The development and generalization of "contingency awareness" in early infancy: Some hypotheses. *Merrill-Palmer Quarterly of Behavior and Development*, 12(2):123–135.

Chapter 9

Brown, A. (1989) Analogical learning and transfer: What develops? In S. Vosniadou and A. Ortony, eds., *Similarity and Analogical Reasoning*, pp. 360–412. Cambridge: Cambridge University Press.

de Haan, M., Pascalis, O., Johnson, M. H. (2002) Specialization of neural mechanisms underlying face recognition in human infants. *Journal of Cognitive Neuroscience*, 14(2):199–209.

Diamond, R., and Carey, S. (1986) Why faces are and are not special: The effect of expertise. *Journal of Experimental Psychology: General*, 115:107–117.

Gauthier, I., Skudlarski, P., Gore, J. C., Anderson, A. W. (2000) Expertise of cars and birds recruit brain areas involved in face recognition. *Nature Neuroscience*, 3:191–197.

Gentner, D. (1983) Structure-mapping: A theoretical framework for analogy. *Cognitive Science*, 7:155–170.

Gentner, D., and Grudin, J. (1985) The evolution of mental metaphors in psychology: A ninety-year perspective. *American Psychologist*, 40:181–192.

Gentner, D., and Toupin, C. (1986) Systematicity and surface similarity in the development of analogy. *Cognitive Science*, 10:277–300.

Gillan, D. J., Premack, D., and Woodruff, G. (1981) Reasoning in the chimpanzee: I. Analogical reasoning. *Journal of Experimental Psychology: Animal Behavioral Processes*, 7:1–17.

Glucksberg, S., and Keysar, B. (1990) Understanding metaphorical comparisons: Beyond similarity. *Psychological Review,* 97:3–18.

Holyoak, K. J., and Koh, K. (1987) Surface and structural similarity in analogical transfer. *Memory and Cognition,* 15:332–340.

Holyoak, K. J., and Thagard, Paul (1996) *Mental Leaps: Analogy in Creative Thought.* Cambridge, MA: MIT Press.

Kotovsky, L., and Gentner, D. (1996) Comparison and categorization in the development of relational similarity. *Child Development,* 67:2797–2822.

Lawrence, D. H., and DeRivera, J. (1954) Evidence for relational transposition. *Journal of Comparative and Physiological Psychology,* 47:465–471.

Medin, D. L., Goldstone, R. L., and Gentner, D. (1993) Respects for similarity. *Psychological Review,* 100(2):254–278.

Oden, D. L., and Premack, D. The foresightful construction of analogies by a chimpanzee (in preparation).

Oden, D. L., Thompson, R. K. R., and Premack, D. (1990) Infant chimpanzees spontaneously perceive both concrete and abstract same/different relations. *Child Development,* 61:621–631.

Premack, D. (1988) Minds with and without language. In L. Weiskrantz, ed., *Thought without Language.* Oxford: Clarendon Press.

Thompson, R. K. R., and Oden, D. L. (1996) A profound disparity revisited: Perception and judgment of abstract identity relations by chimpanzees, human infants, and monkeys. *Behavioral Processes,* 35:149–161.

Thompson, R. K. R., and Oden, D. L. (2000) Concepts in nonhuman primates: The paleological monkey and the analogical ape. *Cognitive Science,* 24:363–396.

Chapter 10

Armstrong, S. L., Gleitman, L. R., and Gleitman, H. (1983) What some concepts might not be. *Cognition,* 13:263–306.

Asch, S. E. (1955) On the use of metaphor in the description of persons. In H. Werner, ed., *On Expressive Language.* Worcester: Clark University Press.

Attneave, F. (1959) *Applications of Information Theory to Psychology.* New York: Holt.

Bartlett, F. C. (1932) *Remembering: A Study in Experimental and Social Psychology.* Cambridge: Cambridge University Press.

Boroditsky, L. (2000) Metaphoric structuring: Understanding time through spatial metaphors. *Cognition,* 75(1):1–28.

Britten, K. H., Shadlen, M. N., Newsome, W. T., and Moushon, J. A. (1993) Responses of neurons in macaque MT to stochastic motion signals. *Visual Neuroscience,* 10:1157–1169.

Cavanagh, P. (1993) The perception of form and motion. *Current Opinion in Neurobiology,* 3:177–182.

Cerella, John (1986) Pigeons and perceptions. *Pattern Recognition,* 19:431–438.

Dasser, V. (1988) A social concept in Java monkeys. *Animal Behavior,* 36:225–230.

Dehaene, S., Dehaene-Lambertz, G., and Cohen, L. (1998) Abstract representations of numbers in the animal and human brain. *Trends in Neurosciences,* 21:355–361.

Gallup, G. G., Jr. (1970) Chimpanzees: Self-recognition. *Science,* 167:86–87.

Goldstone, Robert L. (1994) The role of similarity in categorization: Providing a groundwork. *Cognition,* 52:125–157.

Goodman, N. (1972) Seven strictures on similarity. In N. Goodman, ed., *Problems and Projects,* pp. 437–447. Indianapolis: Bobbs-Merrill.

Greene, S. L. (1983) Feature memorization in pigeon concept formation. In M. L. Commons, R. J. Herrnstein, and A. R. Wagner, eds., *Quantitative Analyses of Behavioral Discrimination Processes.* Cambridge, MA: Ballinger.

Herrnstein, R. J. (1979) Acquisition, generalization, and discrimination reversal of a natural concept. *Journal of Experimental Psychology: Animal Behavior Processes,* 5:116–129.

Hespos, S. J., and Rochat, P. (1997) Dynamic mental representation in infancy. *Cognition,* 64:153–188.

Hodges, A. (1983) *Alan Turing, the Enigma.* New York: Simon Schuster.

Kosslyn, S. M. (1994) *Image and Brain: The Resolution of the Imagery Debate.* Cambridge, MA: MIT Press.

Lakoff, G. (1990) The invariance hypothesis: Is abstract reasoning based on image-schemes? *Cognitive Linguistics,* 1:39–74.

Lakoff, G., and Johnson, M. (1980) *Metaphors We Live By.* Chicago: University of Chicago Press.

Markman, E. M. (1989) *Categorization and Naming in Children: Problems of Induction.* Cambridge, MA: MIT Press.

Medin, D. (1989). Concepts and conceptual structure. *American Psychologist,* 44:1469–1481.

Medin, D., Goldstone, R., and Gentner, D. (1993) Respects for similarity. *Psychological Review,* 100:254–278.

Mishkin, M., Malamut, B., and Bachevalier, J. (1984) Memories and habits: Two neural systems. In G. Lynch, J. L. McGaugh, and N. M. Weinberger, eds., *Neurobiology of Learning and Memory.* New York: Guilford Press.

Munakata, Y., Santoe, L. R., Spelke, E. S., Hauser, M., and O'Reilly, C. O. (2001) Visual representation in the wild: How rhesus monkeys parse objects. *Journal of Cognitive Neuroscience,* 13:44–58.

Murphy, G. L., and Medin, D. L. (1985) The role of theories in conceptual coherence. *Psychological Review,* 92:289–316.

Newell, A. (1990) *Unified Theories of Cognition.* Cambridge, MA: Harvard University Press.

Plyshyn, Z. (1981) The imagery debate: Analogue media versus tacit knowledge. *Psychological Review,* 88:16–45.

Posner, M. I., and Keele, S. W. (1968) On the genesis of abstract ideas. *Journal of Experimental Psychology:* 77:353–363.

Posner, M. I., and Keele, S. W. (1970) Retention of abstract ideas. *Journal of Experimental Psychology,* 104:192–233.

Premack, D. (1983) The codes of man and beasts. *Behavioral and Brain Sciences,* 6:125–167.

Rosch, E. (1975) Cognitive representation of semantic categories. *Journal of Experimental Psychology: General,* 104:192–233.

Rosch, E., Mervis, C. B., Gray, W. D., Johnson, D. M., and Boyes-Braem, P. (1976) Basic objects in natural categories. *Cognitive Psychology,* 8:382–439.

Salzman, C. D., Britten, K. H., and Newsome, W. T. (1990) Cortical microstimu-
lation influences perceptual judgements of motion direction. *Nature*,
174–177.

Sejnowski, T. J., and Nowlan, S. J. (1994) A model of visual motion processing in area
MT of primates. In M. S. Gazzaniga, ed., *The Cognitive Neurosciences*. Cambridge,
MA: MIT Press.

Shadlen, M. N., and Newsome, W. T., (1996) Motion perception: Seeing and deciding. *Proceedings of the National Academy of Sciences of the USA*, 93:628–633.

Shepard, R. N. (1987) Towards a universal law of generalization for psychological
science. *Science*, 237:1317–1323.

Shepard, R. N., and Cooper, L. A. (1982) *Mental Images and Their Transformations*.
Cambridge, MA: MIT Press, Bradford Books.

Singer, W. (1993) Synchronization of cortical activity and its putative role in information processing and learning. *Annual Review of Physiology*, 55:349–374.

Singer, W., and Gray, C. M. (1995) Visual feature integration and the temporal cor-
relation hypothesis. *Annual Review of Neuroscience*, 18:555–586.

Sugarman, S. (1983). *Children's Early Thought: Developments in Classification*. Cambridge: Cambridge University Press.

Tinklepaugh, E. (1928) An experimental study of representative factors in monkeys.
Journal of Comparative Psychology, 8:197–236.

Vaughn, W. L., and Greene, S. L. (1983) Acquisition of absolute discrimination in
pigeons. In R. J. Herrnstein and A. W. Wagner, eds., *Quantitative Analyses of Behavior: Discrimination Processes*. Cambridge, MA: Ballinger.

Wasserman, E. A., Kiedinger, R. E., and Bhatt, R. S. (1988) Conceptual behavior in
pigeons: Categories, subcategories, and pseudocategories. *Journal of Experimental
Psychology: Animal Behavior Processes*, 14:235–246.

Wilson, B., Mackintosh, N. J., and Boakes, R. A. (1985) Transfer of relational rules in
matching and oddity learning by pigeons and corvids. *Quarterly Journal of Experimental Psychology*, 37B:313–332.

Wittgenstein, L. (1953) *Philosophical Investigations*, E. Anscombe, trans. Oxford:
Blackwell.

Xu, F., and Carey, S. (1996) Infants' metaphysics: The case of numerical identity.
Cognitive Psychology, 30:111–153.

Young, M. E., and Wasserman, E. A. (1997) Entropy detection by pigeons: Response
to mixed visual displays after same-different discrimination training. *Journal of
Experimental Psychology: Animal Behavior Processes*, 23:157–170.

Conclusion

Axelrod, A., and Hamilton, W. D. (1981) The evolution of cooperation. *Science*,
211:1390–1396.

Bischof-Köhler, D. (1991) The development of empathy in infants. In M. E. Lamb
and H. Keller, eds., *Infant Development: Perspectives from German-Speaking Countries*, pp. 245–273. Hillsdale, NJ: Erlbaum.

Crawford, M. P. (1937) The cooperative solving of problems by young chimpanzees.
Comparative Psychological Monographs, 14(68).

Dawkins, R. (1976) *The Selfish Gene*. Oxford: Oxford University Press.

Dawkins, R. (1986) *The Blind Watchmaker.* New York: Norton.

Haldane, J. B. S. (1932) *The Causes of Evolution.* London: Longmans Green.

Hamilton, W. D. (1964a) The evolution of altruistic behavior. *American Naturalist,* 97:354–356.

Hamilton, W. D. (1964b) The genetical evolution of social behavior. *Journal of Theoretical Biology,* 7:1–52.

Isaac, G. (1978) The food-sharing behavior of protohuman hominids. *Scientific American,* 238(4):90–108.

McClintock, C. G., and Moskowitz, J. M. (1976) Childrens' preferences for individualistic, cooperative and competitive outcomes. *Journal of Personality and Social Psychology,* 34:543–555.

Marrov, H. I. (1956) *A History of Education in Antiquity,* George Lamb, trans. London: Sheed and Ward.

Olson, D. R. 1996. Toward a psychology of literacy: On the relations between speech and writing. *Cognition,* 60:83–104.

Poulson, D., Kintsch, E., Kintsch, W., and Premack, D. (1979) Childrens' comprehension and memory for stories. *Journal of Experimental Child Psychology,* 28:379–403.

Sofer, E., and Wilson, D. S. (1998) *Unto Others.* Cambridge: Harvard University Press.

Trivers, R. L. (1971) The evolution of reciprocal altruism. *Quarterly Review of Biology,* 46:35–57.

Wilkinson, G. S. (1984) Reciprocal food sharing in the vampire bat. *Nature,* 308:181–184.

Wilson, E. O. (1971) *The Insect Societies.* Cambridge, MA: Harvard University Press.

Index

A

"Accidents," cultural/environmental, 6
"Action-object" rule, 84
Aesthetics, 63–68, 237–240
  in human movement, 67–68
  in infants, 66–67
  and pedagogy, 71–72
  and perceptions of beauty, 63–64
  of physical appearance, 64–66
Africa, 5
Agriculture, 8, 12–13
  and ownership, 9–10
  and seeds, 176
Alphabet, 9
Altruism, 5, 230–231
Analogies:
  chimpanzees' perception of, 182,
    183, 186–200
  and conceptual proportions, 196–197
  functional, 191–196
  and perception of relations, 180–182
  and "same" vs. "different" objects,
    182–183
  and use of labels, 198–199
Animals:
  categorization in, 209–213
  imitation in, 55–56
Arithmetic, 66–67
Armstrong, S., 208
Art, 39, 237–240
Artificial intelligence, 219, 221

B

Atran, Scott, 25
Attention, shared, 117–118
Attractiveness, perceptions of, 214–215
Australian aborigines, 61
Australopithecus, 1–3

B

Baboons, 60–61
Baillergeon, Renee, 20
Barn owls, 102
Bats, 102, 231
Beauty, perceptions of, 63–64
Beavers, 4
Bees, 5, 19, 210
Believing, 125–138
  and comprehension, 126
  and false belief, 148–149
  mental state associated with, 126–128
  and ordinary vs. zealous beliefs, 130
  and perception, 133–136
  in prelanguage child, 130–133
  as pseudo-concept, 126
  and rationality, 128–130
Bennett, Jonathan, 148, 153, 156
Bias, 209, 223
Bidirectional sign, 86, 87
Bilateral symmetry, 65–66
Binding problem, 178
Biology module, 24–29
Birds, 69, 179
Bischof, Doris, 232–234

INDEX

About the Authors

David Premack, Ph.D. is Professor Emeritus of Psychology at the University of Pennsylvania. The Premacks, pioneers in chimpanzee language study, showed why chimps cannot acquire human language. David Premack proposed a theory of reward or reinforcement still used after forty years (the Premack Principle), and introduced the concept of *theory of mind*, a keystone of human social intelligence. His book *The Mind of an Ape*, written with Ann Premack, summarized his work on animal intelligence and was given an award by the American Psychological Association. Ann Premack's *Why Chimps Can Read* was featured in "New and Noteworthy" in the *New York Times* and translated into five languages. She is an editor of *Causal Cognition*, and listed in *Who's Who in the World*.